♦ WINTER 2006 ♦

CONTEMPORARY

LITERATURE

♦ VOLUME 47 ♦

♦ NUMBER 4 ♦

THE UNIVERSITY

OF WISCONSIN

PRESS

♦

CONTEMPORARY LITERATURE

EDITORIAL OFFICE: *Department of English, 7141 Helen C. White Hall, 600 N. Park Street, University of Wisconsin, Madison, Wisconsin 53706.* Manuscripts are returned only if accompanied by a self-addressed envelope with sufficient first-class postage. The editors cannot review manuscripts that are simultaneously under consideration elsewhere and cannot assume responsibility for loss or damage of any work submitted. All details should conform to those recommended by the most recent edition of the *MLA Handbook.*

BUSINESS OFFICE: All correspondence about advertising, subscriptions, and allied matters should be sent to: *Journal Division, University of Wisconsin Press, 1930 Monroe Street, 3rd floor, Madison, Wisconsin 53711-2059.* Website: www.wisc.edu/wisconsinpress/journals

SUBSCRIPTION RATE: One year: $154 print and electronic; $146 electronic only (institutions); print only $42.00 (individuals only; must prepay); add $10.00 surface postage outside U.S.; $35.00 air mail.

Contemporary Literature (ISSN 0010-7484; E-ISSN 1548-9949) is published quarterly by the University of Wisconsin Press, 1930 Monroe Street, 3rd floor, Madison, WI 53711-2059. Website: www.wisc.edu/wisconsinpress/journals. Periodicals postage paid at Madison, WI and at additional mailing offices. POSTMASTER: Send address changes to *Contemporary Literature*, 1930 Monroe Street, 3rd floor, Madison, WI 53711-2059.

CONTENTS

IMMIGRANT FICTIONS

CONTEMPORARY LITERATURE IN AN AGE OF GLOBALIZATION

Edited by Rebecca L. Walkowitz

WINTER 2006 · VOLUME 47 · NUMBER 4

THE UNIVERSITY OF WISCONSIN PRESS

REBECCA L. WALKOWITZ

The Location of Literature: The Transnational Book and the Migrant Writer

"Precisely where is English literature produced?" This is Gauri Viswanathan's question, from an essay about the transformation of English studies in the wake of postcolonial theory (22). Her answer—not only "in England, of course"—focuses on the genealogy of the discipline, its development within the British Empire and other dominions outside England through the education of colonial subjects and the efforts of strangers such as "Jews, Dissenters, and Catholics" (23). But her answer also focuses on the dynamic relationship between "sites of cultural production and institutionalization," the way that "English literature" names a mode of analysis and a collection of works as well as the way that modes of analysis establish collections. In fact, she suggests, there is no "English literature" before institutionalization: only with disciplinary protocols do cultural products become a field (20). "Where is English literature produced?" thus asks us to consider that the location of literature depends not only on the places where books are written but also on the places where they are classified and given social purpose.

In its emphasis on critical geographies, Viswanathan's question remains important to continuing debates about the "national attributes" of literature (21). Yet today we would be likely to ask several other questions as well: *In what language* does English literature circulate? *Where* is English literature read? *Who* counts as a producer (writers, but also editors, printers, designers, publishers, translators, reviewers)? And *how* has the global circulation of English literature shaped its strategies and forms of appearance? These questions turn from production to circulation, and back again, reflecting a new

Contemporary Literature XLVII, 4   0010-7484; E-ISSN 1548-9949/06/0004-0527

emphasis on the history of the book and what Leah Price calls "the geography of the book" within postcolonial studies and world literature ("Tangible Page" 38). This work reinvigorates and reframes Homi K. Bhabha's claim that disciplinary models of comparison and distinction will have to be tested by new ways of understanding community. In *The Location of Culture*, published in 1994, Bhabha argued, "The very concepts of homogenous national cultures, the consensual or contiguous transmission of historical traditions, or 'organic' ethnic communities—*as the grounds of cultural comparativism*—are in a profound process of redefinition" (5). A decade and more later, essays and reports about the future of literary studies assume the heterogeneity and discontinuity of national cultures, and many scholars now emphasize "networks" of tradition and the social processes through which those networks are established (Damrosch, "What Is World Literature" 3; Greene 216–21). Haun Saussy's essay on the state of comparative literature, published with replies as *Comparative Literature in an Age of Globalization*, marks and elaborates this turn. Like Saussy's volume, *Immigrant Fictions* suggests that literary studies will have to examine the global writing of books, in addition to their classification, design, publication, translation, anthologizing, and reception across multiple geographies. Books are no longer imagined to exist in a single literary system but may exist, now and in the future, in several literary systems, through various and uneven practices of world circulation.

Consider, for example, the literary systems represented on the cover of this volume, which displays in miniature the covers of five contemporary works of fiction in English—or, really, the covers of five editions of those works: they are, from left to right, the U.S. paperback reprint of George Lamming's *Season of Adventure* (1999; first edition, 1960), the U.S. paperback reprint of Theresa Hak Kyung Cha's *Dictée* (2001; first edition, 1982), the British paperback translation of Iva Pekárková's *Gimme the Money* (2000; first edition, 1995), the Japanese paperback translation of David Peace's *Nineteen Seventy-Seven* (2001; first edition, 2000), and the U.S. paperback reprint of Monica Ali's *Brick Lane* (2004; first edition, 2003). These editions (as well as several others) are discussed in the volume's essays, which follow *Contemporary Literature*'s stated mission by focusing only on literature in English. But as I have been suggesting, it has become more difficult to assert with confidence that we know what literature in English is. Some of the books depicted on our cover were produced while their authors were living in a place whose principal language is English; but at least two (*Gimme the Money* and *Nineteen Seventy-Seven*) were not. Some of the books are original-language editions, while others are translations of several sorts: a translation into English (*Gimme the Money*, from Czech), a translation into Japanese (*Nineteen Seventy-Seven*, from English), and a multilingual text (*Dictée*, which moves among several languages, including English, French, and Korean). As the essays in this volume attest, Anglophone works of immigrant fiction are not always produced in an Anglophone country; some immigrant fictions produced in an Anglophone country are not originally Anglophone; and some do not exist in any one language at all. These variations test the presumed monolingualism of any nation, whether the U.S. or England, and remind us that there is a (largely invisible) misfit between the national and linguistic valences of the tradition we call "English literature." That misfit is not new, of course: for many centuries, works of Anglophone literature have been produced outside of England (think of Scotland, Ireland, Wales, India, Nigeria, Antigua, the U.S., Canada, and so on); works produced within England have not been uniformly Anglophone (think of Marie de France's lays and Thomas More's *Utopia*); and other important English works have mixed languages (think of James Joyce's *Finnegans Wake* and T. S. Eliot's *The Waste Land*) or were translated from other languages (think of the King James Bible and Rabindranath Tagore's *The Home and the World*). Is today's literary multilingualism different in kind from the literary multilingualism of the past? My account of our volume's cover suggests that contemporary literature in an age of globalization is, in many ways, a comparative literature: works circulate in several literary systems at once, and can—some would say, need—to be read within several national traditions.

The Transnational Book

The contributors to *Immigrant Fictions* affirm that thinking about the migration of writers and about the effects of migration on literary culture will benefit from thinking about the migration of books.

They approach this project variously. In his interview with Tokyo-Yorkshire writer David Peace, Matthew Hart asks what it means, in terms of research and career, to produce strongly regional and historical novels about England while living in Japan. Peace relates that his émigré experience has led him to think all the more carefully about the production and reception of regional texts. In addition, he explains with equanimity the changes he allowed in the recent French translation of his novel about the 1984–85 miners' strike, *GB84*. These changes involved switching the narrative voice of an anti-Semitic character from third person to first, in order to accommodate "the cultural and historical context of anti-Semitism within France" (567). By making substantial textual changes, Peace enters into several literary traditions, French as well as Japanese and English. Strategies of translation are also a concern in Wen Jin's article about *Fusang*, a novel first published in Chinese (1995) and later in English (2001) by the U.S.-Chinese writer Geling Yan. Well-known in mainland China, Yan now writes directly in English as well as in Chinese; she published her first Anglophone novel (not from translation) in July 2006. Examining the textual differences between the Chinese and English versions of *Fusang*, Jin argues that the multilingual circulation of immigrant fiction destabilizes nation-based conceptions of literary culture. She suggests that Asian American studies will need to adopt a more transnational perspective if it is to accommodate the several communities in which cultural products are produced and received. Jin's reading strategies allow us to see that the sexuality of the novel's eponymous character operates differently in Chinese and U.S. literary culture, and that readers' conceptions of the book's achievement often depend on local assumptions about the desires of Chinese women.

Eric Hayot's article about translation and mediation in *Dictée*, by the U.S.-Korean writer Theresa Hak Kyung Cha, and *Becoming Madame Mao*, by the U.S.-Chinese writer Anchee Min, suggests that immigrant fictions often mobilize two or more cultural vocabularies. In the case of Min's novel, this involves Chinese theatrical practice and Euro-American melodrama. Hayot argues that *Dictée* and *Becoming Madame Mao*, despite significant differences in genre and style, can be seen to share in the resistance to what he calls the "ethnic bildungsroman," the novel of successful assimilation. They resist this genre, Hayot contends, by bringing their readers into contact with the media of immigration, both the processes of fiction-writing and those of cultural pedagogy such as dictation and social performance. Directly, as in the case *Dictée*, and indirectly, as in *Becoming Madame Mao*, these texts reflect on the literary and political activities of making, translating, and becoming a work of art.

From the emphasis in the first three contributions on the cultural and linguistic translation of books, the volume shifts to an analysis of mobility's tropes. Věra Eliášová's essay takes up Iva Pekárková's *Gimme the Money*, a novel about a Czech woman who works as a taxi driver in New York City. Pekárková wrote and published *Gimme the Money* in Czech while she was living in the U.S.; she later translated the novel into English after returning to the Czech Republic; she now lives in London. Eliášová presents Pekárková's novel as a book that theorizes its own cultural mobility: she argues that the novel figures migration as a circular movement, like the itinerary of a taxi, rather than as a single journey. In addition, she suggests, *Gimme the Money* has its own complex "multidimensional mobility" because it operates within several literary genres, including the Eastern European immigrant autobiography, the modernist novel about women in the city, and the new writing from postcommunist Europe. The mix of genres and traditions in Pekárková's work, Eliášová suggests, complicates efforts to place her novels within a national geography: because she wrote *Gimme the Money* as a Czech expatriate in New York but now lives in London, Pekárková fits imperfectly in both U.S. and Czech literary cultures.

Like David Peace and Anchee Min, who live in one place but write about another, George Lamming helped to establish the modern Caribbean novel while living in metropolitan London. J. Dillon Brown argues in his essay that the disjunction between the geography of Lamming's production and initial circulation (England) and the geography of his origin and themes (Barbados) helps to explain his work's infamous "difficulty" and its relationship to modernist precursors. Brown argues, moreover, that any analysis of the postcolonial novel needs to take into account its metropolitan development. He suggests that readers must see Lamming in the context of British literary history, as well as in the context of Caribbean literary history. But more specifically he proposes that Lamming's presence within the literary history of Britain gives a different shape to the literary history of the Caribbean. It is not simply a matter of acknowledging Lamming's participation in one more tradition but rather of examining the transnational context of publishing in the 1950s. "Placing Lamming's work into its metropolitan contexts," Brown writes, "allows more space for emphasizing how his novels foreground the practical impossibility of claims for pure cultural absolutism or an unproblematically static, rooted cultural identity." His essay asks, in both literal and figurative registers, what is the *source* of Lamming's fiction and especially of his literary style?

The final essay in the volume, Alistair Cormack's analysis of Monica Ali's blockbuster, *Brick Lane*, asks whether migration has a proper literary form, and whether migration transforms realist fiction. Taking Ali's novel as his test case, Cormack suggests that the struggle with language and subjectivity at the center of many immigrant novels does not fit well with realism's emphasis on individual agency. Cormack argues that scenes of translation in *Brick Lane*, which involve the interpretation of manners as well as of writing, draw attention to the narration's seamless movement between English and Bengali, and between a sense of estrangement in England and a sense of knowledge about that estrangement. For all its *Bildung*, Cormack proposes, Ali's novel fits uneasily within the bildungsroman tradition. "The demands of representing different cultural signifying systems," Cormack writes, "render unstable the novel's transparency." Cormack concludes that the experience of immigration, once it is represented in fiction, alters the way that mimetic genres function. At the same time, Cormack suggests that novels such as *Brick Lane* are exceptionally popular as immigrant fictions in good part because they mostly avoid the analysis of transnational writing and circulating that Hayot, Eliášová, and Brown see in works by Cha, Pekárková, and Lamming.

The Migrant Writer

Not every book that travels is produced by a writer who travels, though today it is common for writers whose works circulate in many areas of the globe to participate in book fairs and tours that take them beyond their original continent and hemisphere. In this limited sense, most successful writers are also migrant writers. The globalization of publishing, which generates immigrating books as well as immigrating writers, is discussed in several of the essays in this volume. But contributors also investigate a kind of immigration that is more familiar and in some ways more old-fashioned: they look at writers who have belonged or who continue to belong to more than one nation, region, or state and who now participate in a literary system that is different from the system in which they were born, educated, or first published. Of course, even this understanding of immigration is relatively new, as Susan Stanford Friedman has argued in a survey of the field, because it reflects a shift from nation-based paradigms to "transnational models emphasizing the global space of ongoing travel and transcontinental connection" (906). Several contributors suggest that it is not simply a matter of leaving one system for another, both because most literary systems rely on networks of publishing and distribution that are international if not global and because one is not always welcomed in new systems; one may not fit comfortably in any system; and one does not necessarily give up past affiliations while forging new ones.

These ways of thinking about the varieties and complexities of literary participation correspond to new ways of thinking about whose lives and which objects are transformed by migration. One of the important turns in the analysis of what this volume calls "immigrant fiction" has been a new emphasis on disciplinary paradigms of tradition, language, and classification. That is, scholars have argued that the political and social processes of immigration shape the whole literary system, the relationships among all of the works in a literary culture, and not simply the part of that system that involves books generated by immigrant populations. This means that "the literature of migration," to use Leslie Adelson's term of art, would have to include all works that are produced in a time of migration or that can be said to reflect on migration. Whether one privileges social contexts or literary content, it is no longer principally a matter of distinguishing immigrant from nonimmigrant authors. "The literature of migration," Adelson argues, "is not written by migrants alone" (23). Conversely, Carine Mardorossian proposes, being a migrant writer or even writing about the experience of migration does not guarantee that one will produce migrant literature. Mardorossian associates migrant literature with an aesthetic program rather than an origin or topic; for her, that program involves rejecting the "opposition between the modern and the traditional, the country of destination and the country of origin" (21). Accordingly, nonimmigrant writers who are engaged intellectually with the movement of people and objects across geographies and cultures, and who articulate in their work a "cosmopolitan, transnational, and hybrid vision of social life," could be producers of immigrant fiction. Likewise, this volume queries the genre it names. Is the immigrant in *immigrant fictions* like the English in *English studies*? Does it name a kind of writer? A kind of book? A kind of writing? A kind of criticism?

Adelson's and Mardorossian's arguments overlap to some extent but not entirely: while Adelson focuses on the transformation of a literary culture, Mardorossian is more concerned with the arguments of individual texts. Both, however, assert that changes in thinking about migration require changes in thinking about belonging, community, and civic recognition. They reject two assumptions: that migrants move "between two worlds" that are distinct and coherent, and that migrants bring with them or enter into literary systems that are unique and strictly local (Adelson 4, 7). These arguments about migration suggest that literary classification might depend more on a book's future than on a writer's past. What has happened to the writer is less important, in these accounts, than what happens in the writing and in the reading, though the biography of the writer may influence the way that books are written and received.

The contributors to this volume also emphasize analytic paradigms of migration and migration's transformation of literary cultures. And the range of authors they consider points to a broad conception of our eponymous term. All of the writers considered in this collection have moved from one place to another at some point in their lives, but the causes and processes of those movements are remarkably different, as are the ways that the writers display mobility in their work. All may respond to immigration, but some do so in a direct manner, by writing about characters who have been transplanted; others treat immigration much less directly, by writing about characters who believe themselves to be very much at home.

Reading beyond the Nation

What happens when the migrant writer reflects on the transnational book? My own approach to this question leads me to look at a range of literary and paraliterary texts—anthologies, essays, memoirs, public lectures, interviews, as well as fiction—and at those examples of *comparative writing* that have sought to preempt or replace national models of literary culture. I share with Franco Moretti, David Damrosch, and other scholars of world literature an interest in the circulation and reception of books, but I examine in addition how writers, translators, and anthologists have helped to shape the field. Consider, for example, Caryl Phillips, who was born in Saint Kitts, raised in Leeds, and now lives and works in New York, London, and New Haven. Phillips mentions these locations on his professional Web site and in the biographies that introduce each of the U.S. paperback editions of his work. The language of the biographies varies slightly, but there are some constants: he emphasizes cities and smaller regions rather more than continents, empires, or nations. Here are a few samples:

> Caryl Phillips was born in 1958 in St. Kitts, West Indies, and went with his family to England that same year. He was brought up in Leeds and educated at Oxford.
>
> *(Higher Ground)*

> Caryl Phillips was born in St. Kitts, West Indies. Brought up in England, he has written for television, radio, theater, and cinema. . . . He divides his time between London and New York.
>
> *(Extravagant Strangers)*

> Caryl Phillips was born in St. Kitts, West Indies. Brought up in England, he has written for television, radio, theater, and film. . . . Phillips lives in New York.
>
> *(New World Order)*

In each biography, Phillips suggests that the book we are about to read has many sources and has been shaped, like Lamming's work, by the interplay among several literary cultures.

A Caribbean-British-U.S. writer, Phillips presents his books both as products and as philosophies of migration. In this doubling, they can seem to stand at once inside and outside the immigrant fiction tradition. His books are products of migration because they are built on literary and political histories that correspond to the several places Phillips or Phillips's family has lived. Building on these histories, they make Anglophone literary culture more inclusive of writers born outside of England. Yet they are philosophies of migration because they seem ambivalent about the process of equating culture with community (literary inclusion as national inclusion) and about the ways that cultural expressivity has been used both to justify and to resist anti-immigrant violence. In his work, Phillips tries to make cultural institutions responsive to migration without simply reproducing the forms and strategies of the nation. What new shapes of collectivity, he seems to ask, can histories of migration help us to imagine?

Phillips's novels, anthologies, and essays offer compelling examples of the new world literature and of what I call "comparison literature," an emerging genre of world literature for which global comparison is a formal as well as a thematic preoccupation. By using the term *comparison literature*, I mean to consider the relationship between the writing of world literature and the protocols of reading we bring to those texts. And I mean to draw our attention to the traditional distinction between the disciplines of national literature, which typically refer to what books are, who wrote them, or where they were produced, and the discipline of comparative literature, which typically refers to what we do with books. Comparison literature implies both of these projects, asking us to understand comparison as the work of scholars, to be sure, but also as the work of books that analyze—as Phillips's do—the transnational contexts of their own production, circulation, and study.

As objects and as containers, Phillips's books function as world literature in several respects: they are written, printed, translated, and read in multiple places; and they analyze the relationship among multiple instances of global travel, not only sampling and collating an array of migration narratives but also rehearsing different strategies of sampling and collating. Phillips's work offers an opportunity to consider the relationship between the production and circulation of world literature because—apart from being read within several literary systems—it is written to make those systems less unique. In his concern with uniqueness,

Phillips is engaged with debates about *historical* distinctiveness, such as whether the Holocaust can be usefully compared to other examples of racism and genocide; and he is engaged with debates about *national* distinctiveness, such as whether works of literature or other cultural products can be usefully classified by the national origin of their makers, however that origin is defined. It would be possible to look at works of contemporary literature that reflect on the geography of their circulation and translation (Walkowitz, "Unimaginable Largeness"), but here I will focus on works that reflect on the geography of classification and promotion.

Over the past two decades, Phillips has published in an extraordinary number of genres, including the stage play, the screenplay, the radio play, the literary review, the memoir, the anthology, and the novel. Even more striking than the variety of his publications, however, is their consistent borrowing from a single genre—the anthology—whose structure and strategies Phillips uses to shape each of his novels and many of his nonfiction works as well. Patently, the anthology form is an odd choice for a writer committed to literary classifications that exceed or abjure the nation. As Phillips well knows, literary anthologies have been used throughout the twentieth century to affirm the expressive cultures of national or micronational communities (Walkowitz, "Shakespeare"). Given this history, the anthology offers an unlikely fit for the discontinuities of migration, and for ideas of community based on social contact and hospitality rather than on collective memory or cultural sameness.

And yet, for Phillips, the anthology is useful because it articulates at the level of form the problems of order, inclusion, and comparison that migration narratives articulate at the level of content. Put another way, thinking about the anthology and migration together allows Phillips to reflect on the intersection between literary and political histories of belonging. Of course, Phillips is not alone in his effort to accommodate migration within the tradition of the anthology. The sheer proliferation of new anthologies of world literature and the new debates about anthologies of national literature are telling. Indeed, one might observe that Phillips has been rethinking world literature through the anthology at the very same time that many editors, including Phillips, have been rethinking the anthology through world literature.[1] Since the 1980s, when Phillips began writing his novels, trade publishers have been producing anthologies devoted to writing by women, writing by African Americans, writing by Jewish authors in Britain and Ireland, and so on. But the substantial revision and diversification of the major anthologies—English literature, American literature, world literature—is a much more recent trend, and it coincides with a critical turn to multilingualism, micronationalisms, postcolonial writing, and migration. In the Norton anthology series, the addition of an anthology of "world literature" to the anthology of "world masterpieces" suggests a new self-consciousness about the rhetoric of timeless value and about the relationship of that rhetoric to histories of imperialism. New thinking about migration has had an effect, too, on anthologies that do not seem to be about language or geography at all: the landmark *Norton Anthology of Writing by Women*, which arguably started the minor anthology trend within major anthology publishing in 1985, now carries the subtitle *The Traditions in English*, a feature that is surely related to a greater awareness about the uneven geography of women's writing. Within the African American literary tradition, which constitutes one of Phillips's touchstones, many writers have also been anthology-makers and have been wary at times of the logic of cultural nationalism that the anthology's tone of celebration often serves.[2]

Ambivalent about the social function of the anthology while relying on its form, Phillips generates a kind of collectivity in his work—but it is a collectivity of negative belonging, what Virginia Woolf famously dubbed a "Society of Outsiders." One of his anthologies brings together nonnative British writers in a book called *Extravagant Strangers*. In that volume, Phillips creates a tradition of very loose affiliation: his contributors have different ways of being "strangers" in Britain, and some only seem to be strangers by technicality, like William Makepeace Thackeray, who

---

1. See Bate, Damrosch, Greenblatt, and King, who engage with this issue in their prefaces. Leah Price offers further discussion in two reviews.
2. See the discussions in Edwards and Mason. See also Walkowitz, "Shakespeare."

was born in Calcutta before moving to England at the age of five. One might say that *Extravagant Strangers* does more to deflate the coherence of other anthologies than it does to assert its own. It includes not only famous English writers who are in some ways strangers in England but also less famous strangers, such as Ignatius Sancho, who made contributions to English prose. Phillips's anthology, from 1997, creates a new order of literary belonging. That belonging is defined by the geography of production, and thus Phillips's collection follows the path of the Longman and Oxford anthologies, which privilege places of making over language and cultural origin.

Phillips's novels and nonfiction works are like anthologies in that they sample and collate stories of racism, slavery, European anti-Semitism, and recent violence against immigrants. But unlike other anthologies, which create a single series, Phillips's books tend to promote various microseries within them. In addition to collating the lives of several migrants, his books also represent the life of any single migrant, including their author, as yet another collated account. In the short biographies that preface each of his books, Phillips mentions the places through which he has moved and continues to move. In a 2001 anthology of his own essays, called *A New World Order*, Phillips describes his collated self as "one harmonious entity" (6). And yet there is something not especially harmonious about the relationship among the parts he names—Africa, the Caribbean, Britain, and the United States—or about the collective stories that these places are meant to represent. Phillips intimates this discord by emphasizing what Theodore Mason has called the "historicity" of anthology production—the procedures of selection, arrangement, and framing that allow one series to emerge rather than another (191). Instead of a single progression through places whose meanings are fixed, Phillips presents multiple progressions through places whose meanings vary according to the framework he establishes for them.

For example, the structure of Phillips's introduction to *A New World Order* presents an autobiographical story of migration that is rather different from the one in his paratextual biography. Emphasizing fantasy and memory rather than legal homes, the introduction begins and ends in different parts of Africa, where in one case Phillips is hosted by a British official eager to display his graciousness toward an African porter; and, in another, he is served by an African waiter who assumes that Phillips, like any other loyal subject of the British Crown, must be mourning the death of Princess Diana. Each of these anecdotes serves to register Phillips's discomfort both with British attitudes toward Africa and with African attitudes toward Britain. And Phillips seems to be acknowledging that there is something limited and perhaps false about identity claims based on a distant past: the slave trade may have transported his family from Africa, but an African local treats him simply as a patriot of Britain. Within the book's introduction, there are additional collections: the collection constituted by classmates from Phillips's childhood school, whose surnames a teacher matches to various geographic origins, though not in Phillips's case; and the collection constituted by new technologies of migration, such as worldwide CNN broadcasts, inexpensive airplane travel, and a tourism industry in the former slave ports of West Africa. These different ways of arranging geography and of arranging the ways that people move through geography today suggest to us the several different anthologies in which Phillips's story takes part. The structure of the chapters of Phillips's book follows yet another order, beginning in the U.S. and moving to Africa, to the Caribbean, and then finally to Britain. Taken as a narrative, the chapters seem to tell the history of Phillips's professional life, whereas the series in the biography and in the introduction display the history of his postcolonial consciousness, the history of his passports, and the history of the African diaspora. *A New World Order*, despite the singular name, offers up many orders of migration. With its multiple framings and allegorical constructions, Phillips's anthology aspires to the ingenuity and artifice of fiction.

His fiction, in turn, hews to the anthology but unsettles the logic of representativeness by introducing comparisons among several narratives and by emphasizing regions and cities rather than nations and continents. Reading beyond the nation in the way that Phillips suggests means recognizing literary cultures and political histories that exceed the nation, and also recognizing those that are narrower than the nation, or those that emphasize alternative grounds of collectivity. Phillips's most recent book, *Dancing in the Dark*, is a fictionalized history of the Bahamas-born, Southern

California–raised minstrel performer Bert Williams, who traveled across the U.S. and throughout England, and who died as a resident of Harlem in upper Manhattan. Presenting Williams as an Afro-Caribbean performer who is taken for an African American performer who is taken for the racist stereotype of a Southern "coon" that he imitates so well, Phillips wants us to understand the regional and international migrancy that complicates the geography of African American culture, which includes not only the story of Bert Williams but also the frame of that story—a novel by Caryl Phillips. *Dancing in the Dark* emphasizes the international and regional journeys that make up the typical artifacts of national culture. In this case, the African American minstrel performer *par excellence* turns out to be a native not of the American South or of a Northern city, but of the Caribbean and the Pacific coast.

Phillips's novel-anthologies eschew two aspects of the anthology tradition: its claim to express a distinctive literary culture based on race or national origin; and its tone of celebration, which has tended to affirm a group's expressivity without acknowledging the violent history of such affirmations. This ambivalence about the celebration of cultural heritage helps to explain Phillips's choice to put a black minstrel performer at the center of a story about the history of African American theater. Phillips's anthologies tend to emphasize violence rather than creativity, and they use various devices of comparison to create a proliferation of overlapping groups. Phillips values the collective, but his communities are made up of strangers whose affiliation is fragile, provisional, and often temporary.

If *Dancing in the Dark* serves to display the international history of African American and U.S. cultural traditions, Phillips's previous novel, *A Distant Shore*, counters stereotypes about British natives and non-British strangers by sounding national histories of violence in both regional and international registers. Engaging with debates about Britain's treatment of refugees and immigrants, *A Distant Shore*, from 2003, sets a story about the strangeness of an English woman in a new housing development beside a story about the strangeness of a man, also new to that development, who is a refugee from genocidal violence in an African country, perhaps Rwanda. By comparing the condition of being a stranger in a village to the more expansive condition of being a stranger in a nation, the novel asks us to think from the beginning about several scales of belonging. The first line of the novel, "England has changed," turns out to refer not to the arrival of immigrants like the man from Africa but to the arrival of gentrification and of people, like the woman from the town, who buy new bungalows outside small, traditional villages (3). It is in some ways disturbing that Phillips would compare the man's experience of racism in this town with the woman's experience of loneliness and ostracism, but this comparison allows Phillips to suggest that the town's exclusion of strangers like the woman is motivated by nativist values that are similar to those that motivate, or at least excuse, the attack on strangers from other nations and other cultures. The novel also seeks to question the cultural heritage that the villagers think they are preserving. Our only initial hint that national histories may have regional variations and that regional variations can complicate assumptions about ethical superiority comes in the novel's first description of the town: a place "twinned," we are told, with a town in Germany that was utterly destroyed during World War II and a village in the south of France where in those same years Jews were deported to extermination camps (4). The identity of the English town seems to depend on its status as a place where bombing and deportation did not take place. But the descriptions of the French and German towns hint at an incongruity that reflects on England. By selecting a victimized town to represent Germany and a victimizing village to represent France, Phillips asks us to consider the difference between what we assume about English hospitality—its comparative liberalism, for example—and what we might learn about the local treatment of strangers.

In *A Distant Shore* and *Dancing in the Dark*, narratives of migration violate the epithets of place ("liberal England," "fascist Germany," and so on) that have allowed us to classify books and, in turn, to classify writers. By creating new anthologies, Phillips tries to modify the way his books will be contained. He does this by troubling the distinction between container and object: his books may seem like objects, but they are full of containers: comparative frameworks that impose new classifications and ask us to question what we know about the location of literature. Within his novels and nonfiction works, embedded anthologies give dynamic form to the history of migration. Instead of suggesting that books by new arrivals expand or simply disable literary histories based on the nation, Phillips suggests that these works can help us to imagine new literary histories, ones whose scale includes the town, the region, and the housing development, and whose object includes not only the production of books but also their translation, circulation, and comparison. It is these multiple scales and multiple objects that reading beyond the nation, if we are to take up such a charge, will have to accommodate.

In the essays that follow, the contributors to this volume examine multiple ways that works of immigrant fiction travel and make their home today. For books, making a home can refer to processes as different as production, translation, circulation, reception, allusion, and curricular adoption; and these kinds of home-making are not necessarily, or now even principally, exclusive or permanent. By thinking about the migration of books, in addition to the migration of writers, this volume urges readers to imagine that the location of any literary work is achieved and unfinished, indebted to a network of past collaborations and contestations, and to collaborations and contestations that have not yet taken place. In this age of globalization, a new work of English literature has its life in many places. The essays collected here show how contemporary writers such as Caryl Phillips, David Peace, Geling Yan, Theresa Hak Kyung Cha, Anchee Min, Iva Pekárková, George Lamming, and Monica Ali have helped to imagine and create that condition.

———————

It is my pleasure to thank the contributors to this volume for their intelligence, camaraderie, and patience. I am grateful to Susan Stanford Friedman, Eric Hayot, Venkat Mani, Thomas Schaub, and Henry Turner for helping me to conceive *Immigrant Fictions* and to Thom Dancer, Eileen Ewing, Mary Mekemson, Taryn Okuma, and Ken Sullivan for helping me to produce it. My thanks also to Graham Huggan and Andrew Thompson for including me in a stimulating conference on postcolonial migrations, which took place at the University of Leeds in June 2006. Parts of this essay received their first hearing on that occasion, and they have benefited from the generous comments of the organizers and other participants.

University of Wisconsin–Madison

WORKS CITED

Adelson, Leslie A. *The Turkish Turn in Contemporary German Literature: Toward a New Critical Grammar of Migration*. New York: Palgrave-Macmillan, 2005.

Bate, Jonathan. General Editor's Preface. *The Internationalization of English Literature*. Oxford: Oxford UP, 2004. Vol. 13 in *The Oxford Literary History*. Gen. ed. Jonathan Bate. Oxford: Oxford UP, 2003. viii–x.

Bhabha, Homi K. *The Location of Culture*. New York: Routledge, 1994.

Damrosch, David. Preface. *The Longman Anthology of British Literature*. Vol. 2. Ed. David Damrosch. New York: Longman, 1999. xxxiii–xxxvii.

———. Preface. *The Longman Anthology of World Literature*. Vol. F. Ed. David Damrosch. New York: Longman, 2004. xvii–xxi.

———. *What Is World Literature?* Princeton, NJ: Princeton UP, 2003.

Edwards, Brent Hayes. *The Practice of Diaspora: Literature, Translation, and the Rise of Black Nationalism*. Cambridge, MA: Harvard UP, 2003.

Friedman, Susan Stanford. "Migrations, Diasporas, and Borders." *Introduction to Scholarship in Modern Languages and Literatures*. Ed. David Nicholls. New York: MLA, 2006. 899–941.

Greenblatt, Stephen. Preface. *The Norton Anthology of English Literature*. Vol. 1. Ed. M. H. Abrams. New York: Norton, 2003. xxxiii–xlii.

Greene, Roland. "Not Works but Networks: Colonial Worlds in Comparative Literature." *Comparative Literature in an Age of Globalization*. Ed. Haun Saussy. Baltimore, MD: Johns Hopkins UP, 2006. 212–23.

King, Bruce. Introduction. *The Internationalization of English Literature*. Oxford: Oxford UP, 2004. Vol. 13 in *The Oxford Literary History*. Gen. ed. Jonathan Bate. Oxford: Oxford UP, 2003. 1–13.

Mardorossian, Carine M. "From Literature of Exile to Migrant Literature." *Modern Language Studies* 32.3 (2003): 15–33.

Mason, Theodore O. "The African-American Anthology: Mapping the Territory, Taking the National Census, Building the Museum." *American Literary History* 10 (1998): 185–98.

McDonald, Peter D. "Ideas of the Book and Histories of Literature: After Theory?" *PMLA* 121 (2006): 214–28.

Moretti, Franco. "Conjectures on World Literature." *New Left Review* 1 (Jan.-Feb. 2000): 54–68.

The Norton Anthology of World Literature. Ed. Sarah Lawall. 6 vols. New York: Norton, 2003.

The Norton Anthology of World Masterpieces. Ed. Maynard Mack. Exp. ed. New York: Norton, 1997.

The Norton Anthology of Writing by Women. Ed. Susan Gubar and Sandra M. Gilbert. New York: Norton, 1985.

The Norton Anthology of Writing by Women: The Traditions in English. Ed. Susan Gubar and Sandra M. Gilbert. 2nd ed. New York: Norton, 1996.

Phillips, Caryl. *Dancing in the Dark*. New York: Knopf, 2005.

———. *A Distant Shore*. New York: Vintage, 2003.

———. *Extravagant Strangers: A Literature of Belonging*. New York: Vintage, 1997.

———. *Higher Ground: A Novel in Three Parts*. New York: Vintage, 1989.

———. *A New World Order: Essays*. New York: Vintage, 2001.

Price, Leah. "Elegant Extracts." *London Review of Books* 3 Feb. 2000: 26–28.

———. "The Tangible Page." *London Review of Books* 31 Oct. 2002: 36–39.

Saussy, Haun. "Exquisite Cadavers Stitched from Fresh Nightmares: Of Memes, Hives, and Selfish Genes." *Comparative Literature in an Age of Globalization*. Ed. Haun Saussy. Baltimore, MD: Johns Hopkins UP, 2006. 3–42.

Viswanathan, Gauri. "An Introduction: Uncommon Genealogies." *ARIEL: A Review of International English Literature* 31.1–2 (2000): 13–31.

Walkowitz, Rebecca L. "Shakespeare in Harlem: *The Norton Anthology*, 'Propaganda,' Langston Hughes." *Modern Language Quarterly* 60 (1999): 495–519.

———. "Unimaginable Largeness: Kazuo Ishiguro, Translation, and the New World Literature." Work in progress.

DAVID PEACE

an interview with

D A V I D   P E A C E

Conducted by Matthew Hart

Born in Ossett, West Yorkshire, in 1967, the English novelist
David Peace lives and writes in Tokyo. Peace first drew
attention as the author of the *Red Riding Quartet*, a
sequence of novels loosely based on the police investigation of Peter Sutcliffe, the serial rapist and murderer known as the
Yorkshire Ripper. The quartet, which was published in Britain and
the United States by the independent imprint Serpent's Tail, began
with *Nineteen Seventy Four* (1999), continued with *Nineteen Seventy
Seven* (2000) and *Nineteen Eighty* (2001), and came to its shocking
and disillusioned conclusion with *Nineteen Eighty Three* (2002). As
the titles suggest, each book is rooted in a particular year of a period
that included industrial unrest throughout the United Kingdom,
something tantamount to civil war in Northern Ireland, the looming
threat of neo-fascist thuggery, a Scottish devolution campaign, punk
rock, recession, the Falklands War, and the gradual emergence of
New Right conservatism as a political way of life. The Yorkshire
plotlines of each novel, which cross and recross throughout the
series, are thus played out against a larger historical screen, where
the local terrors of the Ripper murders join Peace's menacing critique of Thatcherite ideology, alive on the edges of *Nineteen Seventy
Four* but roaring in full voice by *Nineteen Eighty Three*, which claims
"there's no such thing as society" and unleashes xenophobic and
misogynist violence in the name of British individualism.

The *Red Riding Quartet* earned Peace a position on the 2003 edition of *Granta*'s infamous "Best of Young British Novelists" list.
Though some critics are turned off by the bleakness of Peace's

Contemporary Literature XLVII, 4   0010-7484; E-ISSN 1548-9949/06/0004-0547

fiction, the series was more often the subject of laudatory reviews that hailed its mixture of period detail and "Yorkshire *noir*" style. That Peace's style is easily parodied, like the *noir* of old, is evident in these sentences from *Nineteen Seventy Seven*: "Two of the police suddenly ran outside. The other two were looking at me. I had the bag in my hands." Yet despite the stock diction, Peace's prose is imbued with a *Weltschmerz* that is no mere put-on. Rarely sentimental, his novels ask how personal ethical rot legitimates wider social crimes. At the level of the sentence, this inquiry leads to a pattern of allusions and rhythmical associations between the individual and the social, the national and the international, as when a corrupt detective, one of three narrative voices in *Nineteen Eighty Three*, remembers the original sin of his career—a willfully botched investigation into the first of a series of child murders:

> July 1969:
> All across the UK, they're staring at the sun, waiting for the moon—
> *Ann Jones, Biafra, the Rivers of Blood,*
> *Brian Jones, Free Wales, the Dock Strikes,*
> *Marianne Faithfull and Harvey Smith,*
> *Ulster.*
> But here's the news today, oh boy—
> Memo from Maurice:
> *Jeanette Garland, 8, missing Castleford.*

Extracts like these help to show how Peace does much more than give a Yorkshire update to the hard-boiled style. The implication of this paratactic and allusive catalogue, taking in everything from the Beatles to late imperial violence, is that the murder of Jeanette Garland is just the latest "news" in a litany of crimes committed, covered up, and enabled by hard men with secret agendas. In this way, Peace's prose is notable more for its terse and profane formalism than for its subordination to the dictates of the crime genre, as it eschews the institutional realism of the police procedural or the guilty pleasures of the killer thriller for what, in our interview, he reveals to be inventively programmatic formal choices. Though it never lacks narrative energy, a novel like *Nineteen Eighty* sometimes resembles verse more than prose narrative: "A cross to keep the fear away—/ A cross to keep the fear—/ A cross to keep—/ A cross to—/ A cross." These are qualities that newspaper critics can't help but notice. Reviewing *Nineteen Eighty Three* for the *Daily Telegraph*, Simon Humphreys celebrates its "jump-cut prose that perfectly reflects the repetitious rhythms of everyday thought"; David Marley, writing in the *Independent on Sunday*, explains that "the mechanics of detection are almost incidental to the compellingly dark brand of historiography at [the tetralogy's] core."

With his most recent novel, *GB84* (Faber and Faber, 2004), winner of the 2004 James Tait Black Memorial Prize, Peace has exceeded the achievements of the quartet. The novel is a week-by-week history of the 1984–85 Miners' Strike, "a fiction," Peace calls it, "based on a fact." The title features an obvious allusion to George Orwell, whom Peace cites as an inspiration; but Eoin McNamee's *Guardian* commentary points out that it also riffs on Special Air Service founder David Stirling's right-wing paramilitary group, GB75. This combination is fitting, given Peace's interest in how the strike brings together the themes of hard-left unionism, far-right conspiracies, and the intersection of state violence with the forces of the free market. (Indeed, an intriguing plotline in *GB84* concerns an ex-soldier, "The Mechanic," who switches between roles as hired hand to domestic intelligence, anti-union paramilitary goon, and armed robber. Is the shadow state, Peace seems to ask, an early example of privatization?) As a novel, *GB84* combines elements of the political thriller with modernist experimentalism and a tradition of political polemic that stretches back through the Angry Young Men, to the condition of England novels of the nineteenth century, all the way to Milton's allegorical account of the *first* English Civil War. This is state-of-the-nation writing that connects the "occult history" of England to the worldwide defeat of the political left and the violent triumph of neoliberalism.

As Peace explains in our interview, his situation as a strongly regional and historical English novelist living in Japan gives him an unusual slant on the idea of "immigrant fictions." In the first place, his perspective is somewhat backward. He does not, like Samuel Selvon, write novels about immigrant acculturation in a foreign land; nor, like some reverse Kazuo Ishiguro, does he compose ironic dissections of Japanese social life. Until now, he has made a method of his apartness. While he researches and writes a novel like *GB84*,

Peace surrounds himself with the news and media of that time and place, almost to the exclusion of the here and now. This method can exact a toll on everyday life: he alludes in our conversation to the domestic strains caused by holing up with *GB84*; in an interview with New Zealand's *Dominion Post*, he reflected that his "marriage was lucky to survive it." But he also points out that his sort of émigré alienation is not just geographical or linguistic but *temporal*. To write *GB84* he had to travel in time as well as across continents, making imaginative connections with a cast of characters (many of them drawn from real life) who were as estranged from him in time as in their location in a place called "home." Though we tend to think of migration as primarily a geographic act, Peace reminds us that it is a temporal-spatial condition; in this sense it is a historical question and not simply a matter of resetting the Global Positioning System.

This is not to gainsay the cultural dislocation faced by the émigré writer; as Peace puts it, alluding to Gang of Four's song of that name, "at home he feels like a tourist." Nor is it to deny that migration can stir the imagination, trouble ethno-national identity, or license an existing disaffection from one's native spot. It often does all three at once. In Peace's novels, however, we see more of the first and last qualities than of anything suited to the literary-theoretical discourse of self-exile, cultural hybridity, or deterritorialization. After more than a decade in Japan, Peace is now hard at work on a Tokyo trilogy, which puts the sensibility honed on Yorkshire graft to work on the intersection of criminal enterprise and national renewal during the U.S. occupation of Japan. But while he is now more confident of his ability to tackle the history of his adopted country, Peace has not gone correspondingly gooey about Yorkshire. In a 2001 interview with Nicola Upson of the *New Statesman*, he suggests that his small hometown, just outside the increasingly black and Asian cities of Leeds and Bradford, was attractive to incomers "because it's predominantly white, which gives you an insight into [their] mentality." It's safe to say that living in Japan, and fathering two Anglo-Japanese children, has only heightened Peace's interest in the relationship between history's victims and a nation's insider-outsiders. Thinking about the nostalgia of the English abroad, Peace tells Upson: "[L]iving in Japan... you meet a lot of expatriates who say they miss their HP sauce. I've never felt that." He talks of the

English North as a place of "random violence that stalks the streets" and claims that he was "never fond" of many aspects of the region that his novels dissect.

And yet if *GB84* and the *Red Riding Quartet* are the works of an author who swims against the inrushing tide of Anglo-nostalgia, it's not true that Peace writes from a "postnational" perspective. Terry Eagleton's *Guardian* review hails *GB84* as "the literary equal" of the Miners' Strike, which Eagleton called "a showdown that history, or at least the shift to a post-industrial Britain, was going to stage sooner or later." That's putting things in aggressively world-historical terms. Closer to the truth is Andy Beckett's *London Review of Books* essay, which identifies an "intriguing tension between [*GB84*'s] desire, approaching that of a Thomas Pynchon novel, to set wheels turning within wheels, to present a political world of infinite complexity and, ultimately, chaos, and its desire for order, both organisational and moral." That desire for order is crucial, as is Beckett's observation that at the center of *GB84* we find "simply the strike itself: an enormous metaphor for the way Britain works." Beckett worries that "seeing politics in terms of such confrontations has its limits." It's a fair observation; but Peace's strike is no more or less a distortion than the "whodunit" logic of a detective novel—that is, the issue Beckett raises concerns literary genre as much as political strategy. The strike is the answer to the question posed by Conservative Prime Minister Ted Heath in the 1974 election, the question that lies within all Peace's novels: "Who governs Britain?" In 1974, the answer came back, "Not you, Ted"; in 1984, the state demanded a different answer. But for all his dissection of official violence, corruption, and indifference, Peace doesn't turn away from the state as the proper site for addressing questions of social justice. As he remarks in our interview, the July 2005 London bombings—in part the work of youths from West Yorkshire—raise concerns about the role of religious schools in a politics of "being" that degrades the sense of commonwealth embodied in institutions like the system of secular state education. These are curious words from a writer so disillusioned about the actual operation of political and judicial power. And yet this attitude continues even into the coming Tokyo trilogy, which concerns how a sovereign state deals with the messy business of military defeat, foreign occupation, and national renewal. Not all immigrant fictions remain so focused on the matter at hand—rooting narratives of cultural identity in messy bureaucratic histories and ethical questions of institutional address, thousands of miles away, years in the past.

I interviewed David Peace via e-mail between January 14 and February 22, 2006, sending questions one or two at a time. Although I invited him to reply as his schedule allowed, he was unfailingly prompt and generous with his time. I e-mailed a corrected text to Peace, and he reviewed my editorial changes, making only two superficial alterations to his answers. I also edited a few of my questions for length and clarity. Final modifications were made by the editors at *Contemporary Literature* to reflect house style. My thanks to David Peace for being such a great correspondent; to Mat Hollis for help with Faber; and to Rebecca Walkowitz for her interest in this project.

Q.   I'm writing this message from the middle of the United States. You're presumably reading it somewhere in Tokyo. That's a curious fact to remember when, late at night, I'm deep inside the universe of your novels, which paint an astonishingly rich and detailed portrait of Northern England in the 1970s and 1980s. What led you, a writer living and working in Japan, to zero in on the Yorkshire of your childhood and youth?

A.   *Nineteen Seventy Four*, my first published novel, was not by any means the first thing I had written. I had written continuously from about the age of eight—mainly poetry—and then from when I was about eighteen until I was twenty-five I worked on a very, very long novel (in excess of five hundred thousand words). This was initially while I was still living in Ossett, where I was born, but also then in Manchester, where I studied at the Polytechnic and was then unemployed. This book was rejected by every single British publisher in 1992. I then rapidly wrote a play, three screenplays, and another novel. Once again, all were eventually rejected. Following these rejections, the collapse of a relationship, and John Major's 1992 reelection, I fled to Istanbul and, for the first time since I was eight, I wrote nothing for the eighteen months I was there. I came to Tokyo in September of 1994 and, literally, I had a dream. That dream was *Nineteen Seventy Four*, which I then wrote out in exercise books in the tiny flat I then had. I didn't write it for publication. I wrote it for me. But after all the fictions I had written in the past, I wanted to write about where and when I was from, that time and that place—Yorkshire, 1970s to 1980s. This book and all the others, I think, are also a very transparent homage to the writers and books that I have equally kept coming back to: the Angry Young Men such as John Braine, Stan Barstow, Barry Hines, Alan Sillitoe, and David Storey; the detective fictions of both the U.S. and U.K.—for example Dashiell Hammett and James Ellroy, Derek Raymond and Ted Lewis; the postwar avant-gardes, if you like, of William Burroughs and J. G. Ballard; the poetry of, among many others, Dante, Eliot, Ted Hughes, and Tony Harrison; and, finally, there are Orwell and Graham Greene. Obviously, there are many, many more influences—as much from film, music, and painting—but to finally get back to the question, all these books (to me) are as much where and when I am from as the actual time and place. That said, I think the very distance of living so far from Yorkshire gave me the perspective and also the desire (homesickness? loneliness?) to try to write myself back there . . . and also because, even though I had lived there, there are so many, many things that I lived through that I still do not understand—such as the Ripper and the strike—so, I suppose, it was an attempt to get back there to find out what really went on there.

Q.   The focus of this issue of *Contemporary Literature* is "immigrant fictions," and one of the things that's interested me about you from the start is the intensely local and rooted quality of your novels combined with the matter-of-fact way that your biographies refer to your life as an ESL teacher in Turkey and, now, Japan. Do you think of yourself as a migrant? What language do you use to describe your life abroad?

A.   I live in the east end of Tokyo in a traditional, working-class area. There are Koreans and Chinese people living here but no other "Westerners" (that I know or have seen), so I obviously feel a certain "apartness." But I have been here twelve years, and I am married to a Japanese woman, and we have two children, and I do speak and read some Japanese and so can interact, and for the first time since I came here, I have begun to write about Tokyo (albeit in 1946). So I feel a lot less of a "migrant" or "exile" than I did before. To be very honest, though, it actually became a problem during the writing of *GB84*; I was spending every hour of every day in this small study completely absorbed and back in 1984–85, and it wasn't healthy for me or the people around me, and I began to think there was utterly no point being here, that I'd lived in this country for, at that time, almost ten years but had spent all that time back in Yorkshire in the 1970s and 1980s. It was a very, very low point. I then wrote *The Damned Utd*, which is about Brian Clough's forty-four days at Elland Road [the home stadium of Leeds United Football Club] in 1974 and will be published this August [2006] in the U.K. This was a short book, but once again it was about the same time, the same place, but perhaps it brought things full circle—I don't know because there are still two other "Yorkshire" books to come, "UK-DK" and "The Yorkshire Rippers." But now, since I began to research and write this book, "Tokyo Year Zero," I have felt much more connected to here, Tokyo.

Q.   It's great to hear about the new work. I'll come back to that later. For now, I'd like to hear more about the experience of writing *GB84* in that small room in Tokyo. For one thing, I'm interested in learning more about how you do the research that's required for historical writing. Are there resources you can use in Tokyo, or do you have to go back to the U.K.? And then there are the, for want of a better term, cultural elements of that history. I'm thinking about things like the snatches of pop music in all the novels—Bay City Rollers, Sex Pistols, Frankie; the quality of the voices that we hear—and not just the local accents and dialect phrases, but scene-setting elements like the radio news reporters in *Nineteen Seventy Four*; small details like Mrs. Hall's big golden sofa in *Nineteen Eighty*; the types of food people eat, the cars they drive, and so on. Much of what I admire in your work can be found in these details of a time and place that few writers have even bothered to remember, let alone put at the center of their imagined world. Is your ability to endow your prose with this level of local and historical detail remembered or learned? Is it a symptom of homesickness, or affection, or—as you intimated—a desire to understand the place that you come from?

A.   The most important decision I make early in the writing of each book is the number of chapters that the book will have (for example, twelve in *Nineteen Seventy Four* or forty-four in *The Damned Utd*). Once I have decided on the number of chapters (for whatever reason), I then choose the exact time frame during which the story will take place; for example, *Nineteen Seventy Seven* has twenty-five chapters—because of the Silver Jubilee [commemorating Queen Elizabeth II's twenty-five years on the throne]—beginning with an actual murder, so it runs from May 29, 1977, to June 18, 1977. Once these "logistics" are decided, I can then begin the research by going back to the newspapers for that specific period. This research for the *Red Riding Quartet*, *GB84*, and *The Damned Utd* was done in Tokyo at the National Diet Library, using the *Times*, which they have on microfilm. However for *GB84* and *The Damned Utd*, during my summer holidays back in West Yorkshire, I also used the local library in Wakefield for the *Yorkshire Post*. With *GB84*, I also spoke to/interviewed four people who had been involved in the strike itself, one of whom was a union official. During this phase, I am trying to place my own "memories" against what actually happened according to the papers—and it's not only the news and the politics but every single detail from the weather, to the TV, to the gold mine that you can find in the classified adverts and personal columns. At the same time as I am working at the library, I am also reading all the "factual" books on the particular subject. On the strike, for example, most were out of print, but thanks to the Internet I was able to build up a huge library of books, and also a lot of oral testimonies that helped with the striking miners' voices in the columns. Anyway, once I have these basic notes and photocopies, I don't need to leave the room anymore; I can just hole myself up here, submerged in the particular period I have chosen. I also have the music from the time playing, and I read the books of that period and watch the films. I think this "cultural" research helps with the detail of the language, which has changed and continues to change dramatically. Most people who have lived abroad for some time comment on the difficulty of understanding jokes, soap operas, and kids' slang when they do return "home"—"at home he feels like a tourist." Music, books, and film are particularly helpful in bringing back the language of a time and a place, the particular metaphors and references that were commonplace then. I also think the music—like the radio bulletins—adds another layer, or depth maybe, to the text. You do have to be very, very careful though and not burden the story with references. This is what I call the Blue Nun syndrome: nobody in 1974 asked anybody if they would like a glass of Blue Nun; they asked them if they would like a glass of wine. It's easy to get it wrong, and the only way to avoid it is to actually be as far back in that time and place as you can possibly be, so you see it, hear it, smell it, and taste it—because finally, and most importantly, all these "learned" pieces of research will hopefully act as triggers or prompts so my own memories and impressions of that time and that place are reawakened (the big golden sofas, etcetera). Of course, all this went out the window with "Tokyo Year Zero."

Q.   I see what you mean about Blue Nun syndrome. I'm teaching some poems by Hugh MacDiarmid at the moment, and one of the things that people found scandalous about his poetry was his anachronistic use of phrases dug up from dictionaries and stuck next to modern idioms. But what you're talking about is different, the brand reference standing in for the quality of the experience. That *would* be a danger for a historical writer, though it seems like it could lead in different directions—that's to say, to an ironic distance from the past, or to pop cultural nostalgia. Do you think the generally violent and disillusioned tone of your writing has something to do with how you avoid these problems? It's hard to be nostalgic about a mounted police charge, tough to be ironic about murder. Or is this down to a simpler kind of discipline, where you just condition yourself to write "white wine" instead of "Blue Nun"?

A.   Not to cop out here, but I think it's a combination of the two. As you say, it's not possible—or it shouldn't be possible—to feel nostalgic about the time and the place I was writing about and the things that went on there. I very deliberately and consciously, from *Nineteen Seventy Seven* onwards, tried to take the "entertainment" out of my crime writing. There is little humor and no irony in it. As I was writing the books, because I live in Tokyo, I was unaware that there was a booming nostalgia industry in the U.K. in the late 1990s, with TV programs devoted to the particular music and fashion of certain years—such as "I Love 1974." Even though I was, at the time, ignorant of this trend, I did not want to write a kind of "glam rock and flares" history of the 1970s, and I think what I wrote instead was "I Hate 1974." So as I say, I think it is a combination of the subject matter itself and self-discipline.

Q. Let's talk about the new books. I've got some idea, at least, from the superficial evidence of the titles, how *The Damned Utd* and "The Yorkshire Rippers" will connect to the other Yorkshire novels, but what about "UK-DK"? (I've been trying to guess what the "DK" refers to. Disunited Kingdom? Dead Kennedys? Delightful Keighley?) The initials make me think it's part of another series, like the *Red Riding Quartet*, only this time to be read with *GB84*.

A. The "DK" is just a play on "decay," and the combination "UK-DK" was actually used on an old eighties hard-core punk compilation, but it's always stuck with me. "UK-DK" is (structurally and provisionally, at least) based on *Paradise Lost* but set between 1967 and 1979, and it charts the rise of Thatcher's right, as well as the decline of the left. There is quite a bit about Ireland, too. It was once intended to be a sort of prequel to *GB84*, and there may yet be some overlap. However, *GB84*, *The Damned Utd*, "UK-DK," and "The Yorkshire Rippers" will all form a very, very loose quartet of books about Britain from 1967 to 1985 and will be linked by the opening "Arguments," as in *GB84*.

Q. And what about "Tokyo Year Zero"? You've said that your normal research methods went out the window when you started writing about postwar Japan. Is that because there's no way you can "remember" the stuff you're writing about, given that it's so far removed from your historical and geographical "home"?

A. Yes, for me, it's obviously a very different experience writing about a time and a place I didn't live through—but now, in the final months of writing the book, I do feel "there" and I do "remember."

Q. But what is it about Japan in 1946 that's stirred you to write about it now?

A. Having lived here for almost twelve years, being married to a Japanese woman, and now having two children here, I've become increasingly obsessed with the history of Tokyo, particularly in the twentieth century. For example, the area in which we live in the east end of Tokyo was bombed and burnt flat and completely destroyed, this only twenty–odd years after the 1923 Great Kanto Earthquake had done the same thing. I wanted to know much more about this place, the people who lived and died here and who, I feel, still haunt it. I also wanted to understand how Japan, and particularly Tokyo, was able to rebuild itself so quickly after the war. Originally, I envisaged a quartet stretching from 1946 to 1964 (and the final rehabilitation of the Tokyo Olympics), but I found so much in just the American Occupation that, for now, it is a trilogy dealing only with the Occupation years. And as with the *Red Riding Quartet*, I think crime, true crime—and its social and political consequences—is the key to unlock the hidden history. Then the final, final push to write, and to write "Tokyo Year Zero" now—because it had been off and on for a number of years—was Iraq and another occupation.

Q.   What are the correspondences, do you think, between Japan in 1946 and the current occupation in Iraq? I've just been reading about the tremendous amounts of money that have gone missing in Iraq over the last few years—some of it just wasted, some of it flown out of the country into the accounts of this or that Iraqi minister, and some of it gone to pay mortgages or buy cars in Kentucky or New York. It's all very redolent of the institutional corruption you document in *GB84* or *Nineteen Eighty Three*. I suppose this gets to the question of what you call "true crime." Why is crime the lever that opens up unknown histories?

A.   Particularly in the run-up to the invasion and subsequent occupation of Iraq, many figures in the U.S. government referred to Japan as a model of what a successful occupation could do for a defeated and then occupied country. And, as I say, such comments did lead me to think a lot about the whole concept of occupiers and occupied, the victors and the vanquished. The present trial of Saddam also has some interesting echoes of the Tokyo Trials of 1946. But you only have to turn on the TV news any night of the week to see that aside from it being an American occupation of a foreign, sovereign nation defeated in war, there are few other constructive parallels in terms of the actual administration of the two occupations, Japan and Iraq, beginning with the fact that in postwar Japan there never, contentiously, was a "regime change."

    The few English-language fictions that have been written about the U.S. occupation of Japan have been written from the point of view of the occupier. With "Tokyo Year Zero," I wanted to (try to) write from the point of view of the defeated and occupied.

Q.   So is your interest in crime—and in crime fiction—pragmatic? I mean, are you in it for the genre itself, or for what it can do in political or historical terms? Or is that just a false antithesis?

A.   It's both. I was, as a child, drawn to the Sherlock Holmes novels and then Edgar Allan Poe and Agatha Christie, Georges Simenon and Raymond Chandler, etcetera, until finally I arrived at writers such as Walter Mosley and James Ellroy. So I have always had a deep interest in the mystery/crime novel as, if you like, my "genre of choice"—as opposed, say, to science fiction. But even as a child— and this is obviously with a great, great deal of hindsight—I was reading Sherlock Holmes, and, at the same time, I was trying to transpose that kind of narrative order onto the real life "true crime" that I could see around me, namely the Yorkshire Ripper case. As a ten-year-old child my instinct was to try to solve it, to try to catch the Ripper. Failing that I suppose I was then driven to writing about it. So even my very earliest writing was in the style of that genre and it has obviously continued.

But as I have said before, because crimes happen to actual people in actual places at actual times in history, the crime novel has the opportunity to ask why such crimes happen to those certain people at certain places in certain times. I would argue that not only does crime fiction have the opportunity, it also has the *obligation*. Because if you refuse the obligation to examine the causes and consequences of crime—whatever they may be—you are simply exploiting for personal financial gain and entertainment the deaths of other people (even if you fictionalize those deaths, because murder is a fact). This is one reason why I am ashamed of *Nineteen Seventy Four*, which I think simply wallows in the viciousness of the crimes it describes, and I hope, in some ways, *Nineteen Eighty Three* rights/writes that wrong. So I'm not saying any of this from the moral high ground because it wasn't until I wrote *Nineteen Seventy Seven*, which is based on the "true crimes" of the Yorkshire Ripper, that I really began to understand this opportunity and obligation myself. And, I must also say, while I came upon this sense of

obligation independently, I have since found that many other people—notably Orwell, Benjamin, and Adorno—had already said
much the same thing in more eloquent ways.

All that said, the essence of the crime genre is mystery—that is,
who did what and to whom and why—and that adds a very, very
powerful narrative drive to any piece of writing. So as I say, it is
both—the genre itself and what it can do/say/be in political or historical terms—and that is demonstrated in, I hope, the striking contrast between *Tokyo Year Zero* and *Nineteen Seventy Four*, written ten
years apart.

Q.   I'm eager to hear more about the contrast you draw between
Nineteen Seventy Four and *Nineteen Eighty Three*. I remember, when
I first read *Nineteen Seventy Four*, that I found the ending truly shocking. I'm thinking less about the scene in the Strafford pub, where
Eddie Dunford shoots Derek Box and the two policemen, than about
Eddie's descent into the disused mining shaft, where he finds the
child murderer, George Marsh, and into which he shoves Marsh's
wife. That incident was so strange, so occult—like something out of
Dante. And the righteousness of Eddie's rage was flat-out unnerving,
especially when he condemned Mrs. Marsh (who was far from innocent but something less than entirely culpable) to such a lonely death.
Thinking about scenes like that, I can see why you draw a line
between *Nineteen Seventy Four* and the later novels. But this isn't just a
question of subject matter; such scenes recur in the later novels, and
the consequences of Eddie's revenge redound throughout the later
parts of the story, like a kind of hidden apocalypse. And that
Dantesque quality sets the tone for the "baroque" tendencies of your
other novels, which read more and more like a kind of psychogeogra-
phy of the North—or to borrow a phrase from *Nineteen Eighty Three*,
an attempt to reckon with the "ghost bloodied old city of Leodis."
I have a sense that, right from the start, you've tried to depict the historical present as riddled with the ghosts of past violence—and I'm
thinking as much of Neil's fragmentary visions of English Civil War
battlefields in *GB84* as I am about, say, the obviously occult plotline
surrounding the Reverend Laws in the *Red Riding Quartet*.

It's time I formulated all this into a question. I just reread BJ's last
speech in *Nineteen Eighty Three*, where he says "hello" from all the

victims of the quartet but then moves into a consciously political register: "from Maggie Thatcher and Michael Foot, from SWP and National Front, IRA and UDA, from M & S and C & A, Tesco and Co-op and every shopping centre in this wounded, wounded land, from shit they sell and shit we buy, my old mum and Queen sodding Mum." Bits of that sound like BJ, but bits sound like the novel's social conscience writ large. Then, at the very end, John Piggot's suicide is interwoven with Thatcher's second election victory speech— "Where there is discord, may we bring harmony"—which you interrupt with a repeated phrase, "The Hate." Would it be right to say that this kind of political framing of violence is the way you try to avoid the pornographic possibilities of crime fiction?

A.   In a word, yes—but I think the *Red Riding Quartet* also wrestles with a very fundamental question about crime and society, and that is, for want of a better phrase, the nature versus nurture argument. The earliest motive I had for going on from *Nineteen Seventy Four* to write about the Yorkshire Ripper in *Nineteen Seventy Seven* and *Nineteen Eighty* was the basic question, as I said earlier, of why these crimes happened in this place at this time to these people. And by extension, to what extent are/were the people of Yorkshire, and the North in general, culpable in these crimes? What role, for example, did the language or the landscape of Yorkshire in the 1970s play in these crimes, similarly, the political and economic policies of the time? Anything, in short, that could answer the question, "Why the Yorkshire Ripper and not, say, the Cornish Ripper?" Then again, might it simply be—and this goes against my own basic political instincts—that Yorkshire just happened to be, by chance, the unlucky place where a very evil man was born and lived? These are the questions which I feel are at the very heart of the quartet and, I hope, stop the books from simply trafficking in human misery for the sake of entertainment and money.

Q.   It's fascinating what you say about this sense of local responsibility or character. As you know better than I do, Yorkshire has an unusual relationship to the rest of England and, as you show in *Nineteen Eighty*, even to other parts of the North, like Lancashire or Greater Manchester. As far back as the medieval struggle between the bishoprics of York and Canterbury, there's been a sense that

Yorkshire is somehow exceptional, a law unto itself—and this comes out very strongly in, say, your depictions of the "Socialist Republic of Yorkshire" in *GB84*. In the meantime, you've talked about how some of your new work deals with Ireland. How so? And does this come from a desire to escape from the realm of "Yorkshire nationalism"?

A.   I do think there is a tangible feeling of "apartness" in Yorkshire that is most manifest in the strong and "infamous" sense of Yorkshire pride. *The Damned Utd*, being set in the Leeds United Football Club, touches on this. How this all came to be is something, tentatively, I also hope to address in "The Yorkshire Rippers" (but the content and style of this book has changed, and continues to change, on an almost daily basis). But particular periods of Yorkshire history do fascinate me—the Harrowing of the North, when the Norman Army perpetrated what we would now describe as a "genocide" on the people of Yorkshire and the land, and also the Wars of the Roses. Historically, Yorkshire is the place of the defeated, subjugated, and ultimately neglected people of England (and this then might be a link to my interest in Ireland and occupied Japan . . . ?).

As an aside, immediately after the 7/7 London bombs, I was contacted by a number of journalists from France and Italy, who having read the *Red Riding Quartet* wanted to know what my feelings were about the "alleged" bombers and their Yorkshire connections. And if these four men are proven to be the bombers, it may well be worth examining the role "Yorkshire apartness" has had in alienating an already alienated minority. As a further aside, this would be my main argument against the so-called faith schools so popular now in the places where I grew up, which I believe serve only to further alienate and divide. Finally, I'll end this rant just by saying that I do believe the first basic step to end such apartness, such division, is with a strictly secular education system.

Having written the above, I can now see how this all links back to my interest in Northern Ireland—so thank you for helping me articulate something that was previously only felt and not formed!

The war in Northern Ireland, or to use that quaint term, "the Troubles," was something that formed a permanent backdrop to the lives of anyone living or growing up in the United Kingdom or the Republic of Ireland from the late 1960s onwards (and, obviously, for older generations this was nothing new). For me, along with the Yorkshire Ripper and the Miners' Strike of 1984–85, it was another shadow, another dark figure glimpsed out of the corner of your eye as a child: it was always there, but it wasn't; we were at war, but we weren't (like now, like always?). Words, images, names, and places come back constantly: the Shankill Butchers, the faces of the Hunger Strikers, the Miami Showband, and South Armagh. The news from Northern Ireland echoes throughout the *Red Riding Quartet* and also *GB84*.

For me, the two best pieces of writing in the last ten years have been *Lost Lives*, by David McKittrick, Seamus Kelters, Brian Feeney, and Chris Thornton, which is a litany of every single life lost during "the Troubles," and *The Ultras*, by Eoin McNamee, which is a novel (though "poem" would perhaps do it more justice) about the life and death of a British soldier, Robert Nairac, in Northern Ireland. To this list I would also add two films, Alan Clarke's *Elephant* and Ken Loach's *Hidden Agenda*.

In "UK-DK," as I say, I hope to bring Northern Ireland out of the shadows of my other books and set it center stage. But I'm not sure it will be much of an escape . . .

Q.   That strangeness about Northern Ireland was very palpable when I was growing up. I remember being on holiday in Bournemouth during a Tory party conference (this wasn't long after the Brighton bombing, which you feature in *GB84*). Nothing happened, but the council came round, sealing up the manhole covers with tar. Then there was an arms cache found in Macclesfield Forest. And then the 1993 IRA campaign included the bomb in Warrington, just down from my dad's work, which went off in a pedestrian shopping precinct and killed two boys. I'm absolutely not trying to compare my experience to that of a kid from Derry or Belfast; that would be obscene. But you're right—however unreal the Troubles felt, the armed groups did bring the sectarian and political battles of Northern Ireland into the "homeland" (to use the current objectionable parlance), reminding us that, however much we English like to think of the violence as "their" problem, it has its roots in our own imperial ambitions. Either way, do you think you're unusual in your desire to bring Northern Ireland center stage in your novels? For understandable reasons, this has largely been the province of Irish writers. And

yet I sometimes think that English writers depend on the strong contemporary Irish identity (which is surely good in itself) as a way of
letting themselves off the hook about the continuing presence
of Ireland and the Irish in "English" history. The same could be said of
Scotland—that the English can safely "devolve" Celtic history and
politics to the Celts. Do you agree that this is a problem?

A.   I don't actually think it is "obscene" for you to compare your
experience of "the Troubles" to that of a kid growing up in Northern
Ireland. They are simply different. But this, I think, may also be one
of the root causes of what you could call the abdication of modern
English fiction from tackling certain subjects—this obsession, even in
fiction, with the "real," this notion that, somehow, unless you "own"
a place, a time, a memory, or are "from" a particular ethnic group,
"of" a certain sexuality, etcetera, you cannot, or should not, write
about it. And here, as always, I'm as guilty as anyone; up until now,
I have written about times and places in which I grew up, and publishers and journalists make much of my "personal" connection to
the things I write about (as do I). But my mother wasn't a victim of
the Yorkshire Ripper, and my father wasn't a striking miner, and
I don't "own" these times and these places. Even in approaching the
Tokyo trilogy, I have sought to establish my personal connection
(through my wife, my children, where we live) to what I am writing
about. All that said, I do think, for fiction to mean anything, there has
to be an emotional connection—a stake, if you like—between the
subject and the writer; what you are writing about must "matter" to
you; you have to write it out of a compulsion. But that compulsion,
that connection, can be imagined, surely, or gained through empathy.
   Anyway, the point I'm trying (laboring) to make is that this sense
that you have to have somehow "lived through" something or, better yet, "be of it"—Irish, for example—to write about it might then
account for the lack of "English" books about Northern Ireland.
Though, that said, there are a number, *This Human Season*, by Louise
Dean, for example. Last summer, in Edinburgh, I did a reading with
Louise Dean, and because she is a young English woman, living in
the south of France, and not Irish, she got a lot of questions from the
audience about "her right" to write about Northern Ireland, with
the insinuation that she was somehow "exploiting" "the Troubles."

If there were more time, more space, I think there is a lot more to discuss about "rights" and "ownership" of fictions and facts in a capitalist, consumer society, the things that can and cannot be written
about, and who can and cannot write them. I suppose this goes back
to what I was saying earlier about division, that somehow we are
encouraged, forced even, to stay (and think and write) within our
own little boxes. Sadly.

Q. Well, this question of ownership and identity seems to bring us
back to the earliest part of our discussion, where we talked about the
idea of "immigrant fictions" and your position vis-à-vis Yorkshire
and Tokyo. So I want to give you time and space to have your say
about whether or how one can "own" a narrative. On the one hand, it
does seem like a powerful piece of consumer fantasy—the idea, that
is, that one can privatize a story about a time or place. On the other
hand (and I don't happen to agree with this, but it's an argument
I used to hear a lot), you could say that such ownership is all we
have left—that is, in a world without a sense of the commonwealth,
it's only in assertions of identity, or "being of," that a reader or writer
can assert their sense of belonging to some greater collectivity.
What do you think of that kind of defense? And—here's the obvious
question—does your hostility to the notion of cultural ownership
have something to do with your location in an imaginative space
somewhere between Asia and Europe?

A. To read John Braine, Stan Barstow, David Storey, Alan Sillitoe,
and Barry Hines, and later Ted Lewis and Derek Raymond, was
very empowering and inspiring for me—reading about places
I knew in language I heard and spoke every day. But identification,
or recognition, is different from ownership. I see these writers as the
keys to the cell door, not the lock. They are keys because they led me
to other writers and other times and other places and ultimately to
this room in Tokyo; but it wasn't until I left Yorkshire and England
that I was able to write about the times and places I grew up in, and
I think it is important to stress, when we talk about "immigrant
fictions," that it is as much a matter of time as it is of place, and that
the writer is trying to bring the places and the times he or she writes
about "home" to the reader. Whether or not the writer succeeds is

not a matter of ownership or rights, or race or class, but the writing itself: it is the writing that brings the words "home."

Q.   Let's return, then, to the way your writing deals with the theme of belonging. In particular, I'd like to hear about two characters in *GB84*: Terry Martin, the chief executive of the National Union of Mineworkers, and Stephen Sweet ("the Jew"), a businessman and Thatcher disciple who works as a kind of guerilla arm of the government and secret services to undermine the strike. Both of these characters are riddled with self-doubt and the fear of not belonging. Sweet is the victim of anti-Semitism and is clearly marked as a parvenu, even as he ruthlessly exploits, for instance, popular British class prejudices. And Terry Martin desperately wants to be loved and trusted, even as he is ostracized because he's a professional unionist and not the native son of a Yorkshire miner. Why did you decide to structure so much of the action around these insider-outsiders? And did you get any abuse for your use of the epithet "the Jew"?

A.   From the outset, I wanted *GB84* to tell the whole "occult history" of the Miners' Strike—from top to bottom, from left to right— because the strike affected so many, many people, both directly and indirectly. And so I knew the book would need many different characters and many different narrative voices to encompass so many different perspectives. As I researched and read about the strike, real characters obviously acted as inspirations for fictional ones. Terry Martin and Stephen Sweet were based on very real people and were also characters that allowed me to write about the "top" of the strike and, at the same time, explore a number of recurrent themes—as you say, the insider-outsider (aren't we all?), which relates directly to the central theme of the book, which is the division and almost state of civil war that existed not only between the government and the union but within the government and the union themselves. This was why I was so adamant about using "the Jew" as an epithet; obviously, though, it was not something I, or Faber, did lightly. However, one thing that has always interested me is the way in which Thatcher rose to power in a strange coalition between the very far right (the "private armies" of 1974, for example, which will come in again in "UK-DK") and self-made Jewish businessmen. Thatcher surrounded herself, both in opposition and government, with many Jewish advisers and ministers and often held up "Jewish self-help" as a preferable alternative to welfare-state dependence, for example.

In the text of *GB84*, Stephen Sweet appears as "the Jew" only in the Neil Fontaine narrative sections. Neil Fontaine is from a military-—security-service background and has spent time in far-right organizations. Now, for a number of reasons, he is a driver-cum-bagman for Sweet. Neil's anti-Semitism mirrors and highlights the divisions even within the right in their response to the strike. The constant refrain of "the Jew" in the text, hopefully, makes the reader uncomfortable. (At one point, my editor at Faber did wonder about using a more obviously racist epithet—"Yid" or some such thing—but I was against this, as I think there is a certain ambiguity in Neil's usage that, again, reflects the ambiguity of his relationship with Sweet; in the end, Neil, I think, pities him.) Because these sections are all written in the third person, there were (thankfully) questions about the use of the epithet from journalists and readers, but having been given the reasons I have just outlined, people seem to accept the use of the epithet. And, ultimately, while this narrative is in the third person, it is highly subjective; it is only Neil who refers to Sweet as "the Jew." However, in the forthcoming French translation of *GB84*, the Neil Fontaine narrative voice has been switched to the first person for "the avoidance of doubt."

Q.   Did you try to fight that decision?

A.   No, not at all, because I had originally had the Neil Fontaine narrative—and all the narratives—in the first person anyway. However, from past experience with *Nineteen Seventy Seven*, I thought it was probably a bit much to have six first-person narratives in one book. Also, with my French publishers, Rivages & Payot, I have had the same editor and translator since *Nineteen Seventy Four*. They have been very supportive of me, and I do trust their judgment. The cultural and historical context of anti-Semitism within France is, of course, different from that in the U.K.—which is not to say better or worse, just different—and there was a very real concern on the part of my French publisher that in France attention would be directed solely at any perceived anti-Semitism in the book rather than at the strike itself, which is, of course, the reason I wrote the book in the first place.

Q. We're coming to the end of this e-mail conversation, so I want to try and tie up a number of strands of our discussion. One of the things we haven't talked about is the reaction to your recent move from Serpent's Tail to Faber and Faber. I could imagine, if one hadn't actually read the *Red Riding Quartet* and just knew about you as a writer of crime fiction, that one might see *GB84* as "David Peace goes literary"—I mean, it's put out by one of the leading publishers of literary fiction, it juggles six different narrative points of view, it mixes the historical and the occult, it's unembarrassed about its political feelings . . . Have you encountered this kind of prejudice in the wake of *GB84*?

A. I know it seems recent in terms of *GB84* being my last published book and my first for Faber and Faber, but the move itself from Serpent's Tail actually took place five years ago. Initially there were a few such questions, particularly at readings rather than from journalists, about "selling out." But I think for most people who have read the quartet, *GB84* is a natural continuation—in terms of both style and content—in the same way that the previous four books built upon each other. Also, from quite a time ago, I have known the first eleven books I would write, so it's never been the case that I have been influenced or pressured by either my agent or publisher to write anything else or to change style. Thankfully, to date, everyone has been happy to publish what I wanted to write, and there have been no attempts to make me write a children's book. Ultimately, though, I do feel I have been very, very fortunate in my publishers and editors—Pete Ayrton and John Williams at Serpent's Tail, Jon Riley and Lee Brackstone at Faber, and now Sonny Mehta at Knopf—and most of all my agent, William Miller. I am a lucky man.

Q. Lucky or not, it does seem unusual to have those eleven novels planned out so far in advance. That must make you a publisher's dream—no more sleepless nights worrying about where the next book's coming from. I'd love to hear more about how or why you tend to think in such long patterns: the *Red Riding Quartet*, the quartet that begins with *GB84*, and now the Tokyo trilogy. There's something modernist about your interest not just in the long-wave structures between books, but also in the local structure of individual books—for instance, the twenty-five chapters in *Nineteen Seventy Seven*, representing the twenty-five years of the Queen's reign. I'm assuming that you find this programmatic sort of approach very enabling. Why is that?

A.   Well, it is only once I have designed the individual structure of each book—be it the number of chapters or the number of paragraphs within each chapter—that I then feel confident enough to experiment with the language itself, with tense, with grammar, with narrative perspective, and so on. Having the structure gives me that freedom. Similarly, over a quartet or trilogy of books, once that structure is in place, I then feel there is freedom for me to develop characters and explore themes more deeply, making films rather than taking snapshots, getting beneath the surface of times, places, and people, mining the occult.

But in terms of planning out eleven books, I don't think I am actually that unusual because, to some extent, it is the same book, just as, with the artists I really admire—such as Francis Bacon, Paul Celan, Terayama Shuji, or The Fall—it is the same piece of "art" over and over. For me, it is this obsessive pursuit of perfection that makes the "art," the journey, affecting, but that obsession requires structure, discipline, and commitment. It's not "nine to five" or just "when you feel like it": it is day in, day out, over and over, again and again, until there's nothing left.

Anyway, it's not just the structure of each individual book, or only the plan for these eleven books: it is also the way I live my life. Each hour, each day is very, very structured to the point that I can tell you now that on, for example, February 22, 2010, I will be working on "Tokyo Regained," the last of the Tokyo trilogy. The structures in the books and in my life give me discipline, and the discipline, in the books and in my life, allows me to write; as Flaubert said, "Be regular and ordinary in your habits, like a petty bourgeois, so you may be violent and original in your work."

W E N   J I N

Transnational Criticism and Asian Immigrant Literature in the U.S.: Reading Yan Geling's *Fusang* and Its English Translation

Although the name Yan Geling may mean very little to U.S.–based academics, Yan is often commended by scholars in mainland China and Taiwan as one of the most important Chinese-language authors in the United States.[1] Before she came to the U.S. as a student in 1989, Yan had published three novels in mainland China, where she was born in the late 1950s. During and after her study at Columbia College in Chicago for an MFA in fiction writing, she continued to write in Chinese, publishing award-winning short stories, novellas, and novels in the U.S., Taiwan, and mainland China.[2] In 1995, she won a *United Daily News* Best Novel award for *Fusang*, a historical novel set in nineteenth-century San Francisco's Chinatown.[3] The titular figure, Fusang, is abducted from a village in Guangzhou

I thank Paul Breslin, for his perceptive readings of several drafts of this essay, and Dorothy Wang, Betsy Erkkila, and Thomas W. Kim, who provided welcome criticism and advice. I also wish to thank Rebecca Walkowitz and the anonymous readers at *Contemporary Literature* for their encouraging and constructive comments.

1. In transcribing Chinese names, I follow the Chinese custom of placing family names before given names, except in cases where the Americanized form, with the given name preceding the family name, has become the norm in print.

2. Yan is also known as the scriptwriter for the 1992 film *Shao Nu Xiao Yu* (A Young Woman Named Xiao Yu), based on her novella of the same title, and as a co-scriptwriter (with Joan Chen) for the 1998 film *Xiuxiu, the Sent-down Girl*. Another film project, based on her novel *Fusang*, is in the offing.

3. *United Daily News* literary prizes are among the most prestigious awards for Taiwanese writers and Chinese-language writers around the world. Authors in mainland China have also started to compete for the award.

Contemporary Literature XLVII, 4   0010-7484; E-ISSN 1548-9949/06/0004-0570

(Canton), brought to the U.S. on a cargo ship, and sold into a Chinatown brothel. As a Chinatown prostitute, Fusang draws pleasure from all of her sexual encounters without becoming attached to any one of her johns. Presented as an enigma, Fusang solicits competing interpretations from both the various characters in the novel and its diverse audiences. In 2001, the novel was translated into English as *The Lost Daughter of Happiness* and published simultaneously in the United States and Great Britain.[4]

Written in Chinese about the transnational traffic in Chinese women and nineteenth-century Chinatown life, *Fusang* provides a prime example of how Chinese immigrant authors in the United States destabilize nation-based conceptions of literary genealogy, such as "American" literature and "Chinese" literature. As it has been translated into English and read in the country where most of the plot is set, the novel also resists literary categories based on language, such as "Sinophone" and "Anglophone" literature.[5] *Fusang*, like many Chinese-language novels written in the contemporary U.S., is best accounted for by such hybrid categories as Asian American/immigrant literature or Asian diasporic literature, which, though beholden in many ways to nation-based and language-based modes of classifying literary texts, foreground how writings by Asians in the U.S. cross national, racial, and ethnic borders, as material objects as well as aesthetic forms.[6] How do critics, then, interpret an Asian immigrant or diasporic text like *Fusang* in light of, but without being constrained by, the various critical contexts it inevitably travels across? What reading strategies can they use to lay bare as well as intervene in the political underpinnings of these critical contexts? This essay attempts to provide preliminary answers to these questions by considering, in relation to each other,

---

4. According to the translator, Cathy Silber, the English title was suggested by Will Schwalbe, the editor for the translation at Hyperion.

5. According to Emily Gould, an assistant editor at Hyperion, the publisher has sold roughly four thousand copies of *The Lost Daughter of Happiness* in hardcover and another four thousand copies in paperback.

6. If Asian American/immigrant literature still remains differentiated from Asian diasporic literature (the former historically implies a U.S. domestic focus, the latter an investment in transnational movements), the distinction between the two has been questioned frequently since the mid-1990s.

the characterization of the titular figure Fusang, the differences between the Chinese original and its English translation, and the critical responses the novel has generated in different contexts.

In examining the transnational circulation of *Fusang*, this essay is indebted to and in dialogue with scholars who have investigated how Asian American texts give rise to diverse critical discourses in different geographical contexts. Sau-ling Wong's important essays on Maxine Hong Kingston and Nie Hualing have illuminated the ways in which the academic politics of Taiwan and of mainland China shape the criticism of Chinese American texts there. Other scholars have discussed the American or overseas reception of U.S. ethnic authors, such as Filipino American writer Jessica Hagedorn, Pakistani diasporic writer Bapsi Sidhwa, and Korean American/ immigrant writers Chang-rae Lee and Jay San Rhee.[7] My essay uses the example of Yan Geling's novel to further complicate this emerging transnational mode of criticism in two important ways.

First, this essay draws attention to the textual alterations that accompany the novel's entry into different contexts. The English translator of *Fusang* and Yan's editor at Hyperion, for example, agreed to excise or shorten many passages in the Chinese novel, as well as to make the translation read, in the words of Cathy Silber, the translator, more like an "English-language novel."[8] Passages that are removed from or abbreviated in the English translation, most of which contain descriptions (from the narrator's or other characters' perspectives) of Fusang's unruly sexuality, become a kind of constitutive absence that signals the logic of U.S. liberal multiculturalism. Not coincidentally, these passages also play a crucial role, by being either highlighted or ignored, in consolidating mainland Chinese critics' readings of the novel. I give a central position to these passages in my essay as a way of illustrating how translation mediates the transnational circulation of Asian immigrant literature.

---

7. See Lee 75–82, Zaman 210–11, and Kichung Kim 270.

8. Silber informed me during our telephone interview that she was often at odds with Will Schwalbe, the editor for the translation, as to what changes were necessary, although she agreed with him on some alterations that would make the translation read more like an "English-language novel."

Second, while existing scholarship on the global circulation of Asian immigrant and diasporic literature often focuses on a single national context, this essay juxtaposes and compares the different readings of Yan's novel produced in different contexts (mainland China and the United States in particular). It focuses on the divergences as well as confluences between the various interpretations of the central character, Fusang, who seems to accommodate the sexual violence inflicted on her body by embracing and drawing delight from it. Anglo-American critics, with access only to the sanitized, incomplete version of the novel in English, have largely construed Fusang as the proverbial "inscrutable Oriental," even as they argue that the novel subverts the Orientalist imagination of Asian women. In mainland China, Fusang's accommodation of sexual and social violence, presented in an intensified version in the Chinese original, has sparked anxiety in critics mindful of China's colonial and neo-colonial subordination to the West, especially the United States. While the novel is criticized by some for its complicity with the Western feminization of Chinese culture, it is praised by others as the embodiment of a kind of feminine resilience that enabled China to hold its own against its Western enemies during the twentieth century. The interpretations of Fusang generated in the U.S. and in mainland China reveal the operation of two interrelated nationalisms. The U.S. critics' reading of Fusang as opaque is infused with a version of "multicultural nationalism," which solidifies the ideal of a progressive, unified U.S. national culture by simultaneously critiquing and perpetuating the nation's history of racial exclusion.[9] The Chinese critics' anxiety about the novel's possible co-optation by U.S. Orientalism registers a rising tide of Chinese nationalism that constructs itself against U.S. neo-imperialism and the historical legacy of European colonialism. An interrogation of the different critical discourses surrounding the character Fusang helps lay bare the tensions and linkages between these two kinds of nationalisms.

---

9. Minoo Moallem and Iain A. Boal contend that the 1993 transition from the Bush administration to the Clinton administration corresponded to an "emerging form of U.S. identity" which they term "multicultural nationalism" (246). This nationalism functions to manage the tensions between "a universalism based on the notion of an abstract citizenship" and "particularistic claims for recognition and justice by minoritized groups," often by commodifying or naturalizing minority cultures (245).

This essay provides a new reading of Fusang that responds to existent nation-specific ones. Focusing on passages that have been ignored by critics and/or omitted from the English translation, I demonstrate that the novel can be read as a challenge to nationalist discourses and nation-centered critical practices. Instead of reading Fusang as a representative of a racial, ethnic, or national collectivity, I propose that she gestures toward a process of disrupting reified racial, ethnic, and national differences through nonnormative sexual practices. In other words, my reading "queers" the figure of Fusang: by reworking queer theories of sexuality and subjectivity, it seeks to dismantle modes of criticism that help preserve national and racial identity.

My analysis of the critical discourses surrounding Fusang and its English translation and my own reading of both versions of the novel have broad implications for the reenvisioning of Asian American literary criticism in a transnational context. Until the turn of the 1990s, Asian American studies was primarily concerned with forging political and discursive communities among Asians in the United States and supporting these communities' struggles for legal, political, and cultural enfranchisement in the national space. This domestic focus, which implicitly reinforces the separation of Asia and America, reproduces the differential logic by which the U.S nation-state creates its subjects. Taking note of the limitations of a U.S.-centered Asian American studies, Kandice Chuh affirms recent efforts to reconceptualize Asian American studies in a global frame as a "subjectless discourse" that "points attention to the constraints on the liberatory potential of subjectivity" (9). Literary criticism, as Chuh points out, has a crucial part to play in this transnational, deconstructive turn in Asian American studies. By using the example of Fusang, this essay helps imagine the ways in which Asian American studies can be transformed into a transnational discursive space.

Critical Contexts

Roughly one-third of Fusang consists of second-person narration of the titular figure's experience, addressed to Fusang herself. The rest is mostly third-person narration describing the prostitute's interactions with johns as well as with the missionaries trying to rescue her. The novel is also sprinkled with first-person narration in which an embodied female narrator compares her own life with Fusang's. There is certainly no linear narrative to be found in the novel, so at the risk of being reductive, I summarize the plot as follows: Fusang is brought from China to California toward the end of the 1860s and sold into a brothel. She quickly attracts the attention of Chris, a white teenager; Da Yong, a Chinatown gangster; and Chinese laborers forced to live as bachelors because of the immigration restrictions on Chinese women. Fusang becomes Da Yong's possession when she willingly allows him to take her away from the missionaries who are trying to "save" her. Meanwhile, Fusang develops a crush on Chris and initiates sexual contact with him several times, although they do not consummate their mutual attraction. Then a riot breaks out against the Chinese and Chris joins a group of rioters in gang-raping Fusang. At the end of the novel, Fusang turns down Chris's offer of marriage and weds Da Yong just before he is executed for killing a white merchant. She then returns to Chinatown and lives there until an old age.

Fusang is an imagined character based on and yet differing from the descriptions of Chinatown prostitutes available in various historical documents.[10] Although the narrator claims that Fusang is an actual historical figure documented in some of the "one hundred and sixty histories of the Chinese in San Francisco that no one else has bothered to read" (*Lost Daughter* 3), she implicitly undermines this claim by questioning the reliability of historical records, pointing out that they offer reductive or conflicting accounts of Chinatown prostitutes and the people surrounding them (*Lost Daughter* 274). The novel further hints at the ambiguous status of its central character with the

---

10. In his study of Chinese prostitutes in San Francisco from 1849 to 1882, Benson Tong notes that before the passage of the Page law in 1875 prohibited the entry of women for the purpose of prostitution, the majority of adult Chinese women in California declared themselves prostitutes on census forms (30). Most of them had been imported and controlled by *tongs*, secret societies in San Francisco's Chinatown (10). Some of the women who came before 1853 operated as free entrepreneurs, the most notable example being Ah Toy, who arrived in San Francisco in late 1848 or early 1849 (6). Doris Muscatine likewise documents a "lone Chinese courtesan" who arrived in 1849, a "stunning twenty-two-year-old" with a dozen names, the most common of which were Ah Toy and Ah Choy (205). Judy Yung's history of Chinese women in San Francisco focuses mainly on the first part of the twentieth century but refers to an 1892 *Californian Illustrated Magazine* article that condemns nineteenth-century prostitution in Chinatown and cites a few examples of its occurrence.

very name Fusang, which echoes the title of Stan Steiner's 1979 history *Fusang: The Chinese Who Built America*. Steiner explains that "Fusang" appeared in ancient Chinese chronicles as the name of a paradisiacal kingdom east of China discovered by Buddhist priest Hui Shen in 499 A.D.; modern scholars have quibbled over whether the discovery in fact happened and whether the kingdom was an island off Japan or the Americas (3–9). The debates around the meaning of the land of Fusang underscore the slippages between history and myth. By invoking the name of this paradisiacal kingdom, Yan draws attention to the ways in which her representation of a nineteenth-century Chinese prostitute blurs the boundary between history and fiction and questions the presumed stability of historical knowledge.

Most American and British reviewers of *The Lost Daughter of Happiness* highlight the narrator's disavowal of complete knowledge of Fusang's character. Some see this renunciation of narrative authority as an implicit challenge to Western complacency about being able to know the non-West. British reviewer Julia Lovell, for example, points out that by having its subject remain "at all times opaque," the novel subverts the "basic tenet of Orientalism—that the Orient *can* be read." An American reviewer, Jeffrey C. Kinkley, also affirms that the opacity of Fusang's characterization enables readers to exercise their historical imagination and allows the plot to break out of the predictable mold of "white men saving yellow women from yellow men." Some reviewers interpret the lack of a well-defined central character as part and parcel of the novel's attempt to subvert readers' assurance about their own modes of belonging. Rebecca Barnhouse, for example, speculates that the author deliberately frustrates conventional readerly expectations in order to make the reader feel, along with Fusang, the sense of being "displaced in the physical and psychological landscapes we struggle to inhabit." In general, the reviewers of *The Lost Daughter of Happiness* argue that the novel subverts its Orientalist trappings by refusing to make Fusang a transparent object. Their unanimous focus on Fusang's opacity, however, suggests a problem.

While the Anglo-American readings recapitulated above do not reduce Fusang to a transparent racial stereotype, they are nevertheless reductive. In these interpretations, Fusang figures as little more than an empty signifier that warrants all kinds of projections or subjective readings. This problem becomes more serious when we consider the less appealing implications of seeing Fusang as "opaque." Indeed, one critic, Cathleen A. Towey, complains that "Fusang never becomes a fully realized character" and suggests that only readers with a "strong interest in the subject" should pick up the novel. We might say that Fusang's, and hence the novel's, purported opacity is yet another symptom of Eurocentric approaches toward the non-West, which manifest, on the one hand, in subsuming the other as known object and, on the other, in ignoring the other on the grounds of inscrutable difference. By describing Fusang as "opaque," the reviewers seek, arguably, to displace their inability to decipher her. If this is the case, Fusang is not the only Chinese American female literary figure to be denied the status of a meaningful character meriting close attention. Chinese American writer Gish Jen once wondered aloud, during a luncheon-discussion with readers at the Public Square in Chicago, why some reviewers of her novel *The Love Wife* characterized one of its central characters, Lan Lan, a nanny from mainland China, as an opaque figure whom the author does not allow readers to sympathize with or understand. Jen quipped that the reviewers had probably read "right past" the pages and pages of internal monologue attributed to Lan Lan.[11]

For critics in mainland China, in contrast, Fusang becomes an almost transparent signifier. Fusang's experiences as a Chinatown prostitute serve to allegorize Western imperialism and neo-imperial practices in China and the violent racialization of Chinese immigrants in the U.S. from the mid–nineteenth century onward. Her effortless accommodation of forced sexual intercourse signifies for these critics the various ways in which the Chinese people have survived colonial and racial injuries. The critics disagree, however, on the implications of this survival. Teng Wei, a scholar at Beijing Foreign Studies University, argues that in creating the compliant figure of Fusang, the author not only acquiesces to but "takes delight in" the Orientalist fascination with purportedly hypersexualized Asian

---

11. As part of the Illinois Humanities Council, a nonprofit organization, the Public Square hosts readings, lectures, and public discussions of political issues. The occasion for Jen's reading and luncheon-discussion, held on October 27, 2004, was the publication of *The Love Wife*.

women (66). Chen Sihe, a preeminent scholar of twentieth-century Chinese literature, presents an opposing view. He describes Fusang as a Mother Earth figure who absorbs death and regenerates life, a symbol of the "true essence of Chinese culture" that allows China and Chinese people around the world to arise from their historical humiliation. Chen's opinion is echoed in a more recent essay by Lin Cuiwei, who also sees Fusang as an embodiment of "the traditional virtues" of Chinese women as well as Chinese culture (67). Both Teng's and Chen's readings demonstrate how the image of Chinese selfhood, which the critics symbolically map onto the figure of Fusang, relies in important ways on a narrative of China's relation to Western political and epistemological regimes. While Teng emphasizes the danger of being co-opted by a dominant power, Chen expresses confidence in China's ability to survive and rise above that power.

This brief survey of *Fusang*'s reception demonstrates that contemporary U.S. and Chinese national identity are both constructed, albeit in different ways, in relation to the power structure signified by Orientalism. Orientalism is strenuously critiqued, and yet unwittingly perpetuated, to shore up multicultural nationalism in the United States. On the other hand, the critical discourses surrounding Orientalism and postcoloniality, which originated in the Western academy, have given some Chinese intellectuals a vocabulary to legitimize nationalist sentiments as a necessary response to global capitalism. Chinese academics started to discuss postcolonial theory, especially Edward Said's critique of Orientalism, in the mid-1990s. Coupled with China's increasing absorption into world capitalism, exposure to postcolonial thought compelled Chinese intellectuals to reexamine, through the latter half of the 1990s, the relationship between East and West, tradition and modernity, nationalism and globalization. While many of them developed a critical perspective on modern nationalism, some of them articulated strong nationalist yearnings for the economic and political rise of China.[12] This intellectual discourse coincided with both the Chinese government's endorsement of the

---

12. For a well-known manifestation of this nationalist discourse, see Qiang Song, Zangzang Zhang, and Bian Qiao. In their "China Can Say No," these authors decry the Chinese fascination with American culture and call for more awareness of U.S. hegemony in the world.

global revival of Confucianism and a series of popular protests against incursions upon China's national sovereignty.[13] This new, multilayered nationalism did not oppose China's integration into world capitalism, yet it was largely framed in opposition to the legacies of Western colonialism and the presence of U.S. imperialism in the new world order.[14] In their treatment of Fusang as a metaphorical statement about China's position in global culture, the Chinese readings of Yan's novel reflect a range of discourses characteristic of contemporary Chinese nationalism.

How, then, should we view the relationship between the characterization of Fusang and the epistemological and political hegemony of U.S. Orientalism? Does the novel present her as its unknowing victim, or as its unlikely survivor and challenger? If Fusang does challenge what seeks to contain her, does she do that simply by drawing upon her inherent resilience, or by concealing herself behind a veil of mystery? The answers provided in extant readings of the character all depend on suppressing important parts of the novel. In the English translation, this suppression can be quite literal, given the removal of many passages. My discussion of the novel and of the character Fusang will focus precisely on those parts that were deleted or reduced. By paying attention to what has been omitted in the interpretations of Fusang, I aim to reveal the complexity of the novel's narrative structure and characterization. Fusang is an elusive figure not

---

13. In 1994, the Chinese government sponsored an international conference on Confucianism and designated Confucianism an essential component of the nation's patriotic education curriculum; see Liu Kang 172. Popular nationalistic protests in China in the late 1990s and early 2000s included, most notably, the demonstrations following NATO's bombing of the Chinese Embassy in Belgrade in 1999 and the public outrage over the collision between a U.S. Navy spy plane and a Chinese fighter in 2001.

14. For further discussion of these developments, see Dirlik and Zhang, Dai, and Wang. Dirlik Arif and Zhang Xudong point out that the appropriation of postcolonial critique in China "both indicates the heightened awareness of power relations in cultural production and manifests the kind of confidence derived from Chinese economic success in the global market" (13–14). Dai Jinhua notes that the surge of Chinese nationalism in the mid-1990s, often framed in anti-American terms, was closely related to "larger social critiques targeted at globalization, transnational capital, and the economic, cultural, and political imperialism of the West" (177). While Wang Hui takes note of Chinese intellectuals' criticism of nationalist sentiments in the 1990s, he also acknowledges that "[i]n Chinese postmodernism, postcolonial theory is often synonymous with a discourse on nationalism, which reinforces the China/West paradigm" (170).

because she is underdeveloped, but because she is often filtered through different perspectives internal to the novel's narrative.

Suppressed Irony

Two important passages in *Fusang* narrated from Chris's perspective are removed from the English translation *The Lost Daughter of Happiness*. In the first passage, a sixty-year-old Chris remembers how he was surprised when, as a teenager, he first saw Fusang comply uncomplainingly with her johns. He believes that he is now finally able to understand Fusang's inexplicable ability to draw pleasure from forced sexual acts. He concludes that Fusang embodies a "primitive maternity," defined by "eternal suffering, boundless tolerance, and willing sacrifice": "Maternity is the highest level of femininity: the mother opens herself to be plundered and invaded. She does not reject. Her indiscrimination is the most elegant form of wantonness" (*Fusang* 85; my translation). In the second passage, the older Chris reflects on Fusang's attempts to seduce him when she lived temporarily at the missionary house (from which she was soon to be taken by Da Yong). He concludes that Fusang was a "most authentic, most natural" woman because she let everyone "plough" and "sow" her as "a plot of earth" (*Fusang* 114; my translation).

These two passages were undoubtedly what prompted Chinese critics to interpret Fusang as a Mother Earth figure and either criticize her as a thoroughly Orientalized fantasy or commend her as a symbol of Chinese resilience. The removal of these passages from the translation shows not that they were deemed unimportant from the perspective of English-speaking readers. To the contrary, the translator explains their excision from the English translation by saying that these passages are "too sentimental" and "overstated"; they are "telling instead of showing" the reader what to make of the character Fusang.[15] In other words, these passages give the moral of the novel away; their removal ideally leaves English-speaking critics guessing about Fusang's meaning. Reader-critics of the English translation consequently viewed Fusang as opaque, despite all the other suggestive passages thought to "show" rather than "tell about" the character. The

---

15. I obtained this information through my telephone interview with Silber.

Anglo-American interpreters of the novel (including the translator) and the Chinese critics are more similar than different: both base their readings on explicit rather than descriptive passages. They claim a complete understanding of Fusang when she is explained for the reader in what Mikhail Bakhtin in *Dialogic Imagination* calls "extra-artistic" passages (from the perspective of one of the novel's characters) but give up on deciphering her when these passages are absent (262). Both groups of critics, for different ideological and practical reasons that I will discuss, elide the formal sophistication of the novel. One can, in fact, see Chris as a rather unreliable observer. The older Chris's paean to Fusang's "maternity" picks up ironic tones from the novel's self-reflexive turn on his oedipal, Orientalist longing for Fusang.

The narrator attributes Chris's infatuation with Fusang to a convergence of racial and sexual fantasies. When Chris first visits Fusang in her brothel as a twelve-year-old boy, he carries with him all the "fairy tales and adventure stories" he has consumed and the resultant view that the "Orient" is a realm of fascinating mysteries (*Lost Daughter* 15). For Chris, Fusang brings to life a fairy tale, her "cavelike room" figuring as a "distant kingdom." The narrator suggests that Chris approaches Fusang with a set of Orientalist assumptions that fuel his infatuation with her. Chris perceives Fusang's accented, limited English phrases as primitive sounds that "predate human language" (*Fusang* 10)[16] and, in so doing, projects her as an infant or an innocent savage, untouched by civilization. Fusang's bound feet impress him as "fishtails" that signify both "stunted evolution" and cruel mutilation (*Fusang* 11).[17] Thus the younger Chris imagines Fusang as part of a primitive culture that insulates itself from modern civilization and metes out cruel treatment to its women. Chris's imagination is reminiscent of a range of Orientalist discourses and images circulating in the nineteenth-century U.S.,

---

16. The sentence that contains this phrase is missing from Silber's translation. See *The Lost Daughter of Happiness* 13.

17. Here I depart from Silber's translation, which translates Yan's original as "a stage of evolution no one had ever imagined" (*Lost Daughter* 14). Yan's original literally translates as "a stage between evolution and regression" (*Fusang* 11), which I prefer to translate as "stunted evolution."

such as "noble savage" discourse (registered, for example, in Herman Melville's *Typee*) and sensual images of women in harems (reappropriated, for example, in Edgar Allan Poe's "Ligeia"). Yan's novel, therefore, reverberates with contemporary historical and literary scholarship by figuring that nineteenth-century U.S. Orientalism as a contradictory, unstable structure of knowledge that consists of a hodgepodge of images about different parts of what is known as the "Orient" or Asia.[18] Chris's various assumptions about Fusang constellate into a sexualized fantasy of rescue. In the days following his first visit to her, Chris lives in daydreams, as the narrator tells Fusang: "His infatuation with you has left him time for nothing else. In his dreams, he is much taller, brandishing a long sword. A knight of courage and passion. An Oriental princess imprisoned in a dark cell waits for him to rescue her" (*Lost Daughter* 19). The "mutilated points of [Fusang's] feet," again, figure prominently in the boy's fantasy.

The novel figures Chris's unconscious as a repository not only of Orientalist fantasies about white men saving women of color from men of color, but also of patriarchal fantasies about the origin of sexuality, especially the Oedipus complex. In Freud, the Oedipus complex describes a presumably universal psychic pattern: a child between the ages of three and five is sexually drawn to the parent of the opposite sex and sees the parent of the same sex as a rival. In *Fusang*, Chris's Oedipus complex resurges during puberty as he comes into contact with a "sensual," "Oriental" woman. In the eyes of twelve-year-old Chris, Fusang's body is a "fruit heavy with juice," "ripe to the bursting point" (*Lost Daughter* 16), while "[h]er pursed lips and lowered lashes lent her face all the gentleness of a mother" (*Lost Daughter* 12). Chris's desire for thrills turns into that kind of "adoration boys all over the world feel for ripe beautiful women" (*Lost Daughter* 16). While Chris regresses into childhood, Fusang is elevated to the status of a primal goddess, her thick, long hair falling "like water, as black and impenetrable as sky before time began" (*Lost*

---

18. Malini Johar Schueller, for example, provides an analysis of the different constructions of the Orient in U.S. culture before 1890, including the Orientalism induced by the U.S.–North African conflict of the late eighteenth century, Near Eastern Orientalism, and Indic Orientalism (ix).

Daughter 14). By juxtaposing Chris's oedipal infatuation with his heroic fantasy of coming to Fusang's rescue, the novel shows that, for Chris, Fusang is at once a hypersexualized mother who incites penetration and a chaste whore who awaits salvation. Through its representation of Chris, the novel illustrates what Homi Bhabha terms the "ambivalence" at the heart of colonial and racial desire.[19]

Chris's desire for Fusang gestures toward the intersection of sexual and racial difference in the configuration of heterosexual desire in nineteenth-century America. It also shows how infatuation with the racial and sexual other is bound up with fear of the same object. Chris's fascination with Fusang is symbiotic with his fear of the otherness that she embodies, a fear that is mostly displaced onto the Chinese men around her. As he goes through what seem to him Chinatown's shady establishments and becomes exposed to anti-Chinese protests starting to flare up in San Francisco, Chris is increasingly gripped by the conviction that the Chinese, especially the male laborers who account for most of the Chinatown population, are an "inferior race" that should be "wiped out" (*Lost Daughter* 44). At some points, Chris's desire to rescue Fusang seems to be motivated by, or at least correlated with, a different desire—the desire to distinguish himself from, as well as to destroy, "those hideous Oriental buildings, all these grotesque feet and queues," and all those things that he "couldn't understand" (*Lost Daughter* 198). Fusang also becomes a victim of this racial hate in the rape scene.

The novel's Orientalizing of Fusang through Chris, therefore, might arguably be read as what Judith Butler calls, in *Bodies That Matter*, a "critical mime" (47), an act of citing or appropriating dominant discourse so as to expose its foundational violence. Indeed, one can say that the novel mimics Chris's view of Fusang as a way of opening up a conceptual space beyond it. It amply suggests a critical vantage point from which one can see Chris's complicity with the inherently violent racial stereotypes of exotic, passive,

---

19. In his analysis of Edward Said's organization of "manifest" and "latent" Orientalism into one congruent and intentional system of representation, Homi Bhabha critiques the "closure and coherence attributed to the unconscious pole of colonial discourse" (72). Bhabha uses the concept of "ambivalence" to indicate the contradictions in the "polymorphous and perverse collusion between racism and sexism" and in the subjectivities of both the colonizer and the colonized (69).

submissive, and sexually available Asian women.[20] When the younger Chris believes that Fusang's passivity gives her freedom, because she is a "body not ruled over by the soul" (*Fusang* 86), he can be seen as positing an Oriental and feminine other essentially opposed to his own repressed self, brought up on Calvinist teachings against physical desire and prohibited socially and legally from pursuing desire. When the older Chris fantasizes about Fusang as a Mother Earth figure who rises above unspeakable violence through her uncomplaining passivity and "elegant wantonness," he can be understood as enacting what Julia Kristeva terms the ritual of "purifying the abject," which in the case of the novel figures as Fusang's othered, prohibited body.[21]

The Anglo-American and the Chinese interpretations of Fusang, in emphasizing, respectively, her opacity and her transparent symbolic value (as a metaphor for the Chinese nation), elide the ways in which the novel undercuts Chris's perspective. The decision to remove the sixty-year-old Chris's reflections about Fusang from the novel's English translation might have been motivated by a concern that these passages—the ones described by the translator as "too sentimental" and "overstated"—would repel the novel's potential critics and readers in the West, who are presumed to be largely white, middle class, and liberal. Was it feared that they might attribute these two passages to the author and subsequently criticize her for perpetuating an essentialist, exoticizing view of Asian femininity and femininity in general? Chinese and other Asian immigrant literature is expected to adhere to the tenets of multicultural nationalism and stage a critique of *historical* configurations of Orientalism. Yan's Fusang, however, as originally rendered, might upset this

20. For a useful review of the Asian American feminist critique of these stereotypes, see Laura Hyun Yi Kang's *Compositional Subjects: Enfiguring Asian/American Women*, especially the chapter titled "Cinematic Projections." Also see Elaine H. Kim; Wong, "Ethnicizing Gender"; and Espiritu.

21. In *Powers of Horror*, Kristeva defines the abject as what is fundamentally suppressed in the human psyche. The abject, "the jettisoned object," is "radically excluded and draws me toward the place where meaning collapses" (2). The abject appears either as "a rite of defilement and pollution" or as "exclusion or taboo" in various religions; religion and art both devise various means of "purifying the abject" (17). In *Bodies That Matter*, Butler defines the abject more generally as a social and psychic zone of uninhabitability that "constitute[s] the defining limit of the subject's domain" (3).

expectation by seeming to signal Orientalism's continued presence. The deletion of these two passages, then, provides a glimpse of how trade book publishing in the United States shapes Asian immigrant literature by exercising an overt form of censorship. The Anglo-American critics of *The Lost Daughter of Happiness* exercise a more covert form of censorship by refusing to acknowledge parts of the novel that cannot be subsumed into a simple anti-Orientalist reading, dismissing them by describing Fusang as "opaque." While the English translation has been made safe and palatable for mass consumption in the West, it has lost much of the Chinese original's formal and thematic sophistication. The Chinese critics of the original version, in contrast, unquestioningly equate Chris's perspective on Fusang with the novel's, largely to support their allegorical reading of the character as an emblem of Chinese people at home and abroad. As they use the novel to construct coherent narratives of the historical trajectory of China's relation to the West, especially the United States, the Chinese critics fail to consider the possibility that the novel could at once imitate and subvert Orientalist stereotypes in creating the figure of Fusang. Critics on both sides of the Pacific, therefore, converge in reducing Fusang to an unambiguous character and subordinating her to nation-centered interpretive frameworks. Fusang is turned into either a proper ethnic subject embodying the logic of Western liberal multiculturalism or the quintessential modern Chinese subject struggling under Western domination.

Signifying Excision

I have argued that the existing criticism of Yan's *Fusang* and its English translation shows how different audiences, with different cultural and geopolitical affiliations, appropriate Asian immigrant literature in the United States. Equally important, these critical appropriations are anticipated and mirrored within the novel itself, which dramatizes how various characters compete to possess Fusang in both epistemological and sexual terms. While the novel's Chinese laborers and gangsters try to keep Fusang within the social and domestic structure of Chinatown, the younger Chris desires her, as I demonstrated earlier, as a thoroughly racialized and feminized object. One can see strong parallels between the male characters' competing interpretations of Fusang's body and those of the novel's critics. The allegorical readings generated in the Chinese context naturalize Fusang's Chineseness and femininity, as does the heterosexual economy of Chinatown presented in the novel. Just as Chris turns Fusang into a desirable Oriental object by distinguishing her from the "hideous" surroundings of San Francisco's Chinatown, the Anglo-American critics, along with the novel's translator and publisher, are engaged in restaging Fusang as a proper ethnic subject who does not yield willingly to the sexual depravations of Chinatown's male denizens and visitors.

Despite competing efforts to comprehend and possess Fusang, her boundlessly open sexuality continues to fascinate, baffle, and disorient the male characters in the novel. Fusang's at-homeness with forced sexual transactions sets her apart from common tropes of fallen women, such as veteran prostitutes hardened against the world and prostitutes with hearts of gold, who embody moral virtues under a worldly guise. Fusang harbors no bitterness about being turned into a sexual commodity. Surprised by Chris's age during their first encounter, Fusang nevertheless decides not to "cut a single corner with him," instead smiling at him "as if he were a man every bit [her] match" (*Lost Daughter* 15). She also willingly accommodates Da Yong when she comes under his control. When Chris tries to save her by killing Da Yong while he naps, Fusang quietly deters him by continuing to wash Da Yong's hair, as he had demanded.

Many of Fusang's Chinese clients construe her effortless accommodation of their sexual needs as an expression of submissive affection and consequently propose to buy her out of prostitution and marry her.[22] Da Yong quickly overwhelms his rivals and takes possession of Fusang, regarding her as a "pet" the same way he treasures his dog, parrot, and jewelry case (*Lost Daughter* 156). In a scene that literalizes Eve Sedgwick's argument about male homosociality being triangulated through the female body, a brawl breaks out

---

22. The slippage between prostitutes and domestic women, as presented in the novel, is peculiar to early Chinese immigrant history. Chinatowns in the United States had a predominantly male population until after World War II, when the 1945 War Brides Act increased the number of Chinese women allowed to enter the country; see Tong 159.

between Da Yong's gang and a group of white passengers on a ship over the latter's insulting remarks about Fusang and her music (*Lost Daughter* 164). Throughout the novel, the male Chinese characters vie with each other and with the dominant race for control of Fusang, all the while under the illusion of her willing submission. While the novel fully acknowledges the historical, legal, and psychological structures that resulted in the gendered racialization of early Chinese immigrants in San Francisco, it does not romanticize this racialized group. Just as it implicitly subverts Chris's Orientalizing desire for Fusang through a self-reflexive turn, the novel suggests the cost of Da Yong's desperate defense of his own and the other Chinese men's endangered masculinity by showing how it is implicated in the possession of Fusang's body.

Each of the "readers" within the text stabilizes Fusang's implications for a particular shape of racial or national identity by disciplining her seemingly capacious, indiscriminate sexuality. Likewise, as we can see in the competing critical discourses about the novel, turning an enigmatic female figure in Chinese immigrant fiction into a modern national subject is contingent upon interpreting her sexual desire in ways that accommodate the racialized imagination of a particular nation. The interpretive battles both within and around Yan's novel demonstrate how Asian American women's sexuality and subjectivity are defined in conflicting terms by different nationalist discourses that intersect with each other in the Asian Pacific.[23]

Early in the narrative, the novel seems to acquiesce to nationalist readings of Fusang by placing her on the verge of being inducted into racially inflected heterosexual desire. Upon meeting Chris after a long absence and drawing a blank when trying to remember who he is, as she would with any of her johns, Fusang is eventually moved by Chris's persistence at being recognized, realizing that "she'd never forgotten the boy" (*Lost Daughter* 42). The narrator goes on to suggest a parallel between Fusang's feelings for Chris and her own affection for her husband. Just as the narrator feels both infatuated with and

---

23. Leslie Bow makes a similar argument. She contends that "ethnic and national affiliation are determined in part by conflicts over how sexuality is performed, potentially situating the female body as a register of international and domestic political struggle, as a site of national divisions and loyalties" (10).

distanced from her husband because of their perceived "differences" (*Lost Daughter* 43), Fusang develops a heightened sensitivity to Chris by becoming aware of how she is different from him: "You are aware of your strange feet, . . . your cold faux jade bracelet. You are aware of the heartbeat of every embroidered blossom on your peach silk blouse." For a brief moment, Fusang seems to have been interpellated into the racialized economy of heteronormative, monogamous desire that Chris inhabits and to have become a recognizable object of that desire. The younger Chris's erotic gaze puts her through a process of subjectification, turning her into a desiring subject as well as a desired object. This scene, arguably, reifies the racial and sexual differences in which both U.S. and Chinese nationalisms are grounded by naturalizing the heterosexual desire between white men and Asian women.

The novel soon thwarts its own movement toward a standard interracial romance, however. The various legal and social restrictions prohibiting Fusang's desire for Chris do not lead her to take her own life, in the fashion of a betrayed Madame Butterfly; instead, Fusang often figures the possibilities of paring back and transforming the heterosexual, monogamous desire that she can hardly escape from. The novel slowly suggests that Fusang's all-accepting sexuality, characterized as a form of essential, divine femininity by the elder Chris, could actually be a means of dismantling the normative desire that threatens to claim her. It is not a stretch to say that the novel not only mimics and therefore self-consciously critiques the various acts of subjectification imposed on Fusang but also enacts how those acts can potentially be undone and dissolved.

When Chris, as a young man in his twenties, proposes to marry Fusang and move with her to Montana (where interracial marriage is not prohibited), Fusang quietly leaves to prepare and stage a wedding with Da Yong before his execution. Fusang's apparent submission to the institution of marriage signifies just the opposite: her marriage to the dead Da Yong, as the last part of the novel suggests, becomes the best alibi for her not having any real marriage in her life. It can be seen as a final, definitive rejection of marriage. This ending decidedly distinguishes Yan's *Fusang* from Ruthanne Lum McCunn's *Thousand Pieces of Gold*, a biographical novel based on the life of Lalu Nathoy, a nineteenth-century Chinese prostitute who worked in a mining town in Idaho. While McCunn's novel largely revolves around Lalu's love for and marriage to Charlie Bemis, a saloon owner, *Fusang* does not offer the satisfaction of a conventional interracial romance between a white man and an Asian woman.

Although Fusang's rejection of marriage triggers profound confusion in the young Chris and, as he gets older, leads him to think of Fusang as a form of primitive materiality that cannot be socially integrated, it is actually anticipated in a number of long passages that precede this textual moment. In one earlier scene, Chris follows Fusang from the teahouse back to her brothel. Anxious to find out whether she is in danger, he climbs a small tree beneath her window. When he flings himself forward and lands on the window ledge, Chris is greeted by a shocking scene:

> Her body was taking in a man. It was sleek with a faint film of sweat. She wasn't resisting as he had expected, but accommodating herself completely to the man. The way the beach accommodates the tide. . . .
>
> He thought there should be struggle, some sign of suffering. But what he saw instead was harmony. No matter that the man wore a queue, or that his sallow back was covered with grotesque tattoos—the harmony was beautiful.

(Lost Daughter 62)

Fusang's embrace of this experience takes away the foundation of Chris's fantasy of rescue and that of the gendered racialization of Asians in the U.S. (Asian women are seen as hypersexual, while Asian men are seen as asexual.) Whereas Asian bodies are often seen as an undifferentiated mass, their heterosexual unions have rarely been conceived in terms of "harmony." The scene of Fusang drawing pleasure from sexual intercourse with a random Chinese john unsurprisingly astonishes Chris.

But Yan's imagination of intraracial "harmony" in this scene is not a cultural-nationalist proclamation of an erotic bond between Asian men and Asian women.[24] Instead, it presents a snapshot of a nonnormative sexual practice that potentially challenges the

---

24. A recent example of this version of cultural nationalism is Darrell Hamamoto's porn video *Yellowcaust: A Patriot Act*, in which the University of California–Davis professor cast one Asian woman and one Asian man. His express purpose was to "re-eroticize Asian America" and to bring Asian men and women together sexually; see *Masters of the Pillow*, James Hou's documentary film about the making of this video.

reification of sexual, racial, and national differences. Fusang conveys her desire both for the Chinese man and for Chris through seductive, almost phallic body movements:

> Her body was its [the harmony's] basis; she controlled the advance and retreat. . . .
>
> And it [the pleasure] did not reside solely in her; the movements of her body spread it to the man, and her gaze sent it toward Chris.
>
> Chris realized that now he was crying for a different reason. With the onslaught of the mysterious pleasure, his body unfolded and quickened in ways he'd never known. The movements of their bodies drew him into their rhythm.
>
> (*Lost Daughter* 62–63)

Fusang's desire in this passage is not only active but expansive, decidedly nonmonogamous and contagious. At this moment, probably against his will, Chris's murderous jealousy of the Chinese johns, his wish to "rescue the beautiful slave girl on her dying breath" (*Lost Daughter* 61), slides into the pleasure of an imaginary sexual union. Although the sexual pleasure Fusang experiences and helps generate in Chris remains ambiguous, indefinable, and "mysterious," it is clearly differentiated from what Chris sees as the passive submission characteristic of essential femininity.

Fusang's apparently unintelligible sexuality as it is presented in this passage resonates with Leo Bersani's theory of impersonal sexuality, which he developed in a series of writings beginning with "Is the Rectum a Grave?" (1988).[25] In "Sociability and Cruising" (2002), Bersani refines this theory by offering a new interpretation of the seemingly disparaging definition in Freudian psychoanalysis of a male homosexual as one who "cruises the world . . . in search of objects that will give him back to himself as a loved and cared for subject" (17). By loving others as the self, Bersani argues, the gay cruiser

---

25. Bersani points out in this article that while sex is often practiced to create "a hyperbolic sense of self," it also potentially implies "a loss of all consciousness of self" (218); he posits the enhancement of the latter aspect of sex as the aim of radical sexual politics. Bersani builds on this argument in *Homos* (1995), where he considers the possible ways in which male homosexuality provides a "privileged vehicle" for self-shattering sex (10). "Sociability and Cruising" continues this line of thinking, exploring in more detail the psychic resources and labor required for constructing new forms of intimacy dissociated from the fortification of the self.

recognizes that "difference can be loved as the non-threatening supplement of sameness," thus providing an alternative to the normative, heterosexual way of approaching sexual difference. Cruising, therefore, constitutes a form of training in "impersonal intimacy," a term Bersani uses to signify sexual relations that do *not* result in psychic individuation through the simultaneous eroticization and repudiation of the gendered other. Practices of "impersonal intimacy," like cruising, provide a psychic basis for relating to the other in general, on both sexual and nonsexual levels, as supplementary to the self. For Bersani, both heterosexuals and homosexuals can practice "impersonal intimacy," to different extents and at different costs, and, in so doing, challenge normative heterosexual desire organized around reified sexual difference.

Sexual difference, it must be emphasized, claims a unique position in Bersani's theory of "impersonal intimacy." Although he allows that sexual difference should not be "prejudicially sanctified in our psychoanalytically oriented culture as the ground of all difference" (17), Bersani adds that it perhaps "does have a unique epistemological function in human growth as an early and crucial model for structuring difference."[26] In contrast to Bersani's proposition, Fusang's sexuality in this important passage unsettles the normative configuration of sexual and racial difference without arranging these two modes of differentiation in a hierarchy of psychic and social importance. In *Racial Castration*, David L. Eng argues that psychoanalytic theories and queer discourses can be "useful for Asian American and ethnic studies" if we remain sensitive to the ways in which Asian American cultural productions complicate and disrupt these theoretical formations (4). Indeed, the above example from *Fusang* illustrates both the usefulness and the limitations of psychoanalytic and queer discourses for analyzing how Asian immigrant literature questions the construction of difference.

Although Fusang's desire is not homosexual and she, of course, does not cruise the world, Fusang, like the gay man posited by Bersani, would appear to approach the threatening other as the

---

26. This view of sexual difference represents a slight change from the one expressed in the earlier article "Against Monogamy" (1999), where Bersani explicitly parallels sexual difference with "national, racial, religious, ethnic" differences (4).

"non-threatening supplement" of the self. One can therefore simultaneously claim a kind of queerness for Fusang and reinscribe queerness as both a disruption of sexual, racial, and ethnic differences and a process of becoming, rather than a stable component of one's identity. As demonstrated in her interactions with Chris, Fusang manages the trauma of racial and sexual difference, registered on her body in the form of violent penetration, by being hospitable to and drawing pleasure from it. She goes through a ritual of coquetry with any random client, as she does with Chris: she pours some tea, turns to smile at the customer, adjusts her skirt, and then waits a moment (*Lost Daughter* 11–13). In one of the passages omitted from the English translation, the narrator describes, from Fusang's perspective, one of the prostitute's sexual experiences, in which she reaches the acute pleasure lying at the other end of "a vast plain of pain" by treading over "resistance and unwillingness, shame and anger" (*Fusang* 88; my translation). In showing Fusang turning the pain of sexual servitude into pleasure, this passage might unsettle many middle-class American readers, a reason, perhaps, for its having been left out of the English translation. This omission obscures the ways in which the novel appropriates conventional forms of female sexual service, like prostitution, in order to stage new modes of relating to the racial and sexual other. Indeed, this omitted passage shows that Fusang's peculiar form of sexual hospitality not only reconciles her to her violent world but allows her to intervene in it as well. Fusang's vastly expansive desire temporarily dissolves Chris's murderous hatred toward the Chinese johns. The visual pleasure he feels signifies either a cross-racial identification (with the Chinese john) or a cross-gender and cross-racial identification (with Fusang), both of which are foreclosed from the racial and sexual economy of the nineteenth-century San Francisco presented in the novel and, to a lesser extent, from today's America.

As Bersani rightly argues, impersonal intimacy entails both self-extension and self-subtraction. By engaging in sexual acts like cruising, one can learn to refrain from the wish to be individuated from all otherness and embrace one's numerous inaccurate replications in the world, thus extending oneself into the world in a nonaggressive way. Just as Bersani's notion of impersonal intimacy, an expansive connectedness, is predicated upon the work of self-subtraction, Fusang's all-accepting sexuality is based on the stripping away of her sense of an enclosed, autonomous self. Right after the scene discussed above, Fusang gets up and "splash[es] herself with water... to wash off [menstrual] blood" (*Lost Daughter* 64). Watching her from outside the window, Chris is "shocked" at Fusang's "nonchalance" toward the blood. She seems indifferent to, or intent upon dismantling, the difference between inside and outside, private and public. As blood trickles down her leg, Fusang fails to cohere into a female subject with easily recognizable boundaries. She has become a kind of uncountable body inextricable from the world. As the narrator puts it, Fusang's body "didn't count now" (*Lost Daughter* 64). This image emblematizes Fusang's resistance to being counted or categorized as a normative female subject who upholds a specific set of nationalist discourses. The novel's representation of Fusang's open-ended sexuality suggests how acts of survival are continuous with the process of forging new kinds of subjects who do not strive toward autonomy or coherence and new forms of intimacy that do not lie within the bounds of heterosexual monogamy.

The novel stages the most controversial implications of Fusang's sexuality in the gang-rape scene. The description of the race riot that provides the occasion for the rape bears some resemblance to historical accounts of race riots against the Chinese that took place in the 1870s in Los Angeles, Chico, and other parts of the American West.[27] Since the English translation shortens the extensive description and analysis of the rape that are in the original—underscoring, again, how the publisher of the translation would seem to have construed parts of the novel to be potentially unsettling to mainstream American readers—I'll quote mainly from the Chinese original in my analysis. Speaking in second person, the narrator questions the difference between Fusang's experience of being raped and her daily interactions with her johns: "You can't tell the difference between selling your body and gang-rape" (*Fusang* 183; my translation). If one important difference between prostitution and rape is the supposition of female consent, the novel presents this difference as all but nonexistent in the case of Fusang. The novel's equation of rape

---

27. Sucheng Chan provides a discussion of these (48–49).

and prostitution inversely mirrors the analogy Andrea Dworkin draws between prostitution and gang-rape in her essay "Prostitution and Male Supremacy."[28] Both the novel and Dworkin's essay point out that women do not consent to prostitution, just as they do not consent to rape, because they are not legally or socially defined as sovereign subjects in full possession of their bodies. While Dworkin calls for changes in social structures that will enable women to attain subjecthood, however, Yan imagines embodied practices that might help take the aggression out of sexuality by *eroding* the psychic borders that shape an autonomous subject. The novel's indifference to the liberal concept of the sovereign subject would certainly disturb many American readers and is perhaps why the rest of the paragraph that begins with the sentence quoted above was omitted from the English translation. I translate it as follows:

> One can even say that you never felt you were selling your body at all, because you accept the men. There is equality in your interactions with the men: you find pleasure even as you are physically violated, and you take away from the men what you give them. Instinctively, you have transformed the traffic in your body into exchanges between and among bodies. Your body is so hospitable that you never realized that you had had to exchange it for money. Encounters between and among bodies allow different lives to converse with and learn from each other.
>
> This makes me suspect again that you, Fusang, are from a very old time.
>
> (*Fusang* 183)

The last sentence of this passage seems to suggest that the narrator is aligned with the older Chris, who sees Fusang as a symbol of essential, pristine femininity. But if this passage is indeed positing an originary femininity, it departs from the notion, attributed to the older Chris in the novel, that essential femininity lies in a boundless ability to countenance suffering and regenerate life. The passage does not justify rape by implying that it satisfies women's masochistic sexual fantasies—in other words, their proclivities for suffering—nor does it

---

28. In criticizing the tendency among academic feminists to discuss prostitution in abstract, theoretical terms, Dworkin argues that prostitution facilitates unmitigated violence against women, stating, "The only analogy I can think of concerning prostitution is that it is more like gang rape than it is like anything else" (3).

stop at critiquing rape as "traffic in the female body." Instead, it proposes a set of self-subtracting sexual practices, figured as "exchanges between and among bodies," as an antidote to rape. By embracing differently configured bodies without feeling threatened—that is, by practicing a form of impersonal, indiscriminate sexuality—one can start to dissolve the psychic, sexual, and social differences that constitute one's subjectivity. The dissolution of these differences would transform normative sexuality, making impossible the resentment of the other that nourishes such misogynistic practices as rape. The novel's representation of Fusang, as I pointed out earlier, is in conversation with various historical studies of the experience of Chinese prostitutes in nineteenth-century America and with the specific meanings of prostitution and rape in that context. It rewrites conventional historical narratives that cast these women as either victims or agents seeking control of their own lives; this rewriting reverberates with and contributes to contemporary critical inquiries of subjectivity and relationality.

The ideal of an embodied subject seeking disembodiment by circulating itself among other bodies might seem unattainable. But the novel suggests that it could be concretized in the future, and that one possible means of attaining this new kind of subjectivity resides in reflecting on the violence inherent in normative desire. The narrator confides to the reader that Fusang feels her strength drain away and experiences a taste of "humiliation" when Chris joins the rapists yet tries to set himself apart from them by being tender toward her (*Fusang* 185; *Lost Daughter* 225). The "little bit of tenderness" that Chris tries to give her (*Lost Daughter* 231; *Fusang* 189) generates a traumatized reaction in Fusang: she feels humiliated and tries to break away from him. Through Fusang's sense of humiliation, the novel offers a hint at the profound contradictions within the racialized economy of heterosexual desire. Chris's sexual longing for Fusang, expressed through violent penetration in the rape scene, becomes intertwined with an outburst of racial hatred. His attempt to instill some "tenderness" into this sexual act does not offset its violence but instead overlays physical domination with the violence of subjectification. Fusang tries to manage the traumatic effects of this redoubled violence by treating Chris like everyone else, biting off one of his buttons as a reminder of her "peculiar contact" with him (*Fusang* 184; *Lost Daughter* 224). The rape scene suggests that Fusang's resistance to heteronormative, monogamous desire—manifested later in her refusal to marry Chris and in her decision to wed herself to Da Yong right before his execution—derives from her perception of the contradictory and traumatic nature of this desire as well as from the ways she manages this trauma. Both Fusang's social position as a racialized, sexualized object and her refusal to be subsumed into socially instituted desire enable her to become an agent of new modes of subjectivity. Although Fusang's rejection of normative desire does not immediately produce an ideal model of relationality within or outside of the text, it at least suggests a possibility for approaching this ideal.

The novel's radical undoing of normative sexual desire profoundly challenges the tenets of liberal multiculturalism in the United States, in particular the sovereignty and autonomy of the racialized female body, qualities that are often used to measure the significance of writings by women of color. The novel's radical edge is significantly dulled in the translation and all but ignored by its reviewers, none of whom mention the crucial passages I have cited here. The Chinese critics' failure to point out the utopian potential of Fusang's character, as well as their allegorical approach to Chinese immigrant literature in the U.S., including *Fusang*, is fundamentally at odds with the novel's dismantling of the very idea of coherent subjects. A number of Chinese scholars of Chinese immigrant literature have started to consider how this writing interrogates the process of identity formation, but the Sinocentric allegorical approach is hard to break away from in the current climate of ascending Chinese nationalism.[29] My reading of Fusang as a transgressive figure engaged in undoing the normative subject and creating new modes of relationality shows how the novel cannot be easily contained within modes of criticism that use immigrant literature to consolidate sexual, racial, and national identity.

---

29. Rao Pengzi calls for a "multicultural and cross-cultural" approach to overseas Chinese literature that would focus on the subversive configuration of identity and subjectivity in this body of texts (57).

Asian American Literary Criticism in a Transnational Context

As I mentioned in my introduction, this essay illustrates how Chinese/Asian immigrant writings, with their multiple origins and trajectories, open new terrain for Asian American literary criticism and Asian American studies in general. Asian American studies, with its origin in the sociopolitical as well as cultural movements of the 1960s and 1970s, sought to contest institutional racism by, in Eng's words, "claim[ing] ... the space of the U.S. nation-state as enfranchised citizen-subjects" (209). The contestation of homogeneous notions of America in Asian American discourses of the 1980s set the stage for more radical destabilization of U.S. national identity. Since the early 1990s, Asian American studies has given rise to, and in turn become transformed by, a set of transnational projects that focus on the various transnational flows between North America and Asia and the differential workings of U.S. influence in Asia.

The role of literary studies in a transnationalized Asian American studies is yet to be mapped out, but it is certainly crucial that we try to trace the routes along which Asian American literary texts travel, while conducting close analysis of discursive production at various points on these routes. A transnational mode of criticism, which this essay hopes to advance, helps interrogate the discourses of racial, ethnic, and national identity in different but linked national (or local) contexts. Asian women have been central to ongoing discussions in academia and the public sphere about the sex trade, military prostitution, and interracial marriage. While it is crucial to excavate the historical and contemporary experiences of these women, it is equally important to think about how they generate fictions and metaphors in different languages and contexts.

Columbia University

WORKS CITED

Barnhouse, Rebecca. Rev. of *The Lost Daughter of Happiness*, by Yan Geling. *English Journal* May 2002: 97–99.

Bersani, Leo. "Against Monogamy." *Oxford Literary Review* 20 (1999): 3–21.

———. *Homos*. Cambridge, MA: Harvard UP, 1995.

———. "Is the Rectum a Grave?" *AIDS: Cultural Analysis/Cultural Activism.* Ed. Donald Crimp. Cambridge, MA: MIT P, 1988. 197–222.

———. "Sociability and Cruising." *Umbr(a): A Journal of the Unconscious* (2002): 9–23.

Bhabha, Homi. *The Location of Culture.* London: Routledge, 1994.

Bow, Leslie. *Betrayal and Other Acts of Subversion: Feminism, Sexual Politics, Asian American Women's Literature.* Princeton, NJ: Princeton UP, 2001.

Butler, Judith. *Bodies That Matter: On the Discursive Limits of "Sex."* New York: Routledge, 1993.

Chan, Sucheng. *Asian Americans: An Interpretative History.* Boston: Twayne, 1991.

Chen, Sihe. *Dang Dai Zhong Guo Wen Xue Shi Jiao Cheng* [History of contemporary Chinese literature]. Shanghai: Fudan UP, 1999.

Chuh, Kandice. *Imagine Otherwise: On Asian Americanist Critique.* Durham, NC: Duke UP, 2003.

Dai, Jinhua. "Behind Global Spectacle and National Image Making." Trans. Jonathan Noble. *Positions: East Asian Cultures Critique* 9.1 (2001): 161–86.

Dirlik, Arif, and Xudong Zhang. "Introduction: Postmodernism and China." *boundary 2* 24.3 (1997): 1–18.

Dworkin, Andrea. "Prostitution and Male Supremacy." *Michigan Journal of Gender and Law* 1 (1993): 1–12.

Eng, David L. *Racial Castration: Managing Masculinity in Asian America.* Durham, NC: Duke UP, 2001.

Espiritu, Yen Le. *Asian American Women and Men: Labor, Laws, and Love.* Thousand Oaks, CA: Sage, 1997.

Gould, Emily. "Re: The Lost Daughter of Happiness." E-mail to the author, 21 Nov. 2005.

Hamamoto, Darrell, dir. *Yellowcaust: A Patriot Act.* 2003.

Hou, James, dir. *Masters of the Pillow.* Avenue Films, 2003.

Kang, Laura Hyun Yi. *Compositional Subjects: Enfiguring Asian/American Women.* Durham, NC: Duke UP, 2002.

Kim, Elaine H. "'Such Opposite Creatures': Men and Women in Asian American Literature." *Michigan Quarterly Review* 29 (1990): 68–93.

Kim, Kichung. "Affliction and Opportunity: Korean Literature in Diaspora, a Brief Overview," *Korean Studies* 25 (2001): 261–76.

Kinkley, Jeffrey C. Rev. of *The Lost Daughter of Happiness,* by Yan Geling. *World Literature Today* 76.2 (2002): 136–37.

Kristeva, Julia. *Powers of Horror: An Essay on Abjection.* Trans. Leon S. Roudiez. New York: Columbia UP, 1982.

Lee, Rachel. *The Americas of Asian American Literature: Gendered Fictions of Nation and Transnation.* Princeton, NJ: Princeton UP, 1999.

Lin, Cuiwei. "Fusang zhong de Nu Xing Guan" [Femininity in *Fusang*]. *Huawen Shixue* [World literature in Chinese] 62 (Mar. 2004): 65–68.

Liu, Kang. "Is There an Alternative to (Capitalist) Globalization? The Debate about Modernity in China." *The Cultures of Globalization*. Ed. Fredric Jameson and Masao Miyoshi. Durham, NC: Duke UP, 1998. 164–88.

Lovell, Julia. "Chinatown Lady." *Times Literary Supplement* 10 Aug. 2001: 20.

McCunn, Ruthanne Lum. *Thousand Pieces of Gold: A Biographical Novel*. 1981. Boston: Beacon, 1988.

Moallem, Minoo, and Iain A. Boal. "Multicultural Nationalism and the Poetics of Inauguration." *Between Woman and Nation: Nationalisms, Transnational Feminisms, and the State*. Ed. Caren Kaplan, Norma Alarcón, and Minoo Moallem. Durham, NC: Duke UP, 1999. 243–63.

Muscatine, Doris. *Old San Francisco: The Biography of a City from Early Days to the Earthquake*. New York: Putnam, 1975.

Rao, Pengzi. "Haiwai Huawen Wenxue de Xin Shiye" [New approaches to Chinese-language literature overseas]. *Shehui Kexuejia* [Social scientists] 70 (1998): 55–59.

Said, Edward. *Orientalism*. London: Pantheon, 1978.

Schueller, Malini Johar. *U.S. Orientalisms: Race, Nation, and Gender in Literature, 1790–1890*. Ann Arbor: U of Michigan P, 1998.

Sedgwick, Eve. *Between Men: English Literature and Male Homosocial Desire*. New York: Columbia UP, 1985.

Silber, Cathy. Telephone interview. 27 Nov. 2004.

Song, Qiang, Zhang Zangzang, and Qiao Bian. *Zhongguo keyi shuo bu—Lengzhan hou shidai de zhengzhi yu qinggan jueze* [China can say no—political and emotional decisions in the post–cold war era]. Beijing: Zhonghua gongshang lianhe chubanshe [Chinese Industry and Commerce Press], 1996.

Steiner, Stan. *Fusang: The Chinese Who Built America*. New York: Harper, 1979.

Teng, Wei. "Huai Xiang Zhongguo de Fangshi" [The remembering of China in Yan Geling's immigrant literature]. *Huawen wenxue* [World literature in Chinese] 62 (Mar. 2004): 63–69.

Tong, Benson. *Unsubmissive Women: Chinese Prostitutes in Nineteenth-Century San Francisco*. Norman: U of Oklahoma P, 1994.

Towey, Cathleen A. Rev. of *The Lost Daughter of Happiness*, by Yan Geling. *Library Journal* 15 Feb. 2001: 203–4.

Wang, Hui. "Contemporary Chinese Thought and the Question of Modernity." 1997. *China's New Order: Society, Politics, and Economy in Transition*. Cambridge, MA: Harvard UP, 2003. 139–87.

Wong, Sau-ling. "Ethnicizing Gender: An Exploration of Sexuality as Sign in Chinese Immigrant Literature." *Reading the Literatures of Asian America*. Ed. Shirley Geok-lin Lim and Amy Ling. Philadelphia: Temple UP, 1992. 111–26.

———. "The Stakes of Textual Border-Crossing: Hualing Nieh's *Mulberry and Peach* in Sinocentric, Asian American, and Feminist Critical Practices."

Orientations: Mapping Studies in the Asian Diaspora. Durham, NC: Duke UP, 2001. 130–52.

———. "When Asian American Literature Leaves 'Home': On Internationalizing Asian American Literary Studies." *Crossing Oceans: Reconfiguring American Literary Studies in the Pacific Rim*. Ed. Noelle Brada-Williams and Karen Chow. Hong Kong: Hong Kong UP, 2004. 29–40.

Yan, Geling. *Fusang*. Vol. 3 of *Yan Geling Wen Ji* [The collected works of Yan Geling]. 7 vols. Beijing: Dang Dai Shi Jie Chu Ban She [Contemporary World Press], 2003.

———. *The Lost Daughter of Happiness*. Trans. Cathy Silber. New York: Hyperion, 2001.

Yung, Judy. *Unbound Voices: A Documentary History of Chinese Women in San Francisco*. Berkeley: U of California P, 1999.

Zaman, Niaz. "The Americanization of Bapsi Sidhwa." *Bangladesh Journal of American Studies* 7–8 (1994): 197–212.

E R I C   H A Y O T

Immigrating Fictions: Unfailing Mediation in *Dictée* and *Becoming Madame Mao*

· 1 ·

The originality of the Brechtian sign, Roland Barthes once said, comes from its always being read twice. "What Brecht gives us to read," Barthes wrote in 1975, "is, via a kind of disconnect, the look of a reader, not the object of that look; that object only reaches us through the intellectual (alienated) act of a first reader who is already on stage" ("Brecht" 265; my translation). Barthes meant that objects on the Brechtian stage never appear on stage as themselves. They are instead objects—facts, things, people, situations—as someone has perceived them, elements of a story told by an actor who performs a relation to the objects of his regard that subjects them, in advance, to reading. From the edge of the proscenium, the audience sees the reading, not the objects, and sees simultaneously the possibility of reading the objects otherwise. The Brechtian theater thus shows that *an* object is always *someone*'s object, that any given thing, person, or situation has already emerged, prior to any single perception of it, as the "reading" of someone else whose first reading was simply to make this object the object of a look, thereby differentiating it from the seamless fabric of the real.

Like the Brechtian sign, a translated text appears before its audience only after passing through the alienated act of a first reader. There it testifies to the awkward and complex relationship between author and translator, between the translation that appears and the

I am grateful to Christopher Bush, Haun Saussy, and Steve Yao, who commented on earlier versions of this essay, and to Rebecca Walkowitz, whose suggestions substantially improved its final form.

original, authentic text that exists somewhere to ground it. The latter's existence and status as origin can be adequately testified to only by the translator who brings the text into its new linguistic home. For it is the translator who assures readers of the translation that, yes, there exists abroad some text very much like this one, some original to which they could return in order to verify this translation. And yet the translator, like an actor, has a strange relationship to the signs whose passage he or she transmits. There must have been a moment at which she thought, not simply, I *like* this book, but also, I want this book to be translated so that other people will like it. To translate is in this sense always to do something for someone else, or for something else, namely the text. But the sad paradox of translation is that the act of birthing the text into a new space will, by rewriting its language, murder the very thing that made it what it was in the first place. Or at least murder it *enough*, so that it emerges on the other side of the translation through the "act of a first reader."

Just as the Brechtian sign figures translation, translation can figure the Brechtian theater, where the violence done to the sign can be read more broadly as a violence done to traditional notions of character and identification: Brecht's stage, by making its intermediaries visible, hoped to keep its audiences from forgetting the fact of the translation, from imagining that what they saw up on stage were *people* and not actors. That in turn was supposed to keep them from seeing "people"—bourgeois constructs all—outside the theater, to keep them from seeing action as personality, so that they could recognize it, quite simply, as acting. The politics that resulted would consist of the audience's seeing the world not as a neutral fact but as a translation, as a made thing produced by historical actors (human and nonhuman), some with interests in making us forget their role in the production.

Because the translator as figure mediates a passing through or a crossing over, it resembles not so much an immigrant as the mediator—coyote or cargo ship, spouse or corporate sponsor, I–129 visa or Alien Exclusion Act—that frames and establishes the circumstances under which immigration occurs. "Immigrant fictions," if by the phrase one means translations or "world" literature in English, cross the path of a series of literary, capitalized intermediaries (agents or publishers) who judge the texts, rework them, frame them for a new public, review them in the better newspapers, and thereby authorize and ground their presence in the metropole. In these cases, the mediator, like the translator, is supposed to disappear: what one gets in the moment of a translated immigrant fiction should be the authentic and immediate voice of an other, almost always an other allegorizing a national or ethnic location. But any peek behind the curtain of this frictionless fiction shows that the mediations leave their mark: the originality of the origin has been compromised; the immigrant fiction has been modified in the act of immigration.

It's slightly more complicated if "immigrant" in "immigrant fictions" becomes possessive, meaning something like fictions of immigrants, belonging to or about immigrants. Here the category overlaps with that of ethnic American literature, especially those subsets devoted to the problems of racism, integration, and assimilation. Though such texts appear originally in English, their subject matter is the process of mediation itself, and their focus on literature by ethnic authors (as though white people were not also immigrants) is a measure of the cultural roles played not only by ethnicity but also by fiction in the contemporary imagination. The classic ethnic American bildungsroman tends to be read as an autobiography, with the protagonist standing in for the author. Here the *fiction* (rather than the act of translation) is the agent of transformation, and the movement it authorizes between person and protagonist, experience and language is an allegory of the movement of the ethnic subject him- or herself.[1] The ethnic American narrative manages an internal migration, a movement from outside the space of a community or national recognition to its inside, mediated by the act of writing or, more formally, by fictionality and generic form. Caught up in its inevitable reception as an allegory for self- and national transformation, the fiction of ethnic American *Bildung* enacts the very transformation it represents, mediating through fiction the fiction of self-transformation it

---

1. This insistent linkage between authors and autobiography may be culturally particular to the United States. Laura Hyun Yi Kang proposes troubling the "alignment of 'America' and 'Autobiography,'" arguing that the "distinct *autos* of American autobiography may itself have to be socially and historically degraded" (63).

narrates.[2] The dual and mutual translation that ensues—the ethnic subject bending toward "America," the latter adjusting itself ever so slightly to the presence of the new actor on the scene—means that "America" and the self in question produce in their cohabitation the fiction of a resolution on both sides. Call that resolution, with one eye on Brecht, and the other on the INS, a naturalization.

But some fictions know that story is just a fiction, is already a transformation, and so refuse (or can be seen to refuse) the consolations of that final crossing over, the definitive translation. What such fictions tell, like the translator's expert annotations, are never quite the origins they announce themselves to be; and the conclusions they reach, the meaning they finally give, never free themselves enough from the mediation that makes it possible to imagine the ending they dream of. In such texts—call them immigrating fictions—the fiction, like the Brechtian actor, never renounces its claim on the process of the novel; like the customs officer, the literary agent, and the coyote, it demands its cut in the transaction. Two of the major recent texts of Asian American prose suggest that the necessity of that cut in fiction can be understood both as an artifact of ethnic American fictional form and a feature of the literary landscape of cosmopolitan, postcolonial modernity.

· 2 ·

Theresa Hak Kyung Cha's *Dictée* "presents itself ... as a work of passage from one language to another. Thus it deals thematically with the problem of translation, not in its putative symmetrical equivalence of the signification between two languages, but as the work of labor that is required to move from one language to another" (Sakai 26). That labor is visible from the text's first page, on which the physical

---

2. The classic theorization of the relationship between national literature and allegory is Fredric Jameson's in "Third World Literature in the Era of Multinational Capitalism." Jameson's use of "third world" later became the subject of a fairly intense critique by Aijaz Ahmad. But the general argument is recuperable, I think, without the term "third world" at all: American literary criticism's obsessive reading of all American literature as national allegory, for instance, can be thought of as an expression of postcolonial resistance to Empire, an anxiety about the growth of geopolitical dominance and the establishment of in-groups, and as a deep expression of geographic provincialism.

evidence of a French dictation exercise ("*C'était le premier jour point Elle venait de loin point ce soir au dîner virgule...*") appears directly above its own too-literal translation into English.[3] Elsewhere the text incorporates Korean Hangul, romanizations of Greek and Korean names, and Chinese characters, as well as photographs, maps, diagrams, and typed and handwritten documents. This collocation of sources gives the text the feel of an edited archive; the gathering of representations, organized in *Dictée*'s case by a complex but unified narrative voice, aims to trace the voice's own immediate life experience (a childhood spent in French Catholic schools in Korea, a return to South Korea as an American citizen) as well as the international, postcolonial history of a nation-state whose place in the networks of historical and cultural imperialism makes it an unstable or impossible origin for that voice's identity. Caught between personal and historical selfhood, *Dictée* attempts, writes Shelley Sunn Wong, "a new figuration of the dialectic between individuation and ideological interpellation, one which would allow for human agency at the same time that it acknowledged the determinative force of external constraints and impositions" (118).[4]

Readers of *Dictée* have recognized that the book presents a shifting substrate of references whose status as potential origin (of subjectivity, of meaning) is always called into question by the possibility that the entire text is just another dictation. Naoki Sakai, for instance, argues that *Dictée* emerges from the combination of a desire to exist inside the intersubjective work of translation on one hand and the deep wish for a return to a mother tongue on the other. The text embraces its own fragmentation even as it expresses the desire for a definitive origin, but it ultimately "prefers" to remain

---

3. As Shelley Sunn Wong has noted, the first numbered page of the text (on which the dictation exercise appears) follows the book's proper "beginning," which includes a frontispiece containing a photograph of a Hangul inscription found in a tunnel in Nagano Prefecture, Matsushiro City, Japan (108). For more on the history of the inscription, which reads "Mother, I miss you, I'm hungry, I want to go home," see Kang 99n7. Lisa Lowe's reading of this section of the text is masterful (132–35).

4. Because so much of *Dictée* is poetry, because much of it seems to have been written under the literary influence of the French poststructuralism and feminism of the late 1970s (Cha studied briefly in Paris with Monique Wittig, and parts of *Dictée* resemble the latter's 1969 *Les guerillères*), it lends itself especially well to sweeping statements about the instability of identity and political history. As I suggest in what follows, any such reading must account for the text's desire for and suspicion of those categories.

outside either of these solutions.[5] The text's feminism, Wong writes, likewise rejects the solace of origins despite its desire for them: "In telling the mother's story, the daughter/narrator does not seek to reproduce herself upon the authentic ground of the Korean feminine. Rather, the text proceeds with the recognition that the identity of origin, in its ahistoricity, is at best an impossibility and at worst, a delusory consolation" (126). In the refusal of origins, the text also refuses to commit to a form of representation that would generate a stable version of "woman," of "Korean American," or even of "I."

These refusals appear alongside the text's deep investment in precisely the categories of which it seems most suspicious. As Sakai and Wong point out, the text's shifting, unstable language takes place alongside its intense expression of a desire for representational clarity, for a political or gendered or ethnic position from which speech might be possible. Any reading of *Dictée* must account for the presence of that desire in the text, for the degree to which Korea and a feminist genealogy are not simply the arbitrary materials on which the text works out its refusal of consolatory identity but are instead the very things that produce the desire and need for consolation in the first place. It is not, then, that the text's poststructuralist relation to language and representation must be considered apart from its "real" or historically material concerns, but rather that its attempts to work through these concerns confront and are mediated by the text's relation to the reality and historical materiality of the language that has been given to it by the world's history.[6]

---

5. The "mother tongue" in which the text invests so much energy is already multiple, as Sakai suggests: "Mother, you are a child still.... Still, you speak the tongue the mandatory language like the others. It is not your own. Even if it is not you know you must. You are Bi-lingual. You are Tri-lingual... Mother tongue is your refuge" (Cha 45).

6. Elaine H. Kim has argued that the rush to poststructuralist readings erases the novel's historical references: "When post-structuralist critics ignore Cha's Korean heritage, thus denying Korean American identity and gender, it is a case of meaningful omission: they are practicing a kind of reverse Orientalism, according to which we are all the same (white) people" (22). But couple this problem with the degree to which writing by subjects labeled "ethnic" (in relation to some metropole or other) is made inexorably to speak to the condition of its own ethnicity—what Rey Chow has called "coercive mimeticism" (107)—and texts like *Dictée* are caught between a poststructuralist rock and an ethnic hard place, their aesthetic radicalism reduced to a reflection of the instability of their "ethnic" position, so that any act of textual deviation from the realist norm will now simply produce a sense that the writer has adequately "reflected" the fragmentation and radical dislocation of his or her ethnic identity.

In fact *Dictée*, considered as a text and as a physical artifact, must be understood as an attempt to work out precisely this set of problems, as though the text and the book together—that is, the images and words on the pages, and also the physical materiality of the pages themselves—were able to function as an allegory of *Dictée*'s own powerful, incomplete making.[7] One way to read the text is to understand it as a series of attempts to think through the problem of its own literary voice.

The development of those attempts depends, from the book's title page onward, on the idea of dictation. As Sakai points out, the writer of a dictation exercise is meant "to say what she is expected to say *without meaning it*" (27); the writer's body in this sense is designed to be a neutral pass-through for a teacher's voice, with high marks given for faithful reproduction—for reproduction faithful, that is, to the disappearance of the writer as medium. The literal appearance of dictation in the text's opening pages gives way to a series of historical and educational metaphors in which dictation is directly or indirectly implicated: the imposition of the Japanese language on Koreans during Japan's occupation, the prayers and vows of the French Catholic tradition, and the experience of American immigration, education, and incomplete assimilation. The work of these layered metaphors is to suggest, echoing the text's title, that all of *Dictée* might be the result of an extravagant exercise in dictation, an attempt to dictate, to repeat without meaning another dictation, but also to dictate to a reader the network of historical and personal effects that make it possible, finally, for the narrator to write.

Where is the origin or ground of dictated speech? How might a speaker whose language is, in some complex sense, simply the result of a transformation from dictation to dictability find a place from which to begin? Here *Dictée*'s textual machinery comes with

---

7. The temptation is to read the whole of *Dictée* as the anthropomorphic substitute for the subject whose becoming it appears to enact (and whose transformation would therefore be final), allegorizing the physical enclosure of the book as object into the final closure of a coherent and delimited self, making the unity of the text-as-book testify to the completion of another story of ethnic Americanization. But it would be a mistake to read the fact of the book's publication as a sign that its speaking subject has completed and organized itself into a final, definite configuration; the fact of publication is a datum, but not a final one, in *Dictée*'s self-production as book.

the manual printed on the inside. At one point, for instance, the text seems to be working out precisely the problem of beginnings:

> Further, Further inside. Further than. To middle. Deeper. Without measure. Deeper than. Without means of measure. To core. In another tongue. Same word. Slight mutation of the same. Undefinable. Shift. Shift slightly. Into a different sound. The difference. How it discloses the air. Slight. Another word. Same. Parts of the same atmosphere. Deeper. Center. Without distance. No particular distance from center to periphery. Points of measure effaced. To begin there. There. In Media Res.
>
> (157)

"In medias res"—literally, "in the middle of the thing"—describes the literary strategy of beginning a narrative "already in progress," in which the immediate and intense narrative or dialogic action of the story gestures analeptically backward to another, slower beginning ("In the county of Derbyshire, in the village of Perth, there lived a miller . . ."). Such a beginning is always, therefore, a "middle," a place from which the text will later constellate the beginning and ending it requires. But here *Dictée*'s narrator seems to suggest that any such middle must also be a beginning defined by depth and interiority, by its presence in a general atmosphere which contains slight differences that it does not organize into a system: "Points of measure effaced."

The phrase in Latin is correctly written "in medias res," as "medias" is the accusative plural feminine of "medius," middle; in literary historical terms, "in medias res" describes also one of the classic openings of the epic form. The text's replacement of "medias" by "Media" (the accusative *singular* feminine) is, among other things, a failure to respond properly to cultural and linguistic dictation. The "mistake" highlights the degree to which repetition in language depends on and organizes itself around concepts like grammatical number and gender; by reproducing the word "Media" in the middle of things, the text showcases its own investment in the physical form of linguistic or representational transmission.[8] There is no easy way to translate the grammatical error of *Dictée*'s Latin into English ("in the

---

8. *Dictée* includes a number of apparently typographical errors, some of which, like this one, permit extensive reading. For example, in a poem that appears in French and English on facing pages, the word "paragraphs" appears on both sides, though the

middles of things" would literally relate the Latin plural), but it would be equally difficult to translate the pun of "In Media Res" back into Latin. The text's language exists, in some sense, in between the two linguistic media that make it possible, the distance from its center to their peripheries difficult if not impossible to "measure."

Media are always, *Dictée* seems to suggest here, in the "middle of things." This is so at least partly because they inter-mediate the process of the transmission of meaning by acting as the physical surface on which or in which the "message" gets delivered: "Shift. Shift slightly. Into a different sound. The difference. How it discloses the air" (157). The medium's disclosure of message entails, the text seems to say, the production of a slight shift or difference, leaving its mark on the texts that pass "through" it.

Even the physical voice—site of air's shaping and disclosure— can be considered in this sense a "medium," an intermediary between something like intention and meaning. It is in this context that the text's reproduction of a diagram of the human vocal system, complete with subdiagram showing the "Abduction of vocal folds for phonation," mediates or, better, re-mediates the poetic text that appears on its facing page—"Cracked tongue. Broken tongue./ Pidgeon. Semblance of speech"—by making visible the physical medium within which any tongue, any pidgin, will inevitably operate (74–75). *Dictée*'s search for its own literary "voice" turns out to be mediated by the anthropomorphic metaphor of the physical voice. The question that results is not Michel Foucault's "What difference does it make who is speaking?" (614) but, rather, What difference does it make to make the physical system of vocalization a metaphor for the right to produce social meaning? What difference does it make what "speaking" is? That is, to what degree is the text's preoccupation with "voice" already mediated by the anthropomorphism of the metaphor on which a search for voice depends?

French word is "paragraphes." Mistake, or material for interpretation? Likewise, Cha's spelling "correspondance" in a section otherwise in English may be an invocation to involve the body in communication (dance) or a reference to the Baudelaire poem "Correspondances," with its "forests of symbols," rather than a typo, even though the word is spelled "correspondence" elsewhere (33). In a text that plays frequently with translation, typography, and error, reading any given sign as *not* meaning by calling it a mistake feels like a risky strategy.

Characteristically, such a question is not the end of things for *Dictée* but another beginning, as the text presses the subject of voice relentlessly through another mediation. Four pages after the diagram, the text reproduces a map of North and South Korea. A map is, of course, another translation, another dictation authored by the intersection of land's topographical surface and the political, human arrangement of that surface into countries, cities, borders, and demilitarized zones. The fact of two Koreas testifies, also, to the trauma of the Korean conflict, the forced separation of millions of Korean families, and the degree to which the geographical area known in English as "Korea" was, in the early 1980s, the site of a series of conflicts produced by powers that interacted with Korea from both "outside" and "inside" (the latter connected explicitly, in *Dictée*, to the search for political "voice" that produced student demonstrations in 1980 which led to the South Korean army's killing of at least two hundred people and the declaration of martial law).

The map's appearance is perhaps most striking because the vertical arrangement of the Korean peninsula visually echoes the diagram of the vocal system four pages earlier, the bottom edge of South Korea coordinating roughly with the picture of lung and diaphragm, the North Korean border with China figuring—again, roughly—the "Nasal passage" at the top left of the medical illustration. In this fanciful visual translation, the problems of speaking/writing as any given individual subject (and therefore the problems of identity and of the aesthetic that the book so rigorously engages), *Dictée* suggests, reimagine or rehearse the problems of national identity, imperialism, and international mobility that ground the book. Korea's historical role as a "passage" between Japan and the Asian mainland becomes the subject of the metaphor of voice. The nation cannot be spoken as such without speaking geopolitical history. And geopolitical history cannot proceed except by the organization and sequencing of voices, the adjudication of whose relative "authenticity" is one of the fundamental functions of the nation-state.[9]

---

9. Any such adjudication depends, since it will always involve the matching of a manner of speech (an accent, a tone, not to mention content) with a state-sponsored version of reality, on its very own theory of the aesthetic. The notion that deviations from a "realist" aesthetic will necessarily disrupt the realisms of mainstream political power ought to be

But the text does not simply stop there. Instead, the strange parallel of map and diagram highlights the degree to which the comparisons being made here proceed through a medium of their own, namely that of the visual system. The conjunction between human voice and geopolitical history is sustained and mediated by a visual pun that can be described but not directly reproduced in words.[10] Whatever theory of subjectivity one generates from the conjunction of literary, physical, and political voices emerges, therefore, through a visual medium that ignores the question of voice entirely. The problem of political speech appears to us in a vision.

Here we have something like a figure for the text as a whole, in which an initial mediation (of intention, of desire) is turned inside-out by the fact of its being mediated by yet another substance, namely the surface of the physical page that allows it to appear before us. In fact the exercise of dictation can now be understood not simply as an act of repetition, but also of translation across media: the first problem of dictation, almost always the putting down in writing of a spoken text whose meaning is intended neither by its speaker nor its writer, has to do with the translation of sound into writing. Dictation is not a repetition but a remediation, and the written sign it generates is already, in the moment of its inscription, imperfectly doubled by the voice of a speaker who performs it. As the translation of a teacher's vocal cue into *"C'était le premier jour point"* ("It was the first day period") suggests, any attempt to render precisely into writing the sounds uttered by the teacher constitutes a "failure" of the act of writing; the correct response to this dictation is

---

seriously shaken by the Bush administration's recourse to surrealism, myth, and storytelling. The notion that power doesn't have an aesthetic as such (that is, that its aesthetic is "neutral" or "realistic") is just as damaging as the notion that aesthetics have nothing to do with power. What literature and literary scholars have to offer as political critique may well stem from their expertise in understanding how stories are made and told, an argument deducible also from *Dictée*.

10. It is also the case that diagrams and maps are effectively subject to different representational rules and could well be called different "media." The diagram of the vocal system, for instance, must be read as an "illustrative figure which, *without representing the exact appearance of an object*, gives an outline or general scheme of it, so as to exhibit the shape and relations of its various parts" ("diagram, *n.*"; emphasis added). The diagram functions, therefore, as an illustration of a network of relations; what it represents is a *system* and not, like a map, a set of spatial relations.

"*C'était le premier jour.*"—with the sound "*point*" makes turned into a grammatical period. Thus on its very first page *Dictée* has already begun from "the middle of things," foregrounding the medium of dictation that is its major organizing metaphor, and even in this first usage the text shows that it will not blithely follow the instructions of its primary mediating form. Or rather that it will follow them too well, to the letter. How to construe this obedience to the letter—as stupidity or resistance—is the question *Dictée* addresses to the teacher in us.

Lest this play between voice and image, speech and writing, be understood too literally as a language game, *Dictée*, in a section devoted to Yu Guan Soon, a woman whose torture and murder by Japanese forces for her part in the movement of March 1, 1919, has made her a nationalist hero in Korea, connects those themes explicitly to the act of making national, gendered history. Located in the section of the text called "Clio: History," this passage—which appears a few pages after the text reproduces a grainy, captionless photograph of a young woman, facing the inscription "YU GUAN SOON / BIRTH: By Lunar Calendar, 15, March 1903 / DEATH: 12, October, 1920. 8:20 A.M." (25)—considers the difference between national or political history and personal memory:

> Some will not know age. Some not age. Time stops. Time will stop for some. For them especially. Eternal time. No age. Time fixes for some. Their image, the memory of them is not given to deterioration, unlike the captured image that extracts from the soul precisely by reproducing, multiplying itself. Their countenance evokes not the hallowed beauty, beauty from seasonal decay, evokes not the inevitable, not death, but the dy-ing.
>
> (37)

The text's consideration of memory organizes itself around the difference between an image frozen in memory and a photograph, an image frozen on film. In favorably comparing the "memory of them . . . not given to deterioration" to the "captured image" (figuring the Japanese capture of Yu Guan Soon) that reproduces and multiplies itself, the narrator connects the visual exactness of a photograph's mechanical reproduction with "deterioration" and soul-stealing, and perhaps with the degree to which the social reproduction of an image as a photograph is an affront to the image as it is archived in living memory.[11]

And yet if time stops for some, if some do not know age, is that because of a death that comes too early—a question one must ask in the case of Yu Guan Soon—or because the nationalist image subtends the subject's immobility in the narrative imaginary? Who is to blame for the freezing of the image? The text gives no indication that its photograph is of Yu Guan Soon. Instead, this image of an ordinary, expressionless face must be read in the context of its own reproduction and multiplication inside the pages of *Dictée*, as well as in relation to the national myth of female self-sacrifice through which Yu Guan Soon's life is arranged. The text does not reconstruct an image archive that would ground a recovery of the truth of Yu Guan Soon's identity prior to her emergence as a nationalist hero, but it asks what such a life, such an image, might have looked like from a perspective other than the one given by official history. "She is," the narrator writes, "born of one mother and one father" (25). That is, she is, somewhere—but not here, not today, not in this history or in these images—*ordinary*.[12] The text does not so much recover that ordinariness as simply denote its loss.

Here again, then, the text calls up the apparatus of reality and history, as with the diagram and the map, only to undermine its ability to cohere, leaving certain readers with the sense "that modern Korea exists only as a history of found images—even, of dead images" (Cheng 122). But at least one can say, about dead images, that they are there and that they are dead; though *Dictée* may refuse to construct out of such an image or out of Yu Guan Soon's life an ontologically secure theory of what it means to be a Korean woman circa 1919, it nonetheless believes in the value of recording the fact of its presence. And the text goes on to suggest that the fixed image of the photograph—"Time fixes for some" could also refer to the

---

11. For further commentary on Cha's use of Yu Guan Soon, see Kim 16–17.

12. I mean "ordinary" here in the sense that everyone is "ordinarily" subject to a generational discourse of origin and lineage. But it is also the case that Yu Guan Soon is "ordinary" in her heroism, as Laura Hyun Yi Kang has argued: "Being 'marked exceptional' for one's 'self-sacrifice' points to the impossible generic fixation of women within many nationalist narratives. The passage notes the paradoxical historiographic operation that simultaneously privileges the individual as *unique* in her historical context and yet renders her a *generic* figure of self-denial in a broader discourse" (227).

fixing solution used to develop photographic prints—fixes not Yu Guan Soon's death but her "dy-ing," the hyphen marking the text's insistence on process rather than end result. The photographic image itself may be dead, but what it captures is the gerund, which, as William Lily wrote in his 1549 introduction to grammar, "has both the active and the passive signification," a difference irreducible to a certain literalness ("Gerund"). Even a corpse in a photograph is alive, Roland Barthes once noted, if only *as* a corpse: "the living image of a dead thing" (*Camera* 79).

Through the photograph—itself something like a repetition without meaning, a dictation exercise for "what the world might look like in our own absence" (Jameson, *Postmodernism* 248)—*Dictée* reminds readers that what time "fixes" in the photograph can be understood only in relation to the technological demands of its production.[13] The photographic image—like a map, diagram, or metaphor—is a site of mediation, a datum to be translated, interpreted, and organized. It is not the final testimony of the real. In this context, the photograph's lack of a caption places the burden of mediation and interpretation firmly on the reader, who must read it not as origin but as medium, as an object whose interpretation begins from somewhere inside the imperfectly constellated atmosphere of a story "already in progress."

Lisa Lowe writes that *Dictée* "thematizes the failure of translation as a topos of faithful reproduction" (134). I would say that the text's treatment of "translation" in all its possible meanings thematizes, in some sense, the failure of "failure" as a useful concept for describing what translation is or does. The translation that "fails," in *Dictée*, is first of all connected perpetually to the notion of dictation, and therefore to both repetition-without-meaning (as Sakai notes) and repetition-that-is-not-repetition: the dictation exercise, by translating orality into literacy, can succeed only by failing to reproduce precisely and faithfully. Likewise, a map is a map only if it does not precisely reproduce the object it represents; and a voice is a voice only

---

13. In this sense, what Kang says about another of the book's photographs, this one of a Hangul inscription, applies equally well to the photograph of Yu Guan Soon: "its stark framing and odd placement in the text remind us that this is a printed reproduction of a photographic trace of the material inscription, which the readers of *Dictée* must confront in such a multiply mediated form" (233), the "material inscription" in this case being the biological surface of Yu Guan Soon's body.

insofar as it emerges, *Dictée* suggests, from somewhere that is neither the geopolitical map nor the biological system of its possibilities. No one says what they (would like to) mean. Each of these representations is a "failure," but *Dictée* shows failure to be the fundamental intermediary of all representation, all communication. In this sense, what looks like "failure" probably ought to be called something else. In the process of transformation, of production, of expression, and even of living, what comes "In Media Res," as the text has it, never quite ceases to interrupt the process it makes possible, never ceases to be oh-so-slightly unfaithful to the origin and the destination, the source and the target, that imagine themselves on either side (temporally, physically) of its mediation. What begins, "begin[s] there," as the text says (or doesn't "say"), in the middle of things.

· 3 ·

As a concept in narrative form, "in medias res" usefully undermines the notion of linear progress by rubbing the discourse against the story. Whether or not the "real" beginning of a narrative (that is, the first element in the temporal progress of a story) is ever retrieved, the "medias res" beginning at least opens the possibility of a story-beginning abandoned by the needs of a future-oriented discourse. That any such beginning will, of necessity, operate simultaneously as a "middle" (of the story) and as a beginning (of the discourse) simply means that beginning in the middle of things always announces itself as double, as something that is a beginning only in the eye of a particular fiction.

Articulated by a text that also thematizes a concern with geopolitical and personal history, this concern with beginning from the middle/ medium must be understood also as a form of interference with literary genre. The genre I have in mind here is the ethnic bildungsroman, specifically the American version sustained and popularized by a public eager to have stories of successful immigrant assimilation confirm the prejudice of national superiority, and typified in the context of Asian American literary criticism (rightly or wrongly) by the "model minority" novels of Amy Tan.

Dictée's preference for the middle of things makes it profoundly resistant to being read as a bildungsroman of this type; the story arc such a narrative would require depends too heavily on an ending firmly differentiated from a beginning, whereas *Dictée* in some sense never gets far enough past the critique of those concepts to provide the comfort of a plot summary (first, Korea was occupied by the Japanese, then I went to Catholic school, then I came to America, and so on). Though one may therefore read the novel as a critique of the more popular, more obtuse form, reading it as *just* a critique would fail to recognize that *Dictée* confesses or elaborates its deep attraction to and need for precisely the bildungsroman even as it rejects it. It is from the perspective of the book's naming of its own desire, and from the generosity produced by understanding that desire as legitimate, if impossible, that one must begin to read *Dictée*'s relationship to other immigrating fiction.

Lisa Lowe has argued that in the case of Asian American writing, reading bildungsromanlike stories as simple-minded narratives of conversion misses the degree to which the histories such novels include disrupt or mitigate the generic structure they choose. "Even those novels that can be said to conform more closely to the formal criteria of the bildungsroman," Lowe argues, "express a contradiction between the demand for a univocal developmental narrative and the historical specificities of racialization, ghettoization, violence, and labor exploitation" (100).[14] As Lowe goes on to show, with reference to John Okada's *No-no Boy* and Carlos Bulosan's *America Is in the Heart*, the bildungsroman form also serves to showcase a series of obstacles, most often forms of racial or ethnic prejudice, that stand in the way of an America that might successfully reshape itself to accommodate the protagonist's difference; in this sense, the ethnic bildungsroman offers a political and cultural accounting of American society and its limitations. To the degree to which it presents the possibility of overcoming the obstacles it identifies, the ethnic bildungsroman thus functions as a utopian critique, even though, in the hands of certain readers, it appears to confirm the fundamental assimilability of all immigrant or ethnic Americans and the capacious generosity of the U.S. government (full citizenship for everyone!).

---

14. Like Kim, Lowe stresses the dangers of a purely aesthetic reading of textual radicalism. The contradictions derived from the conflict between narrative desire and ethnic history generate "formal deviations whose significances are misread if simply assimilated as modernist or postmodernist aesthetic codes" (*Immigrant Acts* 100).

It is in the doubled context of reception that I would like to discuss Anchee Min's *Becoming Madame Mao*. Min, who was born in Shanghai in 1957, is best known for writing *Red Azalea*, a mildly fictionalized autobiographical account of her life during the Cultural Revolution, which ends with her immigration to the United States in 1985.[15] A quick glance through reviews of Min's work suggests that much of the critical praise she receives depends precisely on the degree to which her novels' portrayals of China, and the implied liberation provided by her move to the United States, reproduce the most Eurocentric, patriotic visions of what ethnic American fiction can do, namely, serving "as a model of panethnic entrepreneurship, selling American society on the value of Asian Americans," as Viet Thanh Nguyen puts it (149). In an interview in *Publishers Weekly*, for instance, Roxanne Farmanfarmaian declares, "Anchee Min herself has emerged from the morass of Maoism cleansed, able to feel and express enormous innocence" (67). And the back cover of Min's *Wild Ginger* features quotations from reviews that give some sense of how Houghton Mifflin intends to market Min's work: "The image she creates of a world marching lockstep is chilling"; "With sly, concentrated power . . . [Min paints] a vivid picture of young people in the grip of ideology . . . [and] reminds us that the passion of youth can be channeled into tragic courses"; "Once again, Min reminds us of the freedoms we take for granted." This last citation, with its sense of the novel as a message from them to us, there to here, suggests that Min's fiction works best in its popular mode as a reminder of how good "we" Americans have it.

But such a reading depends too much on its origins in a single national location and context and therefore misses the transnational complexity of Min's work. Though Min's novels are far less aesthetically challenging than Cha's *Dictée*—indeed, it is precisely Min's formal populism that opens her novels to being read as conventional ethnic bildungsromans—it seems worth trying to read them against the grain of the interviews and reviews (and perhaps even against Min's authorial desire) in order to find expressed there something of the complexity of the transnational politics of form and meaning from which they stem.

---

15. For full readings of *Red Azalea*, see Somerson, Ben Xu, and Wenying Xu.

As in *Dictée*, one of the structural tensions in Min's writing has to do with the movement between a "source" culture that grounds certain important forms of national identity and a "target" culture from which the sexism (and, in Min's case, sexual repression) of the source culture can be criticized. Indeed, one can read her entire oeuvre as an attempt to rework popular nationalist versions of Chinese history by locating in that history the positive presence of sexuality, especially women's sexuality. In a Western context, the notion that women's sexual expression, arousal, and desire constitute a liberating gesture of self-making may not be especially radical, indeed, may simply reinforce the "repressive hypothesis" Foucault has described (*History* 10). In a Chinese context, however, a critique of the Cultural Revolution that makes it a site for repressed or illicit sexual expression, paired with a sense that true liberation and self-development can occur only through immigration to the United States (the endpoint of both *Red Azalea* and *Katherine*, Min's second novel), quite seriously challenges public, state-sponsored notions of Chinese history and Chinese difference.[16]

Nowhere is Min's project to remake Chinese history through a sustained attention to women and women's sexuality clearer than in *Becoming Madame Mao*, which retells the story of Jiang Qing, the wife of Mao Zedong and one of the architects of the Cultural Revolution. Already in *Red Azalea* the Supervisor—an androgynous, anonymous figure the novel suggests may be Jiang Qing, or may be interchangeable with her—remarks on the sexism of Chinese history's judgment of Jiang Qing: "That's Chinese history. The fall of a kingdom is always the fault of a concubine. Why should Comrade Jiang Qing be an exception?" (274). In her interview with Farmanfarmaian, Min repeats that point, noting: "It is the Chinese tradition that every dynasty's downfall is the concubine's fault.

---

16. Wendy Larson has specifically connected the liberatory impulse in Min's work to her American audience, for whom her rewriting of the Cultural Revolution as a crisis in sexual identity reads as a critique of China from the United States: "The interpretation of the Cultural Revolution as nothing more than a time of excessive repression is changed under [Min's] pen, becoming a utopian impetus toward a liberatory future located out and away from China" (443). Larson goes on to argue that Min's work is in this sense typical of a broader movement in post–Cultural Revolution Chinese literature, which aims "to modernize the period through rewriting it as an erotic experience" (448n24).

Madame Mao is considered a white-boned demon. But how could she be all evil?" (66).

Here the author repeats a thought originally published as the speech of one of her characters—originally published, in fact, in a mode of self-defense through the fictional voice of a never-quite-recognized Jiang Qing. As in *Dictée*, where a photograph of Hangul writing precedes the text's official opening, this sort of paratextual material lays the groundwork for a consideration of *Becoming Madame Mao* that recognizes the limits of a book as in some sense arbitrary: sympathy for a fictionalized Jiang Qing as against history's judgment precedes and exceeds the ends of the novel itself. So too in the pages of the novel proper, where an "author's note" on an unnumbered page facing the text's prologue reads, "I have tried my best to mirror the facts of history. Every character in this book existed in real life. The letters, poems, and extended quotations have been translated from original documents," while the last page of the text (also unnumbered) is a works-cited list titled "References." *Becoming Madame Mao*'s narrative is therefore bracketed by a set of historical claims that attempt to ground the novel's aesthetic and narrative structures with the legitimating promise of facticity, documentary reference, and linguistic competence.

That these claims bracket the novel does not, however, exert much influence on its novelistic form. *Becoming Madame Mao* opens with a prologue, printed in italics, which further frames its major narrative:

> *What does history recognize? A dish made of a hundred sparrows—a plate of mouths.*
>
> *Fourteen years since her arrest. 1991. Madame Mao Jiang Ching is seventy-seven years old. She is on the death seat. The only reason the authorities keep postponing the execution is their hope of her repentance.*
>
> *Well, I won't surrender. When I was a child my mother used to tell me that I should think of myself as grass—born to be stepped on.*
>
> (1)

The prologue introduces the novel's most prominent narrative strategy, namely the way the text shifts between third- and first-person narration, which appears here in the difference between the second and third paragraphs. Though the external narration of the first two paragraphs establishes the space from which Jiang Qing's first-person narration emerges in the third paragraph—we assume she is speaking from the jail cell invoked by the external narrator—nothing in the narrative itself, no shift of attention or perspective inside its diegetic space, seems to drive the movement between narrators. Unlike the drifts in free indirect discourse that mark the texts of, say, Virginia Woolf, *Becoming Madame Mao*'s narrative shifts are profoundly unmotivated. In the reading, their effect is to announce, repeatedly, the text's status as fiction, its willful disregard of the realism of the world it represents. The novel's willingness to make seemingly arbitrary shifts in point of view foregrounds the privilege of the fictional author and, particularly given the presence of the first-person narrator, the act of imagination required to generate the novel as a fictional text.[17]

The novel does not accompany these shifts with any shift in tone, syntax, or lexicon—the voice and language of the external narrator resemble in every respect save their grammatical person the voice and language of the character Jiang Qing. Until a reader gets used to this, the combination of shift in narrative person with the familiarity of the textual voice is fairly bewildering, since the similarity in tone and the lack of any paratextual sign of a shift in voice make the change hard to catch; one can get a few sentences into a new paragraph before realizing that the narrator has switched again. The effect is to suggest either that the first-person narration emerges from the imaginative power of the external narrator or that the external narrator might be the projection of Jiang Qing as novelistic character. The impossibility of deciding which particular chiasmatic

---

17. Readers who post reviews at Amazon.com are not the perfect test audience, but a brief perusal there suggests that the technique is as jarring to some readers as one might expect it to be: "first off, min shifts from first-person to third-person with every paragraph. She'll be recounting a point in lan ping's (mao's) life and then in the next paragraph, she IS lan ping, it is often confusing, not to mention pretentious and arrogant"; "The book irked me in one sense though. The writing style—switching between first person and third person every few paragraphs (without any pattern!) made it hard to read. Kinda like listening to a good CD that has a scratch"; "In addition, the constant switching between first and third person perspectives was annoying and puzzling. The third person served no discernible purpose whatsoever." Another reviewer (who liked the book) provides the following critique of the complaints: "If changing perspective is problematic I suggest to a couple of reviewers to try James Joyce."

structure the novel favors speaks, as does the strategy of changing narrators itself, to a wish to confuse imaginative fiction with history, a subjective or fantasized perspective with an objective and factual one. The movement between two narrative voices that speak in the same accent and tone thus offers another answer to the text's opening line: "What does history recognize? A dish made of a hundred sparrows—a plate of mouths." Though the text speaks only in two "mouths," two turns out to be enough to call into question the modes of historical recognition that would be responsible for an "author's note" or a list of academic references.[18]

To say all this about narrative is not yet to have addressed the question of the text's style, which, as in all of Min's work, is straightforward, repetitive English that tends to function as a marker of the text's "immigrant" origins.[19] Wendy Larson has specifically associated Min's style with her approach to historical and psychological realism: "Min's style is direct and simple, with short repetitive sentences forming the bulk of the narrative.... Min...manages to suggest that the story comes directly from the situation and has avoided the obfuscating veneer of civilization and history that makes everything so complex. The story, in other words, presents itself as a real, authentic rendition of something impossibly difficult to represent: the truth of individual subjectivity under Maoism" (434). Though in many ways this assessment strikes me as right—that is, though I agree with Larson that the text's syntactical simplicity has to do with

18. A more extended reading of *Becoming Madame Mao* would have to account for the one moment in the text that adopts—against the tonality and syntax of the rest of the novel—a deliberately academic tone and citational strategy. Discussing Jiang Qing's friend Fairlynn, the external narrator writes, "Although Fairlynn survives the Cultural Revolution...an important compartment in her own conscience bursts as well, as her memoir suggests (written in 1985 and published by South Coast China Publishing in 1997)" (294). This sentence is followed by two lengthy citations from the book.

19. Much is made, in interviews with and articles on Min, of the fact that she began to write *Red Azalea* while learning English in Chicago in the late 1980s. The degree to which Min then comes to model the ideal of Asian assimilation recalls once again the difficulty of reading immigrant fictions outside the ethnic frameworks within which they insistently appear in the public eye. Min's emergence (as a person and author) out of the Cultural Revolution (1966–1976) gives her a historical background that dovetails neatly with the cold war origins of the "model minority" stereotype, through which, as Robert G. Lee argues, "America's anxieties about communism...might be contained and eventually tamed" (146).

the mode of realism it assumes—I am not sure that this simplicity functions as simply as Larson suggests, that one can get directly from something like "simple sentences" to the "real, authentic rendition of something impossibly difficult to represent."

Before saying why, I want to suggest that the writing's syntactical simplicity is matched by a more general characterological and symbolic simplicity, and to propose that the combination of these simplicities allows one to describe *Becoming Madame Mao*'s representational style within a more general historical frame, one that will ultimately return this essay to the question of mediation in immigrating fiction. By "characterological and symbolic simplicity" I mean, first, that the novel consistently includes sentences designed to explain and otherwise make visible the psychological interiority of its characters, so that no thought, emotion, or motivation goes unremarked, and, second, that the novel's own large-scale symbolic interests (even its sense of itself as a potential allegory) are likewise insistently arrayed on the surface of the text. *Becoming Madame Mao* thus leaves its readers with little doubt as to its intended meaning (its "symbolism," simply put), hammering home its major thematic metaphors via a repetition that leaves little room for mis- or noninterpretation. Instead one gets the sense that this novel wants to make sure its readers know exactly what it means.

Consider, for instance, the novel's major metaphor: acting. As a thematic concept, it is diegetically motivated by the facts of Jiang Qing's life: she was an actress in traditional Chinese operas and modern plays (including, famously, Ibsen's *A Doll's House*) before meeting Mao, and in her years at his side took over the entire cultural apparatus of the Cultural Revolution, writing and producing a series of eight model plays that were for a time the only politically acceptable form of public entertainment. From its opening pages, *Becoming Madame Mao* recounts the biographical facts of Jiang Qing's education in the theater, even as the third-person narrator remarks on other events that will eventually work themselves into the model operas ("Madame Mao later uses the incident in both a ballet and opera of the same title, *The Women of the Red Detachment*" [12]). Jiang Qing's entire life, the book suggests, is formed in the crucible of the theater, and her every act must be understood as the playing out of a set of roles within a theatrical framework established by the historical situation in which she found herself (a situation that includes, to be sure, a politics of performed gender). The novel makes this point repeatedly: in an argument with Mao, Jiang Qing cites a line from a play (131); when she changes her name to fit her new position, she leaves behind her "old role" (158); later she is "playing a strange role" (165); another character "continues like a bad actor reciting his lines" (198); she speaks "in a theatrical voice," finding her "line" "stylish and self-moving" (235); the external narrator says, "To history, this is her role. The leading lady of a great tragedy," and "in truth, for Madame Mao, there is no line between living and acting" (275, 284). *Becoming Madame Mao* ends with two paragraphs ventriloquizing Jiang Qing: "It is time to empty the stage.... And don't forget that I was an actress, a great actress.... For those who are fascinated by me you owe me applause, and for those who are disgusted you may spit. I thank you all for coming" (337). No one could get through the novel without grasping this much of the novel's argument. The movement from historical event (Jiang Qing works as an actress) to psychological form (Jiang Qing thinks of herself as an actress even when she isn't acting) is repeated often enough and in important enough places to emerge as the text's single major symbolic idea.

The combined effects of the novel's patent symbolism, simple sentences, collapsed tone and style of the third- and first-person narrators, and open presentation of characterological interiority produce a remarkable flattening of the text's significative topography, as though the novel's third, psychological dimension were only barely managing to keep itself from collapsing into the geometric plane sustaining it. As though, in the words of Peter Brooks, "Nothing is spared because nothing is left unsaid; the characters stand on stage and utter the unspeakable, give voice to their deepest feelings, dramatize through their heightened and polarized words and gestures the whole lesson of their relationship" (4)—in other words, as though the novel were adopting all the generic conventions of a melodrama. Brooks has suggested that the melodrama is driven by a desire to "express all," to lay out on the surface of the text every emotion, every subtext, so that the process of making moral choices can clarify itself (10). Only when one sees that *Becoming Madame Mao* expresses nothing so insistently as its own desire *to be understood*, to make its own meaning absolutely and patently clear—a desire thinkable solely in a world where the text imagines that it will be just as insistently misunderstood—can one grasp not simply its deepest generic identifications, but also its mediated self-doubling.

Understanding *Becoming Madame Mao* as a melodrama allows, for instance, an interesting return to the question that moved Anchee Min to write the novel: how could Jiang Qing be *all* evil? Insofar as this question resists a Manichean conception of good and evil, insofar as it proposes to produce a more complex version of the historical Jiang Qing, as a person rather than a caricature, it can be understood as fundamentally *anti*melodramatic. Indeed, the text's historical self-presentation suggests that the critique of Jiang-Qing-as-melodramatic-figure must begin with clear-eyed historical realism. If the novel has traditionally been a site for the development of the modern sense of what a person is, and if that development has largely proceeded through the invention and representation of "round" characters, then the fundamental premise of *Becoming Madame Mao* could be said to be that the public judgment of Jiang Qing, itself a melodramatic twist on the real, should be corrected via a dual recourse to history and to the novel's power to imagine "character."

And yet *Becoming Madame Mao*'s own formal adoption of the strategies of melodrama—namely the sensational, exaggerated representation of its symbolic structure and its characters' interior language (at one point the narrator says of two characters, "The truth is deeper. They are star-crossed. There is betrayal" [81])—means that its declared attempt to undo the melodramatic judgment of Jiang Qing occurs in the guise of melodrama itself. In other words, *Becoming Madame Mao* reproduces at the level of its own form precisely the generic mechanism that it announces it is its intention to resist.

Before laying out the implications of such a contradiction for the meaning of the novel as a whole, we need to consider the relationship between melodrama and the major metaphorical structure the novel privileges, namely that of theater, or more precisely, Chinese revolutionary opera. Developed in order to stimulate the revolutionary fervor of the masses, revolutionary operas usually featured plots in which a male proletarian hero, often inspired or aided by a female helper, defeats an enemy of the people (bandits, anticommunists, and the like). These dramas were staged with modern costumes and representational sets supplementing Chinese operatic tradition's long-established vocabulary of kinesthetic, visual, and aural signs.

From a Western perspective, Chinese revolutionary opera's "lack" of psychological realism, its emphasis on gestural convention to portray emotional states, actions, and situations (walking in a circle, for instance, to indicate a long journey), has tended to signify as the grossest and most caricatured melodrama, and not just because it, like European melodramas, combines spoken drama with song. Marcelin Pleynet's reaction to the revolutionary opera he saw in 1974 is fairly typical: "The characters are ultra-stereotyped and papier-mâché. . . . Frankly, it's almost unbearable to watch a people, friendly, clearly artful and subtle, being represented by such mannequins" (81).[20] Whether or not Chinese opera is actually "melodramatic"—the question is impossible to answer, since aesthetic categories have cultural origins—Pleynet's reaction suggests something of its *appearance* in the West. The melodramatic style of *Becoming Madame Mao* must therefore be understood within two cultural vocabularies at once—that of a Chinese theatrical practice responsive since the 1920s to the imposition of, or attraction to, the theories of subjectivity grounding Western realism, and that of the historical form of Western melodrama, to which the text's sentimentalism and stereotyping seem to correspond.

The complexity of the novel's style must therefore be understood not simply in relation to its protagonist's particular life history, but also in some sense as an allegory of the cultural translation of form, as an attempt simultaneously to render and to *perform*, for an American audience, the aesthetic style that dominated all Chinese artistic practice during the Cultural Revolution. That allegory

---

20. An introduction to Chinese opera published in Paris in 1955 remarks on the nonrealism of Chinese theater in terms that resemble Pleynet's, but they are positively tuned and recognize the nonrealism of Chinese theater as likely to survive the aesthetic demands of communism: "Also in communist China the problem of realism, touchstone of the arts, has never been confused with the temptations of veridism or the facile notion of naturalism. . . . The leading figures of Chinese theater today understand completely that an art that uses symbols can be realist, and that an art that is a servile imitation of real reality can be absolutely un-*realistic*" (Roy 34; my translation).

interacts uncomfortably with the novel's apparent mission to rescue Jiang Qing from the clutches of history's melodramatic judgment. Because the novel tells us over and over again that Jiang Qing's life was a performance, a play, and that her own contribution to Chinese culture was likewise a series of performances and plays which, the text suggests, were in some sense projections of her personal tendency to imagine power as a *staging*, the style of *Becoming Madame Mao* allows us to imagine the novel itself as a ninth model opera reconstructed from the combination of history and the novelistic imagination. But given that the novel also recognizes the aesthetic of the model operas as a distorting one—given that one of the things the model operas distort into near-unrecognizability is, according to the novel, Jiang Qing's desire—its portrayal of Jiang Qing's life must be understood in turn as a second-order, distorting reflection in the funhouse mirror that was the Cultural Revolution's preferred style.

It may now be clearer why the novel adopts the admittedly awkward strategy of shifting between third- and first-person narration without simultaneously shifting its narrative voice or tone. The movement between Jiang Qing and the external narrator allows the novel to imagine that Jiang Qing is telling her own story in the third person, is in some sense *acting out* her own life in the pages of the novel; and because the text never forces a decision on the issue, it also offers the converse possibility, namely that the novel's first-person subject might be a narrative effect of a third-person consciousness. Is the narrative "I" simply a projection of an objective historical voice, or is the historical voice instead the subjective artifact of a personal imagination? The novel allows for both answers, and in this sense the narrator quite literally "becomes" Madame Mao even as Madame Mao acquires, by the end of the novel, the ability to narrate the curtain call of her own performance. Recalling Barthes, one can say that the novel's reimagined history "only reaches us through the intellectual (alienated) act of a first reader who is already on stage" ("Brecht" 265).

All of this might, in one final turn, be understood within the context of Min's ongoing critique of the Cultural Revolution's sexual politics. Julia Kristeva, returning from a visit to China with Barthes and Pleynet in 1974, remarked that the model operas left "no room for whatever in the psyche, the libido, the imagination, has not been channeled into political sublimation. As if the family, that harbour of the imagination, had consumed itself; and the desires of the community—represented by the desire of the girl—had vested themselves directly in politics, deeply and fully, but not without failure or drama" (155). Indeed, the plot of revolutionary operas frequently hinged on the political intervention of a young woman who, by demanding the right to participate in political action, confirmed the Communist policy of gender equality and, sometimes, shamed less courageous men into joining the revolution. As Kristeva points out— and it is important to note that she does so from the perspective of a post-Freudian West for which sexuality was the most important single component of psychological depth—the effect of the revolutionary operas was to evacuate any sense of sexuality, now understood largely as a system of bourgeois preferences that could only hinder the revolution. The melodramatic flattening of symbol and character proceeded largely through the overwhelming politicization of subjectivity, so that the characters appearing on stage in fact came to reproduce, at least in terms of the relation between inside and outside, the aesthetic strategies of the actors who portrayed them.[21] In some sense, Min's entire body of work can be understood as an attempt to undermine the sexual politics of such a theater from within by insisting that female sexuality was inside the Cultural Revolution all along.

The irony, of course, is that the choice of melodrama as an aesthetic mode in *Becoming Madame Mao* (and its presence more generally throughout Min's work) means that the novel consistently reproduces the aesthetic structures whose strictures it makes responsible for the repression of female sexuality and for the party line on Jiang Qing's place in Chinese history. Melodrama is both the wound and the medicine; the answer to its stylistic demands must be given in the melodramatic terms in which the questions have been asked, as though an intelligible response could not arise from outside the medium but rather had to materialize from somewhere within it.

---

21. As Xiaomei Chen remarks, the "highly stylized movements on [the Cultural Revolutionary] stage initiated offstage imitation leading to conformity. Knowledge was being absorbed through a unique theatrical experience that not only itself resulted from imitating 'real' revolutionary life, but, most important, provided millions of people with a model for more revolutionary behavior in their own 'real' lives. Here was a case, then, not uncommon in those times, of life imitating art rather than the other way around" (137).

The paradox recalls, at last, the question of mediation, since one can now ask how to understand the novel's argument at the level of content in relation to its choice of melodrama as form. The temptation to read the formal choice of melodrama as the insistent return of the novel's repressed is powerful, as doing so would allow us a sense of the novel as a character doomed to endlessly and unconsciously repeat precisely that which it most persistently seeks to criticize. But *Becoming Madame Mao* seems aware enough of itself as a melodramatic fiction for me to want to say, instead, that the return of melodrama is not some unconscious expression of the novel's own unconscious origins, but rather that this apparent "return" or, more generally, the contradiction between the mediating form and what it mediates, is simply the ontological surface of the novel's being. The model opera performed in and by the text, with Jiang Qing playing the parts of both the helper heroine and the enemy of the state, indicates precisely the oscillation between grammatical subject and object, activity and passivity, that characterizes the grammatical gerund. What the text *is* at the level of form cannot be separated from what it *says* at the level of content.

As in *Dictée*, then, the political energy of *Becoming Madame Mao* emerges from that moment at which it seems most contradictory, and that contradictoriness itself means that whatever project it sustains—including the project of rescuing Jiang Qing's reputation—will ultimately be doomed to failure. In this sense the novel's presentation of female sexuality and power inside the Cultural Revolution must also be understood as a "failure," if the fact of its form is to be taken seriously.[22] The novel's evocation of melodrama, already understood as a representational form that aims not to represent reality but to exaggerate it, fails at least partly because its faithful reproduction of, on one hand, the formal conditions of the history it tells (and here it is worth remembering that Jiang Qing's guilt was established by the state in 1981 at a *show* trial) and, on the other, the fictional content of

---

22. To say all this is to say nothing of the gendered history of melodrama as form in the West. Joan Copjec has associated the emergence of melodrama with both a "female logic of failure" and the development of free indirect discourse: "Not only does melodrama center on dramatic situations that elicit tears from its audience, it does so by registering the female logic of failure which makes the cry the inevitable remainder that results from the subtraction of the Other's reply from all that is implied by our address to it" (257).

its narrative (that is, Jiang Qing's history in and with the theater) requires it not to reproduce those things faithfully: it is another failed dictation.

Though *Becoming Madame Mao*, and Min's work more generally, seems far more able than Cha's *Dictée* to generate responses that stage it as the most fully assimilated of immigrant fictions, its melodramatic form can also be read as suggesting that whatever representational victories emerge from the text ("It is interesting to see [Jiang Qing] sketched as a human being and introduced in a vaguely positive light," writes Sheryl WuDunn) can be taken only as seriously as the model operas were, that the "character" of Jiang Qing the novel proposes is at its most accurate only when it represents its own inaccuracy, at its least staged precisely when it most openly presents its stagedness. We do not know whether it tells the truth or a lie. And yet the novel's very existence testifies to its own ability to take the model operas seriously, to make them speak in the present not simply as a form of cultural nostalgia but as an archive of memories and aesthetic forms that can generate new stories.[23] Here, perhaps even more vividly than in *Dictée*, the text gives us an allegory of its own refusal to complete the mediation of its story, its reanimation of Jiang Qing not a completed death but an ongoing "dy-ing" whose absurdly melodramatic goodbye ("I thank you all for coming"), read as a sign presented by the imaginative act of the novel itself, gives the entire historical exercise of the novel (including its claim to reproduce the "facts of history") a comic dimension. Indeed, this is the secret of "dy-ing": caught between the desire for closure and its impossibility, dy-ing generates an ongoing play whose comedy resides in postponing for as long as possible the death of the mediator on whose presence it depends.

· 4 ·

In 1935, Bertolt Brecht saw the Chinese actor Mei Lan-fang perform in Moscow. In "Alienation-Effects in Chinese Theater," written later

---

23. Much contemporary Chinese art strives for just such a goal. Feng Mengbo, for instance, combines scenes from the model opera *Taking Tiger Mountain by Strategy* with images from the video game *Doom* in *Taking Mt Doom by Strategy* (Haggerty Art Museum, Milwaukee, 1997); think here also of Chen Kaige's *Farewell My Concubine*.

that year, Brecht described Mei's performance and introduced his famous concept of the *Verfremdungseffekt*, the technique of alienation that would undergird so much of his epic theater. Brecht used the Chinese model—or, better, his interpretation of that model—as a place from which to critique the sensibilities of the bourgeois theater. Writing that the Chinese actor presents emotional states as *signs* rather than as psychological truths, Brecht argued that the distance thereby maintained between "character" and "actor" destroys the forms of empathic identification that grounded contemporary European theater. The Chinese actor's body, Brecht wrote, remains visible on stage as his *own*; any gesture of the actor's is therefore the act of a subject who is, in that moment, *reenacting* a scene rather than *acting* as a character.

Chinese theater, understood by Brecht as committed to a radical emotional distancing that used conventional symbols to destroy the notion of the actor's psychological interiority, became in the history of European theater one origin of the Brechtian sign, which, as Roland Barthes discovered upon seeing Brecht's *Berliner Ensemble* perform in Paris in 1954, promised "a phenomenon unknown in the West (perhaps precisely because Brecht had learned it from the East): *a theater without hysteria*" (*Rustle* 157). Though Brecht's understanding of Chinese acting did a good deal of violence to how Chinese theater was perceived by Chinese people in China (and was in any case idiosyncratic even among Western observers of Mei Lan-fang's performance),[24] it can nonetheless be read as one potential origin of the mode of reading this essay both pursues and discovers in the work of Theresa Hak Kyung Cha and Anchee Min, the doubled and doubling sign thereby redoubled and redoubling an origin that is not one in any historical or literary sense.

What I have been suggesting all along in my readings is well-captured by this historical irony, in which a European remediation of an Asian representational practice becomes, mediated, one site for the playing out of the poststructuralist concerns with language and form that emerge, half a century later, from ethnic American texts that

---

24. Haun Saussy has been engaged in a lengthy project to recuperate the variety of reactions to Mei's performance, which interacted with the Russian theater world, the aesthetic doctrines of the Comintern, and changes in Chinese theater.

present us with a phenomenon—in this instance the reappearance of a Brechtian sign mediated by the historical and personal fact of immigration and all that it implies—that seems simultaneously "unknown in the West" and "learned . . . from the East." The vertiginous quality of this return ought rightly to produce a suspicion not simply about the categories of West and East, which we have all learned to recognize as profoundly mediated by a dialectics of culture and history, but also about the notion of translation or immigration that would authorize the sense that some idea could arrive in a new place as an "unknown" thing "learned from" elsewhere. What that framing of mediation supposes, first of all, is a theory of mediation or translation in which the new, immigrated unknown can emerge from the process of translation without bearing within itself any difference due to its mediation. As *Dictée* and *Becoming Madame Mao* indicate, each in its own way, the act of acquiring any new thing from elsewhere—be it cultural knowledge, a sense of identity (of the self or of a historical figure), or a sense of the representationality of a literary form—cannot be understood unless one first accounts for the presence of the medium through which that thing crosses over. And that accounting, both texts suggest, can never quite complete itself, since the difference the medium makes means that any putative origin (include the text's own origin-ality) already begins, as Cha writes, in the middle of things; since the medium can never be grasped except through the mediation of another medium (the metaphor of voice translated into a map or diagram, or just into another metaphor of voice), no structure of origin can ever finish what it started, or *where* it started. Instead, what we can do in reading is, perhaps, attend to the presence of the medium itself, recognize the degree to which the medium will, as though in an inaudible hum or a burst of ultraviolet light, continue to mediate in realms outside the immediately sensible.

What my readings of *Dictée* and *Becoming Madame Mao* suggest, then, is that whatever specificity one ascribes to their Asian Americanness (and here it will matter that Cha and Min were born in Asia and immigrated to the United States) must be construed in terms of the texts' investment in the figure of mediation, in how each text folds over into itself the problem of its own language and form so as to make the separation of arbitrariness and ontology impossible. Neither novel offers as a "solution" to the dilemma of its narration the possibility of endless ludic play. Each suggests, rather, that the only place from which to say the very serious things each text attempts to say will be a place whose origin must draw, in some important way, on the intensity of the arguments the text expresses. Though this self-referential generativity cannot, because it never manages to separate its origins from its self, be philosophically "serious" (and therefore ontologically sound), neither is it purely arbitrary. That aporia makes whatever Asian Americanness emerges from the two novels the subject of the same doubled figuration that produces it in the first place, uncovering, perhaps, as Paul Gilroy has argued for the black Atlantic, an "ethics of freedom" outside the racial complicities of "occidental rationality" (56).

Because such a middled and muddled originality seems so often to appear in immigrant fiction—because the real historical conditions that arrange themselves around the fact of immigration, and which arrange in advance its reception, will call to mind the combination of a desire for origin and a recognition of its difficulty or even impossibility, because to say "Asian American" or "African American" is already to denote the presence of two possible origins for a single being—it is tempting to read this doubleness as the final truth of immigrant or ethnic identity itself. But to think this way is to mistake once again the arbitrary for the ontological, to insist too strongly on the fact of ethnic identity as a form of subjectivity that automatically and necessarily resists, if only by its embodiment of contradiction, one hegemony or another. If, as Viet Nguyen suggests in the conclusion of *Race and Resistance*, it "is doubtful that Asian America as a category, a space, or an identity will be adequate in addressing the needs and desires of . . . 'bad subjects' in a future after multiculturalism," it is because in imagining a future that follows the present, Nguyen is able to see that the current constellation, though it may seem ontologically necessary today, will one day be obsolete (171).[25] Managing a relation to that future while respecting the demands of the past whose future

---

25. Wendy Brown has argued that "political identities generated out of liberal, disciplinary societies, insofar as they are premised on exclusion from a universal ideal, require that ideal, as well as their exclusion from it, for their own continuing existence as identities" (65). What Nguyen imagines here is a future in which ethnic identity disappears as a category because the liberal, disciplinary society that sustains it will have been changed—hopefully for the better, but "better" is, of course, a political category.

we are living means doing the work of thinking through the *present*, which is also a medium and which, as *Dictée* suggests, will also take a cut from the transactions it permits.

There is a powerful temptation to read that cut in terms of an ethics of loss, to say that what fictionality teaches, what immigration teaches, what modernization teaches is precisely the experience of the world's inscrutability, an inscrutability compensated for and domesticated when someone attributes it to the Asiatic or the immigrant or even to the fictionality of fiction. The lack of understanding that looks back from the face of the world does sometimes feel like a loss, but only if one expects the world to understand, only if one has imagined an originary plenitude or comprehension that so often is the alleged property of earlier, more innocent eras or places that were truly "home." But why not imagine that such a feeling, too, is historical? Imagine not only that the conjunction of ethnic or immigrant identity with that experience is the product of a particular history of imperialism and globalization, nor simply that the fact of modernization is somehow unusually responsible for a sense of dislocation and lack, but rather that the entire sense of loss that makes the origin of being human something like a foundational trauma, and that regrets without cease the damage done by mediation, might in some other future be understood neither as a loss nor as a gain (which would just reverse things) but as nothing.[26] Imagine that such a feeling of loss might one day disappear and, like Foucault's face drawn in the sand at the edge of the sea, fade into the unremembered and unthinkable.

The interest of the sort of fiction discussed here would not, then, lie only in the fact that it reimagines the historical presence of loss as a generative and necessary force—exposing what I called in the case of *Dictée* the failure of "failure" as an explanatory concept—but that in showing how to conceptualize mediation without thinking of it as loss, these works imagine the possibility of a future (for fiction, for notions of immigration and mediation) that is, however modestly, not our present.

University of Arizona

---

26. Here I think not only of the entire discipline of psychoanalysis but also of the most theological pretensions of the deconstructive enterprise (which emerge partially historicized in the discipline of trauma studies), for which I have great sympathy.

WORKS CITED

Ahmad, Aijaz. *In Theory: Classes, Nations, Literatures*. London: Verso, 1992.

Barthes, Roland. "Brecht et le discours: contribution à l'étude de la discursivité." *Oeuvres complètes tome 3, 1974–1980*. Ed. Éric Marty. Paris: Editions du Seuil, 1994. 260–67.

———. *Camera Lucida: Reflections on Photography*. Trans. Richard Howard. New York: Hill, 1981.

———. *The Rustle of Language*. Trans. Richard Howard. New York: Hill, 1986.

Brecht, Bertolt. "Alienation Effects in Chinese Theater." *Brecht on Theater: The Development of an Aesthetic*. Trans. John Willett. New York: Hill, 1964. 91–99.

Brooks, Peter. *The Melodramatic Imagination: Balzac, Henry James, Melodrama, and the Mode of Excess*. New Haven, CT: Yale UP, 1976.

Brown, Wendy. *States of Injury: Power and Freedom in Late Modernity*. Princeton, NJ: Princeton UP, 1995.

Cha, Theresa Hak Kyung. *Dictée*. 1982. Berkeley: U of California P, 2001.

Chen, Xiaomei. "The Making of a Revolutionary Stage: Chinese Model Theater and Its Western Influences." *East of West: Cross-Cultural Performance and the Staging of Difference*. Ed. Claire Sponsler and Xiaomei Chen. New York: Palgrave, 2000. 125–42.

Cheng, Anne Anlin. "Memory and Anti-Documentary Desire in Theresa Hak Kyung Cha's *Dictée*." *MELUS* 23.4 (1998): 119–33.

Chow, Rey. *The Protestant Ethnic and the Spirit of Capitalism*. New York: Columbia UP, 2002.

Copjec, Joan. "More! From Melodrama to Magnitude." *Endless Night: Cinema and Psychoanalysis, Parallel Histories*. Ed. Joan Bergstrom. Berkeley: U of California P, 1999. 249–72.

"Diagram, *n.*" *Oxford English Dictionary*. 2nd ed. 1989. *OED Online*. Oxford UP. 9 Sept. 2005. <http://dictionary.oed.com/cgi/entry/50063078>.

Farmanfarmaian, Roxanne. "Anchee Min: After the Revolution." *Publishers Weekly* 5 June 2000: 66–67.

Foucault, Michel. *The History of Sexuality: An Introduction. Vol. 1*. Trans. Robert Hurley. New York: Vintage, 1978.

———. "What Is an Author?" Trans. James Venit. *Partisan Review* 42 (1975): 603–14.

"Gerund." *Oxford English Dictionary*. 2nd ed. 1989. *OED Online*. Oxford UP. 9 Sept. 2005. <http://dictionary.oed.com/cgi/entry/50094080>.

Gilroy, Paul. *The Black Atlantic: Modernity and Double Consciousness*. New York: Verso, 1993.

Jameson, Fredric. *Postmodernism; or, the Cultural Logic of Late Capitalism*. Durham, NC: Duke UP, 1991.

———. "Third-World Literature in the Era of Multinational Capitalism." *Social Text* 15 (1986): 65–88.

Kang, Laura Hyun Yi. *Compositional Subjects: Enfiguring Asian/American Women*. Durham, NC: Duke UP, 2002.

Kim, Elaine H. "Poised on the In-between: A Korean American's Reflections on Theresa Hak Kyung Cha's *Dictée*." Kim and Alarcón 3–30.

Kim, Elaine H., and Norma Alarcón, eds. *Writing Self, Writing Nation: A Collection of Essays on "Dictée" by Theresa Hak Kyung Cha*. Berkeley: Third Woman, 1994.

Kristeva, Julia. *About Chinese Women*. Trans. Anita Barrows. New York: Boyars, 1977.

Larson, Wendy. "Never This Wild: Sexing the Cultural Revolution." *Modern China* 25 (1999): 423–50.

Lee, Robert G. *Orientals: Asian Americans in Popular Culture*. Philadelphia: Temple UP, 1999.

Lowe, Lisa. *Immigrant Acts: On Asian American Cultural Politics*. Durham, NC: Duke UP, 1996.

Min, Anchee. *Becoming Madame Mao*. New York: Houghton, 2000.

———. *Katherine*. New York: Berkeley Publishing, 1996.

———. *Red Azalea*. New York: Random, 1994.

———. *Wild Ginger*. New York: Houghton, 2002.

Nguyen, Viet Thanh. *Race and Resistance: Literature and Politics in Asian America*. New York: Oxford UP, 2002.

Pleynet, Marcelin. *Le Voyage en Chine: chroniques du journal ordinaire, 11 avril–3 mai 1974: extraits*. Paris: Hachette, 1980.

Roy, Claude. *L'Opéra de Pékin*. Paris: Éditions Cercle d'Art, 1955.

Sakai, Naoki. *Translation and Subjectivity: On "Japan" and Cultural Nationalism*. Minneapolis: U of Minnesota P, 1997.

Saussy, Haun. "Mei Lanfang in Moscow, 1935: Familiar, Unfamiliar, Defamiliar." *Modern Chinese Literature and Culture* 18.1 (2006): 8–29.

Somerson, Wendy. "Under the Mosquito Net: Space and Sexuality in *Red Azalea*." *College Literature* 24 (1997): 98–115.

Wong, Shelly Sunn. "Unnaming the Same: Theresa Hak Kyung Cha's *Dictée*." Kim and Alarcón 103–40.

WuDunn, Sheryl. "Sympathy for the Demon." *New York Times* 9 July 2000. 8 Mar. 2005 <http://www.nytimes.com/books/00/07/09/reviews/000709.09wudunnt.html?bk0707>.

Xu, Ben. "A Face That Grows into a Mask: A Symptomatic Reading of Anchee Min's *Red Azalea*." *MELUS* 29.2 (2004): 157–80.

Xu, Wenying. "Agency via Guilt in Anchee Min's *Red Azalea*." *MELUS* 25.3-4 (2000): 203–19.

VĚRA ELIÁŠOVÁ

A Cab of Her Own: Immigration and Mobility in Iva Pekárková's *Gimme the Money*

In front of her there was a whole maze of streets crossing each other at right angles, well known to her, made penetrable and available to her as if it was a map of her own head.

Gimme the Money

va Pekárková, a contemporary Czech writer, based her novel *Gimme the Money* (British edition 2000) on her own immigrant experience. After her defection from Communist Czechoslovakia in 1985, Pekárková came to the United States, where she lived in New York for ten years and drove a cab. She published the Czech version of *Gimme the Money* in 1995, shortly before returning to the Czech Republic.[1] Working with her American husband, she later translated the novel into English.

Gimme the Money breaks new ground in ways of reading and writing about immigration by revising the notion of mobility, and by demanding the same mobility for the genre of immigrant literature. When allegorized by a cab, an immigrant's mobility is multidirectional and circular rather than one-directional and linear. In a rendering that hence favors contingency over continuity, Pekárková reconceives one of the basic paradigms of this genre, the immigrant's journey to a new country as a geographical and temporal route from an old self to a new one. At the same time, Pekárková's novel moves like a vehicle across

---

1. In 1993, Czechoslovakia split into two independent countries, the Czech Republic and the Slovak Republic.

Contemporary Literature XLVII, 4   0010-7484; E-ISSN 1548-9949/06/0004-0636

familiar and foreign literary landscapes. It invites a conversation with immigrant as well as nonimmigrant literary works and traditions, including the Eastern European immigrant autobiography of Eva Hoffman, Virginia Woolf's modernist texts, and new writing from postcommunist Europe by Slavenka Drakulić and Dubravka Ugrešić.

Gin, the heroine of *Gimme the Money*, drives a taxi in New York, seeking a new life and identity in her daily encounters with the vibrant and multilayered metropolis. In its daily sequence of fortuitous destinations, the cab's multidirectional movements contrast with a one-directional movement from one location to another, the kind of movement generally thought to characterize immigrant experience. Gin's taxi-driving thus represents a new kind of mobility complicating the given mobility of immigration itself.

Importantly, the mobility of a cab within the mobility of immigration offers a new model for writing about immigrant experience. For Pekárková, immigration is a process that must be constantly renegotiated. Gin is an immigrant who arrives at a new location yet never stops moving. Her new home is located in a vehicle, what taxi drivers call "their four-wheeled homes away from home" (51). As Gin constantly repositions herself vis-à-vis the city, her destinations, as markers on the course of her immigrant experience, are always temporary. Pekárková's text expresses this mobility formally through the trope of circles. These circles convey the circulating life in the metropolis: some chapter titles are "Protective Circles," "The City, Circles," "Cobwebs," and "Return Trips." Within these circles, the characteristics of places and of people overlap, and the coil of the present tense is accentuated. Every moment matters; every moment means an end and a new beginning, a new chance, a new decision. Pekárková terms this new literary form a "taxi story," an open-ended story that is always in the making.

The multidirectional mobility of the cab driver characterizes Iva Pekárková as a writer equally well. It is difficult to place her in a single literary context and tradition. She is claimed by the canon of Czech national literature primarily as a post–1968 émigré writer, because she belongs to the generation of artists and intellectuals who defected from Czechoslovakia after the 1968 Soviet invasion, disappointed by the reimposition of Soviet political doctrine.[2] Among these writers, Milan Kundera is probably the most prominent. Although Pekárková, a much younger writer, left the country later, the continuing restrictions on all freedoms, including freedom of speech and the freedom to travel, were certainly among the reasons for her emigration.[3]

Pekárková questions conventional thinking about "emigrant" and "immigrant" identities, refusing to be bound by either term. She does not fit easily within the male-dominated canon of Czech émigré literature, in which her female voice is unique. But she fits even less well within the context of Czech women's writing: the Czech women writers of her generation who fought communism, such as Daniela Fišerová and Eva Kantůrková, stayed in the country, focusing on resistance from within. Indeed, it is difficult to contain Pekárková within the canon of Czech literature, a territory that is too small for her. In her life and work, she is cosmopolitan, deriving her inspiration from clashes and encounters between cultures. Her work can thus be considered from at least two perspectives. From a Czech perspective,

2. The first wave of political emigration from Czechoslovakia was in the 1950s, after the Communist Party won the 1948 elections and turned Czechoslovakia into one of the satellite states of the Stalinist Union of Soviet Socialist Republics.

3. In her 2001 book-length interview with the journalist Vladimír Ševela, published only in Czech, Pekárková provides a variety of reasons for why she left Czechoslovakia in 1985. Among them was her deep dissatisfaction with the abysmal state of environmental policy at that time, a concern intensified by her background in biology, which she studied at Charles University in Prague. Another was her sense of the all-encompassing grayness of life in Communist Czechoslovakia. Pekárková says that she realized the power of this feeling only after reading Toni Morrison's *Beloved*, where the heroine, during a bleak Ohio winter, craves some color to help her keep her sanity. What seems to have weighed on Pekárková most strongly, however, was the impossibility of traveling freely, certainly the most commonly stated reason for emigration from Communist Czechoslovakia. Traveling was permitted only to an approved list of socialist countries; exceptions were rare and often dependent on the applicant's willingness to collaborate with the state secret police. Yugoslavia, albeit a socialist country, implemented few restrictions on travel and did not watch its borders closely. Many Czech emigrants, including Pekárková, were therefore able to use Yugoslavia as a transit point to the West. In this respect, *Gimme the Money* constitutes the final part of a trilogy, if Pekárková's oeuvre is viewed through the lens of her own route toward freedom. *Gimme the Money* was preceded by the novels *Truck Stop Rainbows* (1989, Czech; 1992, English), featuring a heroine who resists communism by hitchhiking, an activity that provides her with an inner sense of freedom, and *The World Is Round* (1993, Czech; 1994, English), about another heroine's experience in a refugee camp in Austria after she defects from Communist Czechoslovakia. At the end of the novel, she gains permission to immigrate to the United States.

she is an émigré writer; although she did return to her native country, she is seen as someone who spent a major part of her life elsewhere, and whose work is influenced mainly by that experience. From an American perspective, Pekárková may fit the definition of an immigrant writer. When she came to live in the United States, the Iron Curtain dividing the West and the East was still firmly set in place, ruling out the possibility of return. Pekárková reflects on this experience in *Gimme the Money* as the immigrant Gin strives to create a completely new life in a new country. To complicate categories even more, Pekárková now lives primarily in London (after spending several years in the Czech Republic), but her writing is inspired by worldwide travel to countries as diverse as Thailand, India, and Nigeria.[4] It seems that wherever she is, she is already thinking about going somewhere else. In her life and writing, she is exemplary of a postmodern mobility of imagination. The fact that her novels, especially *Gimme the Money*, have found avid readers both at home and abroad proves that the same spark ignites others' imaginations as well.

Pekárková's artistic aspirations and efforts are transnational. By translating her work from Czech to English herself, she strives for a multilingual art that engages a diverse readership. Just like her allegorical cab, Pekárková's writing explores and entwines multiple geographical and generic directions. Like the experience of mobility that *Gimme the Money* describes, reading it requires a multidirectional excursion across diverse literary landscapes. First, the novel can be read as an immigrant autobiography, the genre to which it is most closely related. Pekárková can be seen as following a trajectory outlined by Eva Hoffman, the contemporary Polish-Canadian-American writer, in her autobiographical novel *Lost in Translation* (1989). While Hoffman's narrative only casts doubt on the idea of progress from one home to another as an apt model for contemporary immigrant experience, however, Pekárková's novel completely rejects it. As an alternative, Pekárková offers a mobility typical for the figure of the *flâneuse*, a mobile urban observer who imagines herself anew in

---

4. "Thirty-two Kwan" (2000), "To India Where Else" (2001), and "Naidja, Stars in My Heart" (2004) are works of creative nonfiction based on Pekárková's travels to Thailand, India, and Nigeria, respectively. These works have been published only in Czech. The English versions of their titles here are Pekárková's translations.

the city as she walks around it. In this respect, Pekárková's novel can be read in conversation with literatures that do not address immigration per se.

Second, by drawing on the mobility of the *flâneuse*, Pekárková continues in a long tradition of writing about women in the city, of which Virginia Woolf's works are key examples. Although comparing Pekárková to Woolf entails looking back in time, a look atypical for Pekárková's nostalgia-free sensibility, Woolf's *flâneuse* of "Street Haunting: A London Adventure" (1927) anticipates Pekárková's postmodern heroine Gin, who is divorced from the traditional idea of home and married to a city that symbolizes the world.

Finally, Pekárková imagines Gin as belonging to a collectivity of similarly unanchored subjects, the noncollective collectivity that connects, without constraining, each individual Odysseus of the twentieth century. In this way, the novel engages with contemporary writing about displacement from ex-Yugoslav writers and self-imposed exiles Slavenka Drakulić and Dubravka Ugrešić. Together with these writers, Pekárková explores the possibility of embedding individuality in new forms of collectivity while simultaneously resisting nationalism. By requiring a transnational and transgeneric perspective, her novel moves the boundaries delineating the genre of immigrant fiction. That is why *Gimme the Money* may be termed a new immigrant novel operating at the mutable margins of the genre.

Gimme the Money focuses on the mobility of immigration—the basic paradigm for immigrant fiction—but mobility in a particular form that complicates the protagonist's progress toward acquiring a new immigrant self. Traditionally, the idea of immigration involves a goal, the progress toward which shapes the narrative of immigration. This goal is to find a new identity, a new self adjusted to the changes instigated by the immigrant's arrival at a new home. In the American cultural context, particularly, such a transformation of self has usually required that an immigrant engage in the process of assimilation and the pursuit of the American Dream. However, this tradition has been changing. The idea of progress, which has historically provided the shape of the immigrant story, can hardly suffice to grasp the contemporary immigrant experience today, more than ever characterized by mobility of different kinds and degrees. If we now live in "the age of migration," in Paul White's phrasing, such an increasingly complex mobility necessarily makes new demands on our imaginations. Imagining different forms of movement and displacement, therefore, requires reexamining previous notions of immigration and experimenting with the genre of the immigrant story.

Hoffman's *Lost in Translation* is a prime example of the transition from the traditional story of immigration as progress to the postmodern rendering of it as movement without a clearly delineated direction. Hoffman describes her experiences as a Polish-Jewish immigrant in Canada and later in the United States, starting in the 1950s when she was thirteen years old and continuing to her adulthood. Gradually she overcomes her sense of being "lost in translation" and acquires "a life in a new language," the subtitle of her memoir. Hoffman's work is typical of the genre of immigrant literature in that it presents the story of an immigrant's progress toward acquiring a new self. Even so, Hoffman distinguishes her own autobiography from that written by her Polish predecessor Mary Antin, author of *The Promised Land* (1912). Hoffman interprets the difference between them as one between two Americas with a century between them:

> And what is the shape of my story, the story my time tells me to tell? Perhaps it is the avoidance of a single shape that tells the tale. A hundred years ago, I might have written a success story, without much self-doubt or equivocation. A hundred years ago, I might have felt the benefits of a steady, self-assured ego, the sturdy energy of forward movement, and the excitement of being swept up into a greater national purpose. But I have come to a different America, and instead of a central ethos, I have been given the blessings and the terrors of multiplicity.
>
> (164)

Hoffman discovers that the traditional form of the immigrant story available to her as a precedent is inadequate. She expresses her dissatisfaction with its assumption of a "sturdy energy of forward movement," stating, "I cannot conceive my story as one of simple progress, or simple woe" (164). Although her memoir is structured as a progression—its three parts are entitled "Paradise," "Exile," and "The New World"—she recognizes that assimilation requires her to negotiate multiplicity and mobility: "If I want to assimilate into my generation, my time, I have to assimilate the multiple perspectives and their constant shifting. Who, among my peers, is sure of what is success and what failure?" (164). Thus Hoffman suggests that the meanings of pivotal terms around which the story of immigration revolves are no longer clear. What constitutes "success" or "failure" has changed somewhat with her generation; if these terms blur even more, the generation of writers following Hoffman will need to reconceive an immigrant story more in sync with their contemporary world's movement and instabilities.

This project becomes particularly difficult once neither "old" nor "new" worlds are understood as stable but rather appear to be constantly changing. Indeed, facing this instability is the primary challenge Gilbert H. Muller identifies in works of post–World War II immigrant literature that "reveal a quest for an American Dream or New World Eden that is more fluid than fixed" (22). Muller still sees the pursuit of the American Dream as providing the shape for the contemporary immigrant story, claiming that its new fluidity "becomes the opportunity to retain a bifocal perspective on existence, one that might or might not preserve older cultural habits and beliefs but which assuredly permits a reexamination of identity, an exploration of possibilities in the New Eden."[5] In Hoffman's narrative, however, it is precisely "retaining a bifocal perspective" that proves problematic. The very doubling of perspectives, requiring a constant "translation" between them, entraps Hoffman's persona. In order to experience freely, she needs to get beyond the "double vision" of an immigrant who has left the past and the "old" identity yet not completely assimilated to a "new" one (132). Therefore, she says, she needs "to give up the condition of being a foreigner" and "see the world directly, as the world" (202). When Hoffman claims, "I want to reenter, through whatever Looking Glass will take me there, a state of ordinary reality," she expresses her desire for an undivided perspective. As long as an immigrant remains suspended in the division between past and future, she has no access to present experience. Thus in Hoffman's rendering, the goal of the immigrant's acquisition of a new self is to gain access to the pure

---

5. While examining authors such as Isaac Bashevis Singer, Paule Marshall, Jamaica Kincaid, Bharati Mukherjee, Amy Tan, and Oscar Hijuelos, Muller proposes that "the fiction of the dream—of America as a landscape of possibility—fuses ultimately with the polyglot fluidity of the immigrant heroes and heroines of contemporary fiction as they seek to redefine themselves in this country" (22).

present, free from the burden of the past and anticipation of the future. It takes years, Hoffman writes, before she is able to regain something as simple as a sense of experiencing in the present tense: indeed, the last line of her book reads, "I am here now" (280).

Pekárková's narrative departs from the place where Hoffman's arrives. Gin's story rolls around in the present tense, in "a never-ceasing humongous NOW" (35). Indeed, the difference lies in the continuous present: it can be said that Hoffman's persona arrives at a new self, but Gin keeps arriving. Even the plot of the novel revolves around Gin's continuous encounters with New York City, offering only a frail axis of Gin's temporal development: as if in passing, readers learn that Gin has emigrated from Czechoslovakia and marries Talibe, an immigrant from Mali, in order to get a green card. The plot instead focuses on Gin's interactions with other immigrant characters, mostly taxi drivers, who work for the same garage. Her job enables Gin to observe New York City in ways that are both intimate and wide-ranging. It seems as though Gin will never want to leave New York, because she lives in the city's present moment, which never ceases to fascinate and exhilarate her immensely, but then Talibe dies, shot by a random killer, and Gin has to kill the same murderer in self-defense. After these dark events, the novel ends surprisingly: with her new lover, Gin leaves New York in a stolen cab. Nevertheless, this ending is rendered as a new beginning, as yet another chance for Gin to start a new life.

Pekárková keeps excising Gin out of a temporal progression, rendering her, rather, within the constantly renegotiated present. The novel's beginning is as ambiguous as its open-ended conclusion, with Pekárková allegorizing Gin's arrival in a foreign land as a sudden fall: "Big cities emit gravity, just like big planets. A person seldom decides to arrive in one. Into a big city, you have to fall, usually head first" (1). Thus instead of a processive notion of arriving, Pekárková offers arrival as an accident, quite isolated from the past. Without introducing readers to the place of Gin's origin, Pekárková lets Gin simply fall onto the first pages of the novel, as if from outer space. Unlike some other immigrants, who are "lucky enough to be allowed to slowly, stealthily orbit this or that metropolis" (1), Gin falls to New York unprotected:

The gravity of big cities captures us from the other side of oceans, across nine mountains and nine rivers. Big cities reach out their tentacles like huge octopuses. And when people let themselves be lured and attach themselves to these tentacles, as if they were umbilical cords, very soon they find themselves flying upwards and far away on a silverish spiral, at such a speed that their inevitable butt-falls can be made gentler only by their love for the City; for the unique and thorny planet.

(1–2)

After this prelude explaining, metaphorically, her fall onto the "planet" New York, readers find Gin similarly "climbing up to Manhattan Island on the metallic lace of the Brooklyn Bridge" and then "falling toward Manhattan from a terrible height" (2). Gin's fall to New York—the city that promises contingency rather than progress—is a fall to the present tense. The city means for Gin the "NOW" that "pushe[s] out of her brain...memories only a couple of years or months old" (35). Gin shares with her artist roommate Gloria a fascination with living in the "NOW." As Gloria says, the only "art is the PRESENT TENSE" (60). Gin embraces Gloria's claim that "EVERY slice of time is ART" and that "every crosscut through reality in this City symbolizes something." Taking her own imagined snapshots of the city, Gin continues Gloria's train of thought: "But then art would also be the way in which, on the Lower East Side, the spit-out chewing gums—pink, white, blue and light green—get trampled into the asphalt of the streets," or it would be "the windows of abandoned buildings on 117th Street," "three sleepy-eyed seagulls standing on one leg each in a puddle at Kennedy Airport," "the skyline of Manhattan," or just "that half-rotten rag that has been lying below the curb on 10th Avenue and 46th Street" (61–62). Gin enjoys accumulating imagined snapshots of the city. They are discrete and discontinuous, as they are made and unmade every single moment. This is precisely the kind of experience Hoffman's persona craved—the ability to catch the present moment for herself and relish its rich texture.

Gin's imaginative snapshots of the city lack both temporal continuity and hierarchy. For some, such a lack of order may appear frightening, but Gin embraces the disorderly mass of present moments, without worrying about the future or the past. The pursuit of the American Dream does not seem to interest Gin. Her conception of her "new" world lacks a concrete vision of the future. There is hope, but "[h]opes had the shape of reverse arrows left in the wet concrete by pigeons' toes" (2). Quite evocatively, pigeon-printed "reverse arrows" point away from the future, but Pekárková turns Gin away from the past, too. Gin's Czechoslovak origin figures only intermittently and briefly, as when Gin mentions her original Czech name, Jindřiška, which she does not use because it is too complicated (16).[6] Gin's past is perhaps best symbolized by her old appendectomy scar, "which the doctors back in Czechoslovakia had lousily sewn up with seven stitches" (278). Like her origin, this scar cannot be completely erased; it remains on the surface, carrying no deep significance for her present life. Gin's past seems over, healed and sealed.

Thus Pekárková liberates Gin from the position of eternal translator between "old" and "new" perspectives, the position that Hoffman found troubling. Gin's immigration does not claim the spotlight; it is not even the point.[7] Pekárková has explained, "I wanted my heroine to come to New York, as a completely 'clean slate,' so to speak. I didn't want her to harbor or resist any ideas. I wanted her to have a fresh outlook on things" ("Jumping"). This goal may seem a bit unrealistic; after all, how can anyone be a completely "clean slate"? Pekárková's emphasis on divorcing Gin from the past is striking, but considering the historical and political context of her writing, the dream of a severance of ties, a complete rootlessness, makes sense. For Pekárková, as an émigré from a communist country, it would not be unusual to search for such a form of ultimate freedom. Given that it was exactly the freedom of aimless wandering, both physical (freedom of travel) and imaginative (freedom of speech), that was restricted, Pekárková's desire for chance and intangible horizons has a very tangible explanation.[8] Thus breaking away from history has its

---

6. In the Czech version of *Gimme the Money*, Pekárková does not change the heroine Jindřiška's name to Gin. Although the original and the translation tell the same story, the latter widens the gulf between the heroine's Czechoslovak past and her American present. In the English translation, the heroine's new name, Gin, locates her even more fully in the American present.

7. Pekárková has stated that "all [her] heroines, even though they lived abroad, never quite dealt with emigration as a phenomenon. For example, Gin in New York simply is in New York, we don't know how she got there and why" ("Jumping").

8. Imposed plans—for example, five-year economic plans—characterized life under communism. In her art and life, Pekárková demands absolute freedom from imposed

own history, in which, implicitly, both the heroine and her writer remain rooted.

However, the ideal of the baggage-free state of mind should not be dismissed altogether. Rendering Gin as living without history enables Pekárková to revise the stereotype of the immigrant full of Old World tradition and history. Hoffman has already indicated that the direction of an immigrant story heads toward transcending the condition of being a foreigner. Pekárková continues in this direction away from the stereotype of the immigrant tied down by her "old" self. Pekárková tries to reconceive the immigrant as someone who "belongs" to the New World unequivocally. Perhaps it is only Gin's naiveté that enables her to feel at home in New York. It seems so from Gloria's point of view, at least. She observes:

> Gin BELONGED, and even though Gin's English was simply funny to listen to, Gloria couldn't help herself: she had to envy her her lack of knowledge of the New York world. Gin's naivety . . . made it possible for her to regard the whole colorful palette THE WAY IT WAS, without any prejudice, without filtering all those colors through the sluice of certain private politics that most native New Yorkers had managed to make for themselves; Gin dived into white, yellow, smokey-colored, even bone-marrow-deep black societies with an ease that Gloria could only dream about.
>
> (27)

Although Gin has an advantage in fitting in partly because of her white complexion, this privilege is not solely a matter of color. Gin's "belonging" has less to do with her assimilation, or fitting in, than with her vision of herself as a part of New York, even prior to her arrival there. No matter how imperfect it may finally prove, Gin falls to New York with "love for the City; for the unique and thorny planet" (2). In other words, Gin loves the city even before she gets there. After all, Gloria herself concludes that Gin "belongs" because she lacks "prejudice," knowledge of those rules established in the past that obfuscate the present. Instead, Pekárková imagines her heroine as already beyond those boundaries that imprison an immigrant in a static identity without any possibility of transcending it. Gin neither

---

ways of thinking. In an interview conducted in 2005, she expresses her continuing fear of "writing to conform to party lines" ("Interview" 167). She refuses to satisfy other people's expectations that she should write like a Czech author or a woman author.

absorbs New York's past nor dwells on her identity as a foreigner with a past. Only when her cab breaks down, forcing her to stop and wait to have it fixed or towed away, do "Gin's thoughts [run] away across the ocean and into Europe" (100), and this accidental stasis never lasts.

Gin's living without history may have its pitfalls as well as its opportunities. Being excised from a temporal continuity poses the risk of imprisonment within the present tense, preventing Gin's development beyond the "NOW." What kind of direction can the immigrant story assume if neither going back nor going forth is desirable? Pekárková suggests that the story line is circular, irregular, and jagged and compares its movement to painting a picture. In her cab, Gin "was an artist who was working day after day on a humongous canvas—the Manhattan Island—creating yellow pictures on it with jerky motions of her brush. Her tires stroked the surface of it, leaving their imprint, and Gin, day after day, was choosing again and again how to make her opening brush stroke" (63). Each of the turns taken leads to an end and, at the same time, to a new beginning. Gin's tire strokes, transformed into the brushstrokes of her imagination, thus correspond to her discontinuous experience, expressed in a likewise disorderly narrative form. It can be said that Pekárková "paints" Gin's story as an accumulation of "opening brush stroke[s]." Pekárková suggests that an immigrant story constantly forks into different directions that correspond to different chances. In this way, Pekárková steers away from propelling Gin's story in one direction only; every turn means a new beginning.

Every turn Gin takes in her cab leads to a new crossroads and proliferates into a new set of chances: "Every day Gin with EVERY action of hers was choosing a single one of the possibilities of a certain moment, branching her day into the Tree of Decision" (64). One chapter, entitled "The Tree," is organized as a list of chances, numbered from 1 to 614. These chances correspond to left and right turns Gin takes as she is driving, as well as to the turns of events during one of her night shifts. Thus chance number 6 reads, "Straight across 10th," and number 12 says, "Gin takes that lane on the left" (67). Other chances, in contrast, involve miniature events, such as describing encounters with different kinds of customers as well as bits of conversation that Gin holds with them. Some of these conversations are superficial, concerning simply their intended destination or the traffic situation. Other conversations are more interesting, such as the one in numbers 20 through 22, in which a customer is so surprised by seeing a female cab driver that she forgets to tell Gin where to go.

Importantly, the list of chances remains incomplete. Missing links in the metaphorical chain of chances mean that Gin's story cannot be reassembled into a temporal continuum. But even if the chances did create a continuum, the picture would still remain incomplete. In Pekárková's rendering, chances cannot be understood as beads on a string, events leading one to another. Instead, every chance forks into at least two new possibilities, corresponding to two new directions that may or may not be explored:

> Chances were chained one after the other—and Gin was painfully aware that with every YES she loses a NO, with every RIGHT TURN she loses a LEFT TURN or KEEP GOING STRAIGHT, that behind every chance there is a whole mob of other chances hiding, chances that had escaped Gin forever.
>
> (63)

Although some of the chances remain unexplored, these losses are not lamented. Chances are abundant in each present moment; after all, there is always a whole "mob" of them (and the number 614 is by no means definite) awaiting Gin at every turn.

Finally, Gin espouses chance itself, embodied by her lover, whom she decides to call the Tree. His name and identity remain undisclosed because he carries a deeply symbolic meaning for Gin's life. His name is inspired by his hair, which Gin compares to "winter branches" (274). His metaphorical name corresponds to the other "tree" metaphors in which the novel abounds, such as "the Tree of Decision" and "the tree of possibilities" (64, 63). It can be said that, just like Gin, he is a rootless and routeless Tree, always en route. That Gin leaves New York with the Tree implies the continuation of her story. In the story that Gin writes and in which she is being written, even commitment does not mean settling down; there is neither a completely happy nor unhappy end.[9]

If an end leads to other chances, then leaving New York may also mean a new beginning. In the final chapter of the novel, the

---

9. I am grateful to Iva Pekárková for drawing my attention to the penultimate chapter of the novel, where Gin almost falls off the Kosciusko Bridge. This chapter can be interpreted as providing an alternative, tragic end to the novel (E-mail to Věra Eliášová).

Holland Tunnel turns into "a concrete birth canal through which Gin was coming into the world" (276). In this powerful scene, Gin's mobility means the possibility of her rebirth. This last chapter is evocatively entitled "There Are More New Yorks Than Just This One" and hence anticipates a new arriving. After all, "There's Paris in Texas, Manhattan in Kansas, Moscow in Idaho, Rome and Athens in Georgia, Venice in California, Berlin in Wisconsin.... If we drive far enough, we're bound to find a New York!" (277). Or there is yet another direction in which to take the story's ending: the Tree comforts Gin, "I'll be your New York!" (276). In this way, they will inevitably "carry it with [them] everywhere" (277). If Gin and the Tree embody New York, then they never leave it. Thus the final lines of the novel read as if Gin has begun to narrate her story anew. In fact, the novel opens and closes with an identical pair of words, "big cities."[10]

Gin's story is thus always to be continued and thereby corresponds to the notion of immigrant identity as subject to constant reimagination. Instead of anchoring Gin in a new home, culture, or language, Pekárková destines her to rounds of self-negotiation. The trope of circles turns up frequently in Pekárková's narrative, implying the repetitiveness of this imaginative process that is also the process of Gin's writing of the self. These circles are both external and internal. When circling the city, Gin observes that "New York neighborhoods—or hoods—seldom have well-defined boundaries" and thus "resemble circles" (162–63). Simultaneously, the city's "plasma circled in [Gin's] veins" (34).

Elsewhere, Gin's thoughts circle in a whirlwind, mixed with urban debris:

> Scraps of her thoughts rambled around in the form of flown-away broad-sheets, printed with stock prices, news, disasters, murders, horrors, pictures of whores and politicians, personals and advertisements, and eyewitness' testimonies, flying in little circles right on the corner of 7th Avenue and 34th Street, pretty close to Penn Station.
>
> (20)

10. Here, too, I would like to thank Iva Pekárková for pointing out this narrative strategy to me: using the same phrase to begin and end her novels is her own "lucky charm" (E-mail to Věra Eliášová).

The city's "plasma," made of debris in Pekárková's rendering, turns into Gin's lifeblood. Gin circulates in the city and the city circulates in her. Gin's mind overlaps with the frightening newspaper content as well as its chaotic, disordered pages. Like her scattered thoughts, her immigrant self seems impossible to pin down, circulating, like her cab, on and on through the streets.

The circle metaphor serves as the basis for Pekárková's articulation of a new form of the immigrant story as nonlinear and open to chance. In search of such a new form, Pekárková would perhaps endorse Janet Wolff's proposition that "displacement (deterritorialization) can be strikingly productive" because "the same dislocation can also facilitate personal transformation, which may take the form of 're-writing' the self, discarding the life-long habits and practices of a constraining social education and discovering new forms of self-expression" (*Resident Alien* 9). While this would explain how Gin's instability works as an invitation to "'re-writ[e]' the self," it is important to add that for Pekárková, the process of rewriting is continuous. Pekárková does not seem interested in finding a lasting result that could finally be secured as the truth about one's self. While Wolff maintains that the process of "becoming a stranger" represents "a crucial liberating step in self-discovery" (2), Pekárková implies that there is no such final "discovery"; being "a stranger" is a persistent state of identity.[11]

Pekárková proposes that the new kind of immigrant experience she describes in her novel is modeled on the form of taxi drivers' engagements with the city and thus can be called a "taxi story." As Gin says, "[e]very real taxi story is like a short-short mystery novel with the first and the last few pages torn off" (118). The lack of both an opening and closure seems to energize the taxi driver's imagination,

---

11. Pekárková's project resembles a proposition made by Julia Kristeva in *Strangers to Ourselves*. Kristeva argues that the state of foreignness cannot be cast as a difference from the familiar because it has always been a part of it: "Strangely, the foreigner lives within us: he is the hidden face of our identity, the space that wrecks our abode, the time in which understanding and affinity founder. By recognizing him within ourselves, we are spared detesting him in himself" (1). Thus Kristeva calls for embracing the foreignness that is never only external but always internal as well. Pekárková shares with Kristeva a recognition that the need to embrace the foreign as a constitutive part of our identity increases in a globalized world, where clashes between the familiar and the foreign are no longer the privilege or the curse of the immigrant.

turning a taxi driver into an artist who makes up stories from observed fragments: "even though [the taxi driver] knows neither the beginnings nor the ends of stories that get revolved on the back seat of his taxi night after night—he could easily dream them all up. Which makes it even more interesting, of course" (120). Thus Pekárková suggests that her "taxi story" is perpetually being written and is permanently unfinished.

The open form of a "taxi story" corresponds to an immigrant's openness to chance, chance that can change his or her life, at any moment, for good or for bad. A cab driver, according to Gin, must understand "[t]hat it's, after all, quite possible to get shot, thrown next to the sewer, discovered, autopsied and buried without anybody reading about it in the paper" (120). Gin, however, embraces the unpredictability, feeling excited to think that anything can happen. Although she may be scared, Gin says that "for some reason, these goose bumps feel kind of sweet" (120). This embracing of chance, bordering on the absence of fear, distinguishes Gin from Hoffman's persona, who feels threatened by her lack of knowledge of the cultural environment and states, "As long as the world around me has been new each time, it has not become my world; I lived with my teeth clenched against the next assault of the unfamiliar" (278). Gin, on the contrary, is energized by the unpredictable. Each turn, after all, may turn out for the better rather than the worse. Even after Talibe dies and Gin herself must kill, she does not give up on chance.

Paradoxically, a "taxi story" does not fit the criteria of the story form. A "taxi story" cannot be easily told, because it resists being contained in time and taking a permanent shape. A "taxi story" is always happening in the present tense, and always happening to all who drive taxis. For example, Gin's fellow cab driver Ashraf always offers to tell his taxi stories: "Oh boy, I could tell you things, oh boy.... What I seen with my own eyes, stories you wouldn't believe" (122). But when asked to proceed with his narrative, Ashraf never gets beyond the already stated prelude; he repeats the same words like a mantra: "I could tell you things, oh boy." It can be speculated that Ashraf's stories cannot be told because they are too fragmentary; his experience resembles Gin's motley crowd of strokes, turns, and chances. Moreover, Ashraf's taxi stories overlap, in both form and content, with those of other taxi drivers, and since they are shared by others, they cannot be related as separate stories. This is suggested in the passage where Gin conceives of all taxi stories as concentrated into one living story that stands for all of them: the city "thicken[s] in taxidrivers' heads," she observes, so that "just ONE BIG STORY gets saved in their heads, a long, tangled, mixed-up one" (53). The taxi-driving experience is so concentrated that it is as hard to separate individual taxi stories as it is to separate the past, present, and future experiences within them.

Pekárková turns to New York City in order to imagine the immigrant identity as an identity-in-movement, thus replacing the narrative of the immigrant's journey from an old to a new home with that of an immigrant's cruising around the city. In the city, Gin reimagines herself in relation to a multiplicity of chances. Pekárková treats the present moment as an explosive mixture of ramifying chances, because every moment has the potential to expand its chances infinitely.

In this respect, it is useful to read Pekárková in light of Virginia Woolf. Woolf considered London to be an essential influence on her experimental fiction, in which she explored the impact of the modern metropolis on female subjectivity.[12] Like Pekárková, Woolf sees the city as a reservoir of chances and encounters. As Woolf writes in her essay "Modern Fiction," "an ordinary mind on an ordinary day" in a city receives "an incessant shower of innumerable atoms" that stimulates the imagination (150). Consequently, the city offers women, at every step, a chance to reinvent themselves in response to this "shower."

This is evident, for example, in Woolf's well-known essay "Mr. Bennett and Mrs. Brown," in which a chance encounter with an anonymous woman sitting in the same train compartment leads

---

12. Woolf views a specifically urban effect as essential for her artistic creation. In "A Sketch of the Past" she declares that it is "the shock-receiving capacity . . . [that] makes [her] a writer" (71–72). In an excellent study of Woolf's relationship to London, Susan Squier points out that London is central to Woolf's thinking through the question of women's writing. Squier focuses on the contrast between Woolf's figures Judith Shakespeare and Mary Carmichael, arguing, "[t]he London she portrayed shifted from an environment hostile to women (like the city Judith Shakespeare encountered) to a later city like that experienced by Mary Carmichael, which at least held the possibility for the emergence of authentic female—even feminist—voices and values" (4).

the narrator to try to imagine the woman's identity and fabricate her story. Drawing on the figure of the female urban walker and observer, the *flâneuse*, Woolf shows how the reservoir of chance encounters can ignite the imagination.[13] Unlike the prototype of the male *flâneur* as he is depicted in the work of Charles Baudelaire and Walter Benjamin, Woolf's narrator does not eroticize and thus control the image of the observed woman but instead builds her own story on the recognition that both she and Mrs. Brown are part of the same fiction.[14]

It may at first seem surprising to look at Pekárková in terms of Woolf, for there is obviously a wide chasm between them. Their work is different in terms of historical period, aesthetics, nationality, language, and location. Different also are the kinds of dislocation they imagine: Woolf's *flâneuse* of "Street Haunting: A London Adventure" traverses her home city, and her dislocation is temporary, while Gin traverses continents, and her sense of dislocation is persistent. Finally, the mode and speed of their mobility vary: while Woolf's *flâneuse* walks, Gin drives a cab.

But in spite of the differences (and my list is by no means complete), the ways in which the two employ the *flâneuse* figure exhibit a striking continuity. Woolf's female urban peregrinator, like Pekárková's taxi driver, draws on the city to free her imagination from the constraints of

---

13. The *flâneuse* is the female counterpart of the male *flâneur*, representing the consciousness of an urban walker and observer of urban modernity. Perhaps the most famous essay on the *flâneur* is Charles Baudelaire's "The Painter of Modern Life" (1863). Walter Benjamin's well-known analysis of Baudelaire and urban culture brings the *flâneur* to the twentieth century and shows his continuing relevance for examining the modern mass culture of spectacle (*Arcades*; "Some Motifs"). Deborah L. Parsons, in a comprehensive examination of the *flâneuse* in modern English literature, focuses on modernist women writers for whom the city represents "a constituent of identity, and who translate the experience of urban space into their narrative form" (7). Parsons understands the figure of the *flâneur* in broad terms: "Once an idle observer of the Parisian *demi-monde*, for contemporary theory he is an increasingly expansive figure who represents a variety of 'wanderings,' in terms of ambulation, nationality, gender, race, class, and sexuality" (4).

14. In his essay "Some Motifs in Baudelaire," Benjamin analyzes Baudelaire's poem "To a Woman Passing By" as an urban encounter that becomes erotic. The fleeting nature of such encounters precludes the cultivating of an affair with any woman whom the *flâneur* catches sight of and leads to his idealizing the woman's image while lamenting the impossibility of loving her. Benjamin describes this modern urban phenomenon as "love—not at first sight, but at last sight" (125).

familiarity and focuses on the possibilities that the present moment offers to her. "Street Haunting" serves as an excellent example. Its *flâneuse*-narrator rambles the streets of London on the pretext of going to buy a pencil, implying that in order to compose a story, the writer needs a walk in the city as much as she needs the pencil.[15] This trip beyond the walls of her familiar house also involves leaving the familiar boundaries of the self. In the city, she says, "[w]e are no longer quite ourselves" because "we shed the self our friends know us by" (20). Like a taxi driver, the *flâneuse* of "Street Haunting" is willing to exchange security for unpredictability if it brings her a new turn of events to inspire her writing. In the process of walking and observing the city, the *flâneuse* finds that she can reimagine herself: instead of relating her self to her home, she can relate it to the city's streets.

Woolf imagines the narrator of "Street Haunting" in temporary exile, a move that sheds light on the kind of displacement without nostalgia that Pekárková expands. Although Woolf's narrator does not leave her home city, Woolf defamiliarizes the setting as much as she can, exiling her *flâneuse*, at least temporarily, from her familiar surroundings and the self that inhabits them. For Woolf, these moments of temporary homelessness and mobility are crucial, because they allow one to see the world from a new perspective, one stripped of personal and familiar meanings. This defamiliarized perspective holds the potential for rewriting the self, whose form is otherwise modeled by the walls of home and personal identity: "The shell-like covering which our souls have excreted to house themselves, to make for themselves a shape distinct from others, is broken, and there is left of all these wrinkles and roughnesses a central oyster of perceptiveness, an enormous eye" (21–22). Having escaped its previous containment and separation, the self as eye roams the city freely.

Glimpses caught at separate moments present to the eye different kinds of selves. This experience leads the narrator to pose a series of intriguing questions:

---

15. I interpret Woolf's narrator as female, given that she refers to herself as wearing pearls, although the narrator's gender is never stated and indeed is obscured by Woolf's use of the collective pronoun "we" and her move toward dissolving the boundaries of an individual and individually gendered self.

Is the true self this which stands on the pavement in January, or that which bends over the balcony in June? Am I here, or am I there? Or is the true self neither this nor that, neither here nor there, but something so varied and wandering that it is only when we give the rein to its wishes and let it take its way unimpeded that we are indeed ourselves?

(28–29)

The narrator arrives at a new vision of her "self" as multiple and discontinuous. Importantly, there seems to be no pressure to commit to any one of these selves. Liberated from the idea of the self as singular and functioning within a temporal continuity, the narrator leaves the question of the self open; or rather, she leaves the self in the form of a question. Such a freedom of choice is only temporary, however. In contrast to Pekárková's postmodern *flâneuse*, who keeps moving away from home, Woolf's modern wanderer returns home, intact. Within the walls of a familiar house, the self regains its singular shape:

Circumstances compel unity; for convenience' sake a man must be a whole. The good citizen when he opens his door in the evening must be banker, golfer, husband, father; not a nomad wandering the desert, a mystic staring at the sky, a debauchee in the slums of San Francisco, a soldier heading a revolution, a pariah howling with scepticism and solitude. When he opens his door, he must run his fingers through his hair and put his umbrella in the stand like the rest.

(29)

Although Woolf returns the *flâneuse* home, and thus to her familiar self, it is important that the *flâneuse* can again open the doors of the house and experience an unfamiliar self. This experience, as Woolf suggests, changes profoundly the idea of a "good citizen" whose self is "whole." Woolf imagines that a "good citizen" can leave this wholeness behind, that a coherent self is as much a fiction as becoming "a nomad," a "mystic," a "debauchee," "a soldier heading a revolution," or a "pariah." Through these vivid metaphors, Woolf paints a new kind of subjectivity that can escape from the stable, socially sanctioned self molded by the home. Woolf encourages women to imagine the kind of subjectivity that would not leave its wandering, nomadic aspects out of doors but instead invite such qualities to cross the thresholds into their imaginative dwellings.

Woolf thus anticipates the kind of immigrant whom Pekárková depicts. Woolf implies that a woman's perspective on the world must involve her experience of freedom from home. In this way, Woolf opens the door to an imagining of the postmodern wandering self, a self that questions its own status and affiliations, a self that forms its shape in relation to the contingent nature of urban life. Importantly, the narrator of "Street Haunting" does not order or judge the different kinds of selves that can be made and unmade on each of her walks. Woolf's idea of the "varied and wandering" self that is "neither this nor that, neither here nor there" is typical of a postmodern imagination and sensibility (although her writing here confirms that it is not, per se, a postmodern invention).

Woolf foreshadows later discussions of a rootless, postmodern subjectivity in offering the list of metaphors for rootlessness. Symbolizing mobility and change, "nomad" in particular has become a prominent critical term for describing the postmodern self. In *Nomadic Subjects*, for example, Rosi Braidotti suggests that the nomad symbolizes a postmodern subjectivity that rejects stasis, one that "has relinquished all idea, desire, or nostalgia for fixity" (22). Similarly, Iain Chambers describes postmodern mobility with the term "migrancy," which "involves a movement in which neither the points of departure nor those of arrival are immutable or certain" (5). This concept corresponds to a mobile sense of "home," of our "being in the world," that requires us to imagine ourselves in constant motion, or in Chambers's words, "to conceive of dwelling as a mobile habitat, as a mode of inhabiting time and space not as though they were fixed and closed structures" (4).[16] While images of postmodern rootlessness certainly

---

16. Along similar lines, Carine M. Mardorossian argues for a "paradigmatic shift from exile to migrant literature," or the literature of postmodern movement (15). In migrant literature, "the world inhabited by the characters is no longer conceptualized as 'here' and 'there.' Because of her displacement, the migrant's identity undergoes radical shifts that alter her self-perception and often result in her ambivalence towards both her old and new existence. She can no longer simply or nostalgically remember the past as a fixed and comforting anchor in her life, since its contours move with the present rather than in opposition to it. Her identity is no longer to do with being but with becoming" (16). Mardorossian distinguishes migrant literature from exile literature according to the representation of movement. While an exile moves between fixed points of reference—"here" and "there," "old" and "new"—these stabilities no longer hold up, and hence the term "exile" does not suffice in the face of contemporary "movement, rootlessness, and

reflect aspects of the contemporary world, the world of and in movement, the idea of a dislocated, vacated, and "becoming" self does
not fit everybody. Mobility is not always a matter of individual
choice but often a consequence of poverty, war, or political per-
secution. Feminist critics, such as Janet Wolff, point out that an indiscriminate embrace of mobility is risky, because "we do not all have
the same access to the road" (128).[17] Nonetheless, it is worthwhile to
examine the benefits Woolf and Pekárková gain by embracing mobility and homelessness. As Woolf shows in "Street Haunting," the temporary forgetting of a familiar location frees the self from its familiar
shape, thus enabling a woman to see herself from a new perspective. Woolf encourages her *flâneuse* to see her own city afresh, focusing her attention away from the regular lines of self and toward
irregular urban stimuli and passersby. Similarly, Gin's subjectivity expands toward the city, where she becomes rooted. These roots
work as new routes toward her new self, a self incorporating the
urban collectivity. Both Woolf and Pekárková use this move: they
free a subject from her stable location of subjectivity, that is, from
her home, so that she can reimagine herself when making connections to others.

Woolf's and Pekárková's homeless figures are unanchored in
terms of a domicile. Their new home is the city itself, where they
surround themselves with an alternative family, as each becomes
part of a collectivity of urban dwellers. Woolf's narrator in "Street

---

the mixing of cultures, races, and languages." Mardorossian's emphasis on "becoming"
certainly corresponds to Pekárková's understanding of an immigrant self as an always
unfinished project.

17. Wolff speaks against romanticizing metaphors of displacement, such as that of the
nomad, and argues that although metaphors of mobility are certainly useful, every
"destabilizing has to be *situated*" (128). Thus she finds it problematic to use metaphors of
mobility without simultaneously paying attention to the particularity of each moving
subject: she warns, "The problem with terms like 'nomad,' 'maps' and 'travel' is that they
are not usually located." Wolff's concern that the metaphors of mobility do not apply to
everyone is representative of feminist criticism's call for always acknowledging the location from which one speaks, as articulated in Adrienne Rich's "Blood, Bread, and Poetry,"
where Rich shows that every woman is specifically located in multiple social positions.
Rich's politics of location reflects the particularity of each individual woman and her
experience. Similarly, Caren Kaplan holds that "[a]ll displacements are not the same" (2),
and Heike Paul states that the immigrant "needs to find out *where* she is in order to find
out *who* she is" (26).

Haunting" says that after we "shed" the self, we "become part of that vast republican army of anonymous trampers, whose society is so agreeable after the solitude of one's own room" (20–21).[18] The narrator explains that, before returning home, an individual self turns into a collective one; leaving the familiar self behind leads to "indulg[ing]" in "the illusion that one is not tethered to a single mind, but can put on briefly for a few minutes the bodies and minds of others" (20, 35). Such a strategy, although it may be only an "illusion," enables the narrator to see herself as a part of an urban collectivity of those whose "bodies and minds" she imaginatively puts on. For example, the narrator observes a dwarf woman entering a shoe shop, the sight of whom diverts her attention away from herself; she asks, "What, then, is it like to be a dwarf?"(24). Importantly, the imaginative exercise of the narrator's trying on the dwarf woman's identity transforms not only the narrator but also the dwarf woman and the street crowd: "Indeed, the dwarf had started a hobbling grotesque dance to which everybody in the street now conformed" (25). The relationship that the narrator forms in her chance encounter results in a collective change.

Like Woolf, Pekárková draws on urban plurality in order to construct an individual yet collective identity, imagining Gin's subjectivity as always related to the city and its dwellers. New York has an ongoing impact on Gin's imagination, interlacing the individual with the collective ever more tightly. Living in New York means spinning in a vortex of nationalities and languages. There are, for example, Gin's husband Talibe from Mali, her Russian-speaking boss Alex, and her Cuban roommate Gloria. But Gin feels part of the urban collective that reaches well beyond the immediate circle of her acquaintances: "she felt she belonged . . . to something, to the secret brotherhood of blue distances perhaps, to the brotherhood of those who DARED" (19). Pekárková suggests that even though the members of this "brotherhood" may remain anonymous to one another, they are connected by the mobility of their "daring"

18. In her analysis of "Street Haunting," Rachel Bowlby stresses that the "pleasant companionship" found in the modern city is, interestingly, "to be found out of doors and among the 'anonymous'" (210).

imaginations, which take them away from their homes and toward "blue distances."

Thus Pekárková depicts the urban collective as sharing an imagination focused on transgressing boundaries. By naming this collectivity "the secret brotherhood of blue distances," she implies that its members strive to imagine themselves beyond already explored horizons and beyond their own limitations. These imagined places might be "the sky-blue THERE that the homeless Randy liked to talk about" or simply a new street that Gin drives through (20). Moreover, the members of the brotherhood imagine themselves beyond their individual identities. As immigrants, they cross geographical distances, but they also cross those distances that separate them from each other. Once they enter the fabric of New York City, their subjectivities are woven together.

The city makes up both the exterior setting and the interior landscape of Gin's mind: "Late at night, toward morning, Gin's thoughts were spread like a map on the gray asphalt and concrete, her thoughts, adventures, memories and hopes included" (2). But Pekárková goes beyond merely comparing Gin to New York; she starts overlapping them. From rendering Gin "like" the city, Pekárková makes Gin "become" the city. Thus Gin's "[m]emories and adventures became those beer caps, flattened aluminum cans or glass shards forced deep into the asphalt by numerous tires" (2). Instead of gliding on the surface of the city, Gin "becomes" the city as she goes into its depth, "forced deep into the asphalt," which symbolizes the primal matter of the city. In short, Gin becomes "a building block, a cell, a molecule in that humongous, colorful, crazy mosaic" of New York City (34).

Thus Gin spins in the urban vortex together with other people equally comprised of the city's elements. Gin's roommate Gloria creates artworks that portray, even embody, New York: she mixes 365 dead roaches into a painting titled *A Year of Poverty*. The car mechanic Ramon wears "filthy overalls" that "became one mass with his skin, melted together into the shape of something that lay on the sidewalk all winter long, covered in slush and dogshit" (30). Ramon sleeps on the oil-soaked garage floor with newspaper as his bedding, and Gin observes that his body merges with the newspaper, so that "his body on paper looked like another New York disaster, one which they forgot to write about in *The Post*" (31). Along with Gin, these characters create a collectivity of similarly unanchored immigrants, whose very bodies have undergone a metamorphosis: instead of flesh and blood, they are made from the primal matter of the city.

For Pekárková, an individual identity is unimaginable without a collective one. The territories of individuals' subjectivities are constantly transgressed as they overlap with one another. Their interactions leave imaginative imprints on each other, expanding individual mental spaces into spaces that encompass others:

> The interference of thoughts, opinions, ideas and heads, however, penetrated through the entire City.
>
> ALL the heads here left their signatures on one another; all the opinions, loves, hates, happy and unhappy thoughts, ideas, emotions, inspirations— absolutely everything that ever took place in human heads got reflected in the heads of all the others, whether they liked it or not, like rainbow-color interference stripes—
>
> (33)

In this passage, Pekárková experiments with punctuation to make her point: a period is supplanted by a dash, indicating that an individual fragment—whether it is a thought, a sentence, a taxi story, or even a self—inevitably connects to something beyond its own boundaries. Thus she suggests that the writing of Gin's individual self cannot be rendered separately from all the "interfering" sides of the picture. Gin simultaneously "reflects" and is "reflected" by others. As she says, "as an individual you simply couldn't exist, live or create here because the interference from all those other heads took your concentration away from you" (34). Gin, as an individual, is unimaginable without these mutual reflections, which cement her sense of "belonging" to the "brotherhood" and the city: "the more people in the same situation Gin met in the streets, the stronger, better and more real this feeling of belonging was" (19–20). Gin even imagines that "the souls of all the immigrants merged together into one huge megasoul" (20).

Pekárková emphasizes that these connections among immigrants work on a visceral level. Metaphors of such interactions among people in the city permeate the novel. For example, Gin imagines individual people as "bubbles" whose fragile, even fluid, membranes allow her to articulate different kinds of interactions:

"—the bubbles scratched and hurt one another, they penetrated one another and sometimes, for a spell, they merged together in a scream of empathy and passion; they destroyed one another and burst in spasms of pain; they didn't fit into this City, there were too many of them—" (33–34). Contacts between individuals might be damaging but also healing. Because of their fragility, they "scratched and hurt," even "destroyed one another," but the elasticity of their boundaries also enables their "merg[ing] together," fostering a sense of "empathy and passion." These individual "bubbles" can hardly stay intact or alone in an urban crowd. Their permeability and interpenetration are, once again, visually emphasized by the punctuation Pekárková uses. She opens and ends this sentence with a dash that symbolizes the links between urban dwellers.

In order to strengthen the visceral nature of these interactions, Pekárková uses tactile metaphors when describing contacts within the urban collective. The city attracts people with prehensile feelers: "Big cities reach out their tentacles like huge octopuses," and "people let themselves be lured and attach themselves to these tentacles, as if they were umbilical cords" (1). At the same time, Gin observes that "[a]ll over the surface of her body visual sensors sprouted like she was a rainworm. Tentacles emerged from her belly like she was an octopus, and their gentle suction cups stroked the whole world. The world stroked her back" (19). Interestingly, Gin has the same tactile organs as the city. Using the image of an octopus for both of them, Pekárková depicts Gin and New York as similar organisms, their bodies equipped with tactile organs and permeated with "tactile cells" (21). The sense of touch thus serves as a metaphor for reciprocity as the principal relationship between the individual and the collective.

Pekárková's focus on collectivity is unique given her cultural and sociopolitical background. A contemporary Czech writer would not be expected to write about collectivity at all. In Central and Eastern Europe, there is an understandable tendency to imagine identity as strictly individual, far from anything that might resemble the infamous communist collectivity.[19] For example, in *Café Europa: Life*

---

19. Madelaine Hron discusses the tendency of postcommunist Czech women writers to reclaim the individual and argues that these writers are painfully entrapped by the

After Communism, the Croatian writer Slavenka Drakulić expresses deep discomfort with her own lingering tendency to write in the first-person plural; her introduction to this collection of essays is titled "First Person Singular." Drakulić "hate[s] the first-person plural" because it is connected to her memories of state-imposed collectivism (2). She explains that "the difference between 'we' and 'I' is to me far more important than mere grammar. 'We' means fear, resignation, submissiveness, a warm crowd and somebody else deciding your destiny. 'I' means giving individuality and democracy a chance" (4). Due to the bad reputation of collectivity, such a view is widely shared in Eastern and Central Europe. Pekárková, however, sees that in contemporary multicultural society, an irreconcilable divide between the individual and the collective cannot hold.

While Drakulić believes that claiming one's individuality must start with saying "no" to "we," Pekárková shows that such a no should not be said hastily, because not all collectivities are the same. Pekárková's rendering of the urban collectivity shows that individual freedom must allow for the possibility of productive interactions between the individual and the collective. Saying no to the "interfering" collectivity would mean excluding those who are already part of oneself as well as denying the part of oneself that dwells in others.

Pekárková's voice, calling for the imagining of self beyond one place and one country, is not solitary. In *Three Guineas*, Woolf writes, "as a woman I have no country," because "my country is the whole world" (109). In this famous statement, Woolf anticipates future women writing beyond national boundaries and encourages them to

---

current imperative of individualism: "in postcommunism, 'the Word became Flesh': the shift to a market economy, private property and democracy favored a turn to individualism, material concerns, and emphasis on the body—materializing the former symbolic abstractions into localized, individualized particularity" (19). Hron points out that the current trend toward reclaiming individuality, albeit understandable given the forty years of state-imposed collectivism, takes a disturbing turn toward marking the individual body with violence. Hron refers in particular to Pekárková's previous novel *The World Is Round*, whose heroine is gang-raped after her escape from the communist East to the democratic West. Hron sees a horrible paradox in the heroine's escape from the oppressing communist collectivity only to find another imprisonment within her own body. That is why she calls attention to a problem facing contemporary Eastern and Central European writers, "the dilemma of how to act so as to be set free, not from one's material prison but from the prison of self that sets one apart from one's companions" (40).

form a new collectivity, the famous "Society of Outsiders." Similarly, Hoffman calls for the kind of imagination that accounts for a post-modern world, where "[d]islocation is the norm rather than the aberration" (274). Living in a world that is no longer "vertical" but "horizontal, made up of the endless multiplicity of events going on at once and pressing at each moment on our minds and our living rooms," Hoffman comes to the conclusion that contemporary "multivalent" experience requires an equally multivalent imagination, "even in the unlikely event that we spend an entire lifetime in one place." She writes that there is not one center but many: "New York, Warsaw, Tehran, Tokyo, Kabul—they all make claims on our imaginations, all remind us that in a decentered world we are always simultaneously in the center and on the periphery, that every competing center makes us marginal" (275). All these cities interfere with the rest of the world, like Pekárková's bubbles. And their interferences create our present; they make us who we are.

Interestingly, bringing together multiple cities in order to determine who we are is a proposition Drakulić can share in. Despite her rejection of collectivity, Drakulić's national allegiances are plural. In the same volume of essays in which she tries to resist the stifling form of a communist collectivity, Drakulić addresses the major contemporary challenge of building a new European collective identity. Arguing that Europe cannot preserve the same old dividing lines between its centers and peripheries, she holds that the war-ridden city of Sarajevo must remain at the center of Europe's imagination as much so as Paris or London.

Importantly, Pekárková's voice resonates with the voices of exactly those contemporary Central and Eastern European women writers who fight against nationalism. Besides Drakulić, there is Dubravka Ugrešić, who has refused to permit her citizenship and art to be eclipsed by the onset of nationalism in Croatia following its separation from Yugoslavia in 1991. Still considering herself Yugoslav, a multinational designation obliterated by the recent bloodshed, Ugrešić opposes a nationalistic discourse that would appropriate writers as its emblems in her essay "A Short Contribution to the History of a National Literature: The Top Ten Reasons to Be a Croatian Writer." One of these reasons is "Because of difference." She ironically observes:

> The most important reason to be a Croatian writer is because that means you're not a Serbian writer. The same holds true for Serbian writers—the best reason to be one is so as not to be Croatian. In fact, all of the top ten reasons for why it's good to be a Croatian writer apply to Serbian writers. And to Bosnian writers. And others as well.
>
> (123)

Here Ugrešić ridicules the compartmentalization of national literature that has accompanied the parceling out of the former Yugoslavia. As a Yugoslav writer, she has always felt part of more than one nation and culture—Croatian, Serbian, Bosnian. Ugrešić still feels this way even though Yugoslavia as a multinational country no longer exists.[20] Thus forced to reexamine where she now belongs, Ugrešić proclaims her allegiance to an utterly different kind of collectivity: "If I have to belong to someone, then it's to my readers. Wherever they may be" ("Glossary" 272). As a writer, Ugrešić ties her own imagination to her audience of readers worldwide. Although the members of this audience may be anonymous to one another, as in Pekárková's "secret brotherhood of blue distances," Ugrešić's links to them nurtures her individual imagination and creativity while simultaneously keeping her connected to others.

In Pekárková's view, the binary of immigrant and native is no longer meaningful, since it fails to account for the complexity of the contemporary immigrant experience. Together with Woolf, Hoffman, Drakulić, and Ugrešić, Pekárková emphasizes the need for a personal affiliation to many centers, many countries, and many collectivities. Certainly, Pekárková's work demonstrates that she finds inspiration in international collectivity. Twice in interviews she has disavowed her affiliation to any one national literature; her writing arises from cosmopolitan contingencies rather than national continuities.[21] Pekárková sees herself as an outsider to any one particular tradition,

---

20. Sadly, because of their "lack" of patriotism, both Drakulić and Ugrešić have been accused of betraying Croatia and labeled "witches" in the nationalistically oriented Croatian press.

21. In a 2006 interview, Pekárková expresses her dissatisfaction with "being thrown into a box," adding sardonically, "I was told that every Czech author must write about beer, so I felt very guilty that I didn't. I just couldn't bring myself to write about beer. Perhaps there are things that make me part of Czech literature, but I found out about them after I wrote my books. Perhaps there is such a thing as a national character, but

because only this perspective allows her to see the whole world. For this reason, Gin finally cannot remain faithful to one city only. In the novel's aforementioned final chapter, bearing the evocative title "There Are More New Yorks Than Just This One," we do not learn whether Gin will succeed in breaking away from New York in her imagination. After all, she and the Tree take New York with them. But clearly Pekárková makes sure that Gin heads toward new cities, seeking new horizons that may bring new chances, new selves, and new stories.

Importantly, seeking these new horizons does not require traveling across continents.[22] After all, home may not be a stable place, and Pekárková's experience provides a case in point. She left Czechoslovakia and returned to the Czech Republic, a country half its original size and engaged in a multifaceted process of transformation from totalitarianism to democracy, a free market, and membership in the European Union.[23] These changes have been rapid, radical, and massive. Both a returning immigrant and a native who never left may feel equally like foreigners in their own home. Reflecting on these unforeseen and complex challenges, Pekárková ironically speculates, "It may be easier to live in exile" ("Interview" 165).

Eradicating the distinction between immigrant and native motivates Pekárková's creative process. As a writer, Pekárková resists being pinned down. Her travels, her commitment to self-translation, and the bilingual conception of her novel are active gestures of excising a desire for stasis, and nationalism as one of its most dangerous forms, from our imaginations. In all these ways, Pekárková turns her cab into "a room of our own" for the twenty-first century. It provides a mobile imaginative space that simultaneously provides an opening to the world. It is a mobile space of "interferences" between self and others as well as between traditions and contexts of writing and

---

when I am writing, I am not aware of it" ("Interview" 166). In a 2001 interview, she emphasizes, "One of the things that interests me most is mixing of cultures, and various clashes of cultures, opinions, ideas or races. That's why New York was so right for me; I could watch all that" ("Jumping").

22. In a 2006 interview, Pekárková claims that traveling can be done even from the comfort of one's own home—for example, by surfing the Internet ("Interview" 163).

23. The Czech Republic joined the EU in 2004.

reading. At the same time, these multiple "interferences" characterize Pekárková's mobile place in contemporary immigrant literature. *Gimme the Money* resists being conceptualized as contemporary immigrant literature in relation to a national canon. Thus the novel escapes, for example, Gilbert H. Muller's characterization of contemporary immigrant fiction as "emblematic of the transformation of our national mythology and of its literary canon" (x). For the same reasons, the novel exceeds what has been termed the "final stage of the migration-literature model," defined by the editors of *Writing across Worlds: Literature and Migration* as one where "[l]iterature no longer simply sheds light on migration processes, but migrants, or writers born out of the migrant experience, play an increasingly prominent role in shaping the development of erstwhile 'pure' national (and international) literatures" (King et al. xii). *Gimme the Money* moves well beyond this "final stage" defined in relation to national literatures.[24] Pekárková's allegorical cab breaks ties with one national tradition, either Czech or American, and moves us into a space of "interferences" among national literatures and between immigrant and nonimmigrant literary genres. In this space, immigrant fiction engages with nonimmigrant forms of writing across countries and centuries. By generating an international and intergeneric conversation, or "interference," among Pekárková, Hoffman, Woolf, Drakulić, and Ugrešić, the novel expands the frontiers of immigrant literature.

Does *Gimme the Money* then mark a new "stage" of immigrant literature, one in which an immigrant novel breaks free from national traditions, and even from the genre of immigrant literature? Some may argue that international and intergeneric "interferences" may preclude the novel's designation as "immigrant." But I contend that the novel still belongs to this genre, although its place is on the genre's frontiers. Besides offering a story of mobility, the novel is part of the immigrant story through its own material existence in the

---

24. For the same reason, Pekárková's novel does not fit Muller's conceptualization of how contemporary immigrant fiction shapes American literature: "Immigrants have always engaged in nation-building, and the immigrants we encounter in postwar American fiction are emblematic of the transformation of our national mythology and of its literary canon. Such fiction argues for a polyglot nation, transnational connections, and new forms of cultural authority" (x).

world, as it participates in transnational processes of production and consumption that involve writing, translating, reading, circulating, and contextualizing. Just like a taxi story, this genre keeps recasting its own boundaries. Some pages at its front and back are "torn off" (118). Without beginnings and endings, Pekarkova's novel, like the immigrant genre of which it is part, continues to evolve.

Rutgers University

WORKS CITED

Austin, Mary. *The Promised Land*. 1912. New York: Penguin, 1997.

Baudelaire, Charles. "The Painter of Modern Life." 1863. *The Painter of Modern Life and Other Essays*. Trans. and ed. Jonathan Mayne. London: Phaidon, 1995.

Benjamin, Walter. *The Arcades Project*. Trans. Howard Eiland and Kevin McLaughlin. Cambridge, MA: Belknap-Harvard UP, 1999.

———. "Some Motifs in Baudelaire." *Charles Baudelaire: A Lyric Poet in the Era of High Capitalism*. Trans. Harry Zohn. 1968. London: Verso, 1973. 107–54.

Bowlby, Rachel. *Feminist Destinations and Further Essays on Virginia Woolf*. Edinburgh: Edinburgh UP, 1997.

Braidotti, Rosi. *Nomadic Subjects: Embodiment and Sexual Difference in Contemporary Feminist Theory*. New York: Columbia UP, 1994.

Chambers, Iain. *Migrancy, Culture, Identity*. London: Routledge, 1994.

Drakulić, Slavenka. "Introduction: First Person Singular." *Café Europa: Life After Communism*. 1996. New York: Norton, 1997. 1–5.

Hoffman, Eva. *Lost in Translation: A Life in a New Language*. 1989. New York: Penguin, 1990.

Hron, Madelaine. "Word Made Flesh: Czech Women's Fiction from Communism to Post-Communism." *Spaces of Identity* 2.1 (2002): 19–43.

Kaplan, Caren. *Questions of Travel: Postmodern Discourses of Displacement*. Durham, NC: Duke UP, 1996.

King, Russell, John Connell, and Paul White, eds. Preface. *Writing across Worlds: Literature and Migration*. New York: Routledge, 1995. ix–xvi.

Kristeva, Julia. *Strangers to Ourselves*. Trans. Leon S. Roudiez. New York: Columbia UP, 1991.

Mardorossian, Carine M. "From Literature of Exile to Migrant Literature." *Modern Language Studies* 32.2 (2002): 15–33.

Muller, Gilbert H. *New Strangers in Paradise: The Immigrant Experience and Contemporary American Fiction*. Lexington: UP of Kentucky, 1999.

Parsons, Deborah L. *Streetwalking the Metropolis: Women, the City, and Modernity*. Oxford: Oxford UP, 2000.

Paul, Heike. *Mapping Migration: Women's Writing and the American Immigrant Experience from the 1950s to the 1990s*. Heidelberg: Universitätsverlag C. Winter, 1999.

Pekárková, Iva. E-mail to Věra Eliášová. 19 Sept. 2005.

———. *Gimme the Money*. Trans. Raymond Johnston and Iva Pekárková. London: Serpent's Tail, 2000.

———. "An Interview with Iva Pekárková." Conducted by Věra Eliášová and Simona Fojtová. *Contemporary Literature* 47 (2006): 155–69.

———. "Jumping into Another Life." Interview. Conducted by Madelaine Hron. *Central Europe Review* 3.15 (2001). 15 June 2006. <http://www.ce-review.org>.

———. "Můj život patří mně [My life belongs to me]." Interview. Conducted by Vladimír Ševela. Praha [Prague]: Mat'a, 2001.

———. *Truck Stop Rainbows*. Trans. David Powelstock. New York: Farrar, 1992.

———. *The World Is Round*. Trans. David Powelstock. New York: Farrar, 1994.

Rich, Adrienne. "Blood, Bread, and Poetry: The Location of the Poet." *Blood, Bread, and Poetry: Selected Prose*. New York: Norton, 1986. 210–31.

Squier, Susan M. *Virginia Woolf and London: The Sexual Politics of the City*. Chapel Hill: U of North Carolina P, 1985.

Ugrešić, Dubravka. "Glossary." *The Culture of Lies: Antipolitical Essays*. Trans. Celia Hawkesworth. University Park, PA: Pennsylvania State UP, 1998. 269–73.

———. "A Short Contribution to the History of a National Literature: The Top Ten Reasons to Be a Croatian Writer." *Thank You for Not Reading: Essays on Literary Trivia*. Trans. Celia Hawkesworth. Normal, IL: Dalkey Archive, 2003. 115–23.

White, Paul. "Geography, Literature and Migration." *Writing across Worlds: Literature and Migration*. Ed. Russell King, John Connell, and Paul White. New York: Routledge, 1995. 1–19.

Wolff, Janet. *Resident Alien: Feminist Cultural Criticism*. New Haven, CT: Yale UP, 1995.

Woolf, Virginia. "Mr. Bennett and Mrs. Brown." 1924. *The Captain's Death Bed and Other Essays*. New York: Harcourt, 1950. 94–119.

———. "Modern Fiction." 1925. *The Common Reader*. London: Harcourt, 1984. 146–54.

———. "A Sketch of the Past." 1939. *Moments of Being*. 2nd ed. London: Harcourt, 1985. 61–159.

———. "Street Haunting: A London Adventure." 1927. *The Death of the Moth and Other Essays*. London: Harcourt, 1942. 20–36.

———. *Three Guineas*. 1938. London: Harcourt, 1966.

J. DILLON BROWN

Exile and Cunning: The Tactical Difficulties of George Lamming

Let us never cease from thinking—what is this "civilization" in which we find ourselves?

Virginia Woolf, *Three Guineas*

George Lamming is one of an important group of pioneering Caribbean novelists, commonly called the Windrush generation, who are given credit for the efflorescence of West Indian fiction in the 1950s.[1] Like those of his contemporaries, Lamming's novels—contemporaneous with political independence movements across the region—were strongly invested in establishing a specifically anticolonial regional-national cultural identity. The criticism that has subsequently grown up around his work has accordingly focused on issues relating to its Caribbean contexts and resonances. While such examinations have clear importance (and certainly comply with Lamming's intentions of exerting social and political influence at home), they tend to overlook an important aspect of the novels' production: these foundational West Indian novels were written and published in London, the metropolitan capital of the British Empire. Although it may seem counterintuitive to discuss such polemically anticolonial literature in its metropolitan context, the importance of this context should not be overlooked. Indeed,

---

1. Other novelists in the group include Edgar Mittelholzer, Samuel Selvon, Roger Mais, Jan Carew, John Hearne, and V. S. Naipaul. The term "Windrush" comes from the *Empire Windrush*, the ship that carried some of the first West Indian emigrants from the Caribbean to England in 1948.

Contemporary Literature XLVII, 4   0010-7484; E-ISSN 1548-9949/06/0004-0669

Lamming himself ruefully acknowledges in *The Pleasures of Exile* that in the postwar years he had no real West Indian audience but instead wrote "always for the foreign reader" (43), as the circuits of capital, criticism, and publishing seemed to necessitate an engagement with the imperial culture against which he was committed to writing.[2] Thus, although the normative critical approach to Lamming's work is to see it as exilic, postcolonial literature and hence to return it to its "rightful" (West Indian) place, I propose to read Lamming's novels as immigrant literature, as works that are not simply out of place but also firmly situated in a new context—addressed to a foreign (English) reader. This type of reading, itself "immigrating" into alien territory within the discipline, provides an important vantage point on one of the least understood and critically disputatious elements of Lamming's writing: the turbid difficulty of his prose style. In a West Indian context in which literacy, let alone literariness, could hardly be taken for granted, Lamming's difficulty can be (too) easily dismissed as an elitist, politically incoherent gesture; however, placed in the context of postwar London, "difficulty" takes on the guise of a potent political strategy that helps articulate a sense of Caribbean nationalism and anticolonial protest.

From virtually the beginning of his publishing career, Lamming's writing has been described as difficult. As early as January 4, 1948, in the first *Caribbean Voices* program dedicated exclusively to Lamming's work, editor Henry Swanzy's introduction of Lamming captured the ambiguous effects of his writing, with Swanzy asserting that in the poems about to be read, "one finds a strange, oblique, violent, passionate emotion, which I feel, somehow, may prove of importance to the Caribbean" (*Caribbean Voices*). His qualifying "somehow" betrays doubt in his own ability to gauge the precise meaning and import of Lamming's work, an uncertainty explicitly articulated in his commentary after the first poem is read: "We start with that rather mysterious poem because it seems typical of this writer, who never

---

2. In analyzing the contribution of the BBC radio program *Caribbean Voices* to the creation of a West Indian literature, Lamming evocatively articulated the economic, political, and cultural constraints of his position as a colonial writer, observing that the BBC "played a role of taking the raw material and sending it back, almost like sugar, which is planted there in the West Indies, cut, sent abroad to be refined, and gets back in the finished form" (*Conversations* 62).

says, straight out, exactly what he means." Swanzy thus introduces difficulty as an identifying characteristic of Lamming's work, while maintaining with cautious imprecision that the work is, "somehow," meaningful and important. Such critical evaluations of Lamming as difficult—many, indeed, negatively critical—have continued until today. More recent books on Lamming by Simon Gikandi, A. J. Simoes da Silva, and Supriya Nair note his difficult style, while Rudolf Bader sees fit to begin his entry discussing Lamming's work in the encyclopedic *International Literature in English: Essays on the Major Writers* with the caveat that "many readers find George Lamming's novels difficult" (143). For his part, Lamming seems to welcome the critical consensus that he is a "difficult" writer, saying, "This means that I have to be read more slowly than would be the case with some writers, which I think is a good thing" (Interview 11).[3]

Lamming's view of the salutary effects of reading more slowly provides a key to the formal aspect of his intentions regarding difficulty— a hallowed, modernist effort at "interrupting the 'realistic' processes of habitualized communication" (Eysteinsson 238). This interruptive motivation behind Lamming's prose style has been articulated very eloquently by David Scott, who argues in the preface to his interview with Lamming that the latter's novels entail a confrontation with "this obligation: to pause, to doubt, to question, to wonder out loud about the assumptions, the conditions, the terms, the conventions, the values in relation to which, at any given moment, we pursue the projects we pursue" (Lamming, "Sovereignty" 74). In a similar vein, George Steiner's theoretical examination of literary difficulty, "On Difficulty," identifies the primary aims of difficulty as "forcing us to reach out towards more delicate orderings of perception" and "drawing attention . . . to the inertias in the common routine of discourse" (40).[4]

---

3. Immediately following this comment, Lamming acknowledges the complications of this attitude if one wants a large audience, particularly of Caribbean peasants, as readers. Charges of elitism, of course, animate much of the critique of Lamming's difficulty, and throughout his career Lamming has been both aware of and sensitive to such charges while remaining unwavering in his commitment to avoiding simplification.

4. These characteristics are attributed to the third category of difficulty that Steiner identifies, the "tactical." Lamming's difficulty indeed seems to function mainly in a way that Steiner would call tactical. Steiner notes, "it may be no accident that tactical difficulties crop up where poets consider their métier" (38), thus suggesting that tactical

Lamming clearly sees his writing in these terms—as a stimulus to the reordering of discourse via an interruption of habitual thought patterns. In a talk commemorating the work of Sam Selvon, Lamming relates an anecdote that underscores the type of reordering he sees as necessary. The story involves querying an Englishwoman about the arrival of a letter; she responds that no letters have arrived, though she has been checking carefully for "black stamps." Lamming interprets her comment thus:

> She meant stamps marked Africa or India, China or the West Indies. One kind, honest and courteous old woman had fixed almost two thirds of the World's population with one word. You might say that the woman was a simple example of ignorance but I maintain that ignorant or not it has fundamentally to do with a particular way of seeing.
>
> ("Coldest Spring" 6)

Resisting the simple, dismissive interpretation of the woman as ignorant, Lamming analyzes her speech as a fundamental effect of her (colonizer's) perception, which *The Pleasures of Exile* consistently identifies as "an inherited and uncritical way of seeing" prevalent on both sides of the colonizer/colonized divide (76). Indeed, Lamming takes the term "colonized" to apply to people who have "found models and texts which they . . . embraced uncritically" ("Sovereignty" 177), and he asserts that colonization can often be understood as "simply a tradition of habits that become the normal way of seeing" (*Pleasures* 157). It is against these stubborn, ingrained, and effectively naturalized routines of perception that Lamming positions his literary difficulty: he wants to oblige his audience to read his works more slowly, with more consideration, paying more attention, as Steiner would have it, to the "inertias in the common routine of [colonial] discourse" and thus recognizing the importance of reordering one's perceptions with careful attention to the interests influential in directing them.

While this formalist reading of the uses of difficulty can shed important light on the *general* functions of Lamming's opaque literary style (and on ways in which difficulty might converge with postcolonial and immigrant literature's interests in counterdiscursivity writ large),

---

difficulty is an important part of modernist technique, which is generally seen to be overtly self-conscious with regard to the elements of its own medium.

undue focus on such an abstract level risks occluding how such a label functioned in the social and literary milieu in which Lamming's novels were created and received. More recent critical considerations of difficulty have pinpointed its relevance and interpretability less in the work itself, as Steiner's account generally assumes, than in the intertwined relationships among text, reader, and the publishing and critical arenas. Bob Perelman's *The Trouble with Genius* effectively reads difficulty as reflecting a shifting struggle over the social role of the artist vis-à-vis a perceived split between the social and aesthetic spheres; Leonard Diepeveen's *The Difficulties of Modernism* focuses on a similar extratextual significance, arguing that difficulty is based in the social relationship between author and reader, with cultural and class concerns (expressed particularly by psychological feelings of anxiety and inadequacy in Diepeveen's account) at the foundation of difficulty's effects. These more sociological accounts of literary difficulty suggest a fruitful methodological approach to Lamming's puzzling literary technique that resonates with the specific issues of immigrant writing: determining how the label "difficulty" worked within the postwar London literary world in which Lamming wrote provides instructive insights into some of the strategic negotiations adopted by migrant novelists from the British Commonwealth as they lay the foundations of what is today understood as the postcolonial novel.

Lamming's choice to write "difficult literature" appears on the surface to be somewhat mysterious, given the general publishing and critical trends in London at the time. In these postwar years, difficulty was indissolubly associated with the prewar writers now thought of as high modernist, an experimental style that was steadily losing influence and esteem in the world of English letters. The rising generation of native-born writers such as Kingsley Amis, Philip Larkin, John Osborne, and John Wain were vociferous in their hostility to the intellectual, internationalist, and explicitly self-conscious techniques of their modernist predecessors; the emergently dominant tenor of the literary opinion of the period is succinctly conveyed by the title of Rubin Rabinovitz's 1967 study, *The Reaction against Experiment in the English Novel, 1950–1960*.[5] Indeed, experimental writing was

---

5. The case for antimodernism should not be overstated, as James Joyce, Virginia Woolf, and D. H. Lawrence had their defenders, most prominently in the universities, as

commonly linked with notions of exile and an outsider status, which were becoming particularly suspect in a time of national consolidation. In light of the anti-immigrant journalistic furor—vividly presented in Mike and Trevor Phillips's *Windrush: The Irresistible Rise of Multi-Racial Britain*—over the incoming thousands of West Indian immigrants, Lamming's aesthetic decision to enunciate his racial and national difference seems to fly in the face of any sound strategy for a young, West Indian writer looking to be published without the standard social network or Oxbridge education.[6]

If one takes into account Lamming's migrant status and his generation's commitment to dissecting and diffusing colonial power through cultural means, on the other hand, his affiliation with the role of modernist writer becomes much more comprehensible. As a black West Indian immigrant, Lamming was already clearly recognized as an outsider in a still almost monolithically white postwar England and was thereby seemingly ready-made to fit into a category (modernist writer) often associated with difficulty. Contemporaneous racial discourses surrounding West Indians, however, insisted on their essential primitiveness, lack of culture, and childlike status, with the implication that high cultural achievement from the Caribbean was simply not in any way conceivable. These poles of "outsider" and "primitive" are crucial, and they find a close conjunction with the twin dangers of assimilation and exoticism that Peter Hulme identifies as the main pitfalls in reading (what he terms) third-world literature from the metropolis. The parallels between these sets of terms are provocative, and within them Lamming's modernist difficulty can be read as a quintessential migrant strategy—an assertive literary-political gesture aimed at preserving a West Indian (racial, political, cultural) difference while countering an English exoticism that tended to read West

---

well as in important arbiters of literary taste such as the *Times Literary Supplement*, but almost all cultural and literary accounts of the period—such as those by Blake Morrison, Alan Sinfield, and Randall Stevenson—note a pronounced rejection of the stylistic precedents set by modernist writers in both the literature and the literary criticism of the fifties.

6. Of course Lamming's status as "new" (that is, ethnically other) could be construed as an advantage in the publishing competition: Lamming was frequently reviewed together with not only fellow Caribbean authors, but also with African American and African writers such as James Baldwin and Amos Tutuola, and the market for books written by people of African descent—targeted mainly toward the guilty liberal British conscience—was certainly expanding throughout the fifties and sixties.

Indians as simple, unthinking (and unworking) residents of a tropical paradise.[7] The category of (modernist) outsider functions to allay the threat of assimilation, while the invocation of a highly intellectualized cultural tradition (modernism) strategically disrupts, on several levels, the dismissive reduction of West Indian artists to simple, natural creatures of merely anthropological interest.

The reviews of Lamming's early novels consistently place him in a lineage descending from high modernism. The *Times Literary Supplement* review of *In the Castle of My Skin* (1953) muses that "one is tempted to rename this book, 'The Portrait of the Artist as a Young Barbadian.' It recalls James Joyce of the *Portrait* and certain scenes of *Ulysses*, not by virtue of imitation but in a curious similarity of vision." Arthur Calder-Marshall, the author of this review, makes exactly the same comparison in his *Caribbean Voices* review of the novel. The anonymous *TLS* review of *The Emigrants* (1954), "In Search of a Future," makes a similar parallel, noting the novel's resemblances to *Ulysses*.[8] The reviewer for the *Spectator* also notes Lamming's technique, making like comparisons: "Mr. Lamming does not restrict himself to straightforward narrative and description but at moments of extreme tension, moves into dramatic dialogue, into poetic incantation, and into the sort of stream-of-consciousness writing that Joyce has made us familiar with" (Jennings 411). The *Observer*'s Francis Wyndham brings in the example of William Faulkner to elucidate Lamming's prose, while Michael Swan in *London Magazine* places Lamming squarely in an experimental European tradition (epitomized by, perhaps exasperatingly, *Ulysses*), just as critics on *Caribbean Voices* did when describing Lamming's poetry as essentially surrealist. In the end, it seems evident that

---

7. It is important in this light to recall Kingsley Amis's 1958 review of West Indian novels in the *Spectator*, "Fresh Winds from the West," in which Amis clearly associates the broad category of "West Indian prose" with the notion of experimental writing. Amis, of course, roundly dismisses the validity of experimentalism while at the same time emphasizing the "otherness" of this new group of writers in relation to what he takes to be contemporary English literature.

8. The review further notes an "intrusion" of the influence of Sartre, perhaps viewed as reprehensible for both its foreignness and its politicizing tendency. Jean-Paul Sartre was a favorite whipping boy at the time for essentially conservative pro-aesthetic, antipolitical advocates, and indeed this review asserts that both the Joycean (formalist) and Sartrean (political) influences "interrupt" what Lamming has to say.

whether or not they approved (and at the time many did not), Lamming's contemporary British literary commentators identified him as a writer in the old high-modernist tradition, someone whose prose, in the words of another anonymous *TLS* reviewer, is "heavy and dense," "whose style jarred and confused the reader" ("Time and Change" 669).

This aligning of Lamming with Joyce might seem discordant, given postcolonial criticism's traditional characterization of modernism as an important facet of imperialist ideology. In a special issue of *Ariel* devoted to a discussion of the postcolonial-postmodern divide, for example, Stephen Slemon names these avenues of inquiry "the two critical discourses which today constitute themselves specifically in opposition" to modernism, which is conceived of as founded on "the wholesale appropriation of and refiguration of non-Western artistic and cultural practices" (3). During his lifetime, of course, Joyce himself was frequently figured as a provincial outsider assaulting the respectable environs of English literature, and the fervent 1990s "postcolonizing" of Joyce's work (exemplified by works such as Enda Duffy's *The Subaltern Ulysses* and Vincent J. Cheng's *Joyce, Race, and Empire*) suggests a recent revaluation of the previously overlooked potential of his novels to provide a critique of empire and imperial discourse.[9] Indeed, Joyce and Lamming both seem to use their status as English-speaking subjects of empire as a launching point for examining the deception inherent in language and rhetoric, and they employ similar techniques of interruption to make their critique.[10] The two authors' works share a suspicion of naive nationalism as well, as the myopic narrator, the Citizen, of Joyce's "Cyclops" chapter in *Ulysses* finds an equally devalued counterpart in the unthinking black nationalist certainty of Trumper in *In the Castle of My Skin*. The

---

9. Cheng's later article "Of Canons, Colonies, and Critics: The Ethics and Politics of Postcolonial Joyce Studies" provides a useful overview of this newer strain of Joycean criticism, analyzing the advantages as well as the prospective dangers of shifting Joyce studies into the postcolonial arena.

10. Joyce makes the point of the linguistic alienation of the colonized in *Portrait of the Artist as a Young Man* by recording Stephen's thoughts during his conversation with the English Dean of Studies: "The language in which we are speaking is his before it is mine. His language, so familiar and so foreign, will always be for me an acquired speech. I have not made or accepted its words. My voice holds them at bay. My soul frets in the shadow of his language" (189).

postcolonial readings of Joyce, which decisively re-place him into the context of Anglo-Catholic Irishness, represent a counterpoint to reading Lamming into postwar London: both approaches work against institutional tendencies and disciplinary assumptions, and taken in tandem, they move each author closer to the other, suggesting a rarely acknowledged kinship between modernist and postcolonial writing. While there are clear and persuasive reasons for postcolonial critics to be wary of modernism due to its potential institutional, European, metropolitan, and colonial attachments, the linking of Joyce and Lamming in these early reviews reveals that many of the salient features of modernism—such as the strong fifties perception of modernism as a practice opposed to traditional notions of authority and power—have been removed from consideration by contemporary critics in favor of a more reified concept of modernism as always, unchangingly, a parasitic colonial practice.[11]

Accompanying the critics' association of Lamming with Joycean modernism was their recognition of Lamming's efforts to avoid assimilation into the contemporary cadre of British realist writers. The *New Statesman* review of *Of Age and Innocence* (1958), penned by V. S. Naipaul, notes that while Lamming "has devised a story which is fundamentally as well-knit and exciting as one by Graham Greene...he is not a realistic writer" (327). V. S. Pritchett's review of *In the Castle of My Skin* in an earlier issue is even clearer in making the distinction, arguing that Lamming's novel "makes our kind of documentary writing look conventional and silly" (460).[12] While Lamming's style could be comfortably compared to that of older modernist writers, it was not easily allied with that of his British contemporaries. The reviewers also had difficulty assimilating the meaning of Lamming's novels, pointing with particular discomfort and incomprehension to his style. The *Observer* review of *The Emigrants* is typical—"The author switches

---

11. A collection of essays edited by Howard J. Booth and Nigel Rigby, *Modernism and Empire*, seeks to problematize this reflexive dismissal of modernism as inherently imperial. The critical work of Neil Lazarus and Elleke Boehmer also frequently addresses the intersections between postcolonial and modernist literary practice.

12. Pritchett's choice of possessive pronoun reveals much: although encouraging its colonized population to consider themselves British, the home country was in fact quite removed from this ideal of national solidarity. In literary reviews of the time, there is a symptomatic oscillation between differentiating and claiming the writing of the Commonwealth.

from scene to scene and period to period for no obvious reason, is elliptical without excuse, and obscure where everything is plain" (Muir 13)—as is the *London Times* when it excoriates *Of Age and Innocence* for being "badly confused by [Lamming's] method of narration which includes extracts from diaries, flashbacks, and other devices which ... do not provide clear and coherent readings" ("New Fiction"). Such arguments reveal themselves as one side of the consistent pattern of disagreement over literary difficulty observed by Diepeveen—in essence, the prevalent fifties manifestation of the pro-realism pole in a caricature of the Georg Lukács–Bertolt Brecht debates over the political efficacy of modernist art. From a literary historical perspective, the reviews express a growing, if untheorized, awareness that formal experimentation's social efficacy was certainly on the decline, its formative texts firmly entrenching themselves in the establishment canon with newer versions relegated to the category "derivative." Nevertheless, Diepeveen's observation that while difficulty can inspire a number of responses, "the option that the difficult text does not encourage is that of half-consciously rubbing one's eyes over hundreds of pages" (234) speaks to what is clearly one of Lamming's goals as an author: to change the habit of instrumental, unengaged reading into a practice of "reading for exploration and discovery" (*Pleasures* 49).[13] It is precisely the British request for clarity and coherence that Lamming wants to resist, because it is the British narrative, "clear and coherent," that has in Lamming's view naturalized at an almost unconsciously deep level "the habitual weight of a colonial relation" and all its cumbersome consequences (*Pleasures* 25).[14]

A perhaps obvious but still illustrative example of Lamming's antipathy toward mechanistic and familiar ways of processing narrative occurs in his first novel, *In the Castle of My Skin*. The event it hinges on is the landlord Mr. Creighton's party, when Trumper, Boy Blue, and the sometime narrator, G., sneak into the yard and are almost caught after stumbling onto a soldier trying to seduce the

---

13. In such a context, it is also useful to note Diepeveen's assessment that antidifficulty arguments almost always employ a language of normativity in which "difficulty is presented as an abnormal state of affairs" (74), making difficulty an appealing trait if one is seeking distinction of some kind.

14. Edward Said's *Orientalism* is a fundamental and originary postcolonial text in delineating how organized (and thus easily internalized) the effect of colonial discourse can be.

landlord's daughter in the darkness. The chapter dealing with the boys' near disaster is a first-person account, and it is followed immediately by a more traditional, third-person account of Ma and Pa, the characters representing the archetypal peasant tradition of the island. The focal point of this chapter is Ma's discomfort at relating to Pa the story she has heard from Mr. Creighton, which emerges eventually as the landlord's narrative of events the night of the party. It is expressly noted that the "landlord's story was incredible" (187), that it is one Ma "wouldn't have believed were not the source of information beyond suspicion" (184). When the landlord's predictably self-serving narrative does emerge—that the boys had attempted to rape the young woman—both Ma and Pa placidly accept its truth, the rote nature of their imperturbability emphasized by Lamming's presentation of it in dramatic dialogue, with the implication that they are simply acting out their prescribed roles in accepting an account the reader knows to be fabricated. Elsewhere in the novel, Lamming explicitly describes this logic of uncritical absorption, emphasizing its linguistic, literary basis: "The language of the overseer. The language of the civil servant. The myth had eaten through their consciousness like moths through the pages of ageing documents" (27). The image is one of passive decay, the dissolution of the force of language by unthinkingly accepted ideology, and it seems, indeed, that the major task *In the Castle of My Skin* seeks to perform is a reversal of this submission to discourse. The depiction of Ma's and Pa's relationship to narration illustrates how much "the pattern has absorbed them" (32), suggesting that the colonial subjects of the Caribbean suffer from a state in which the "meaning was not clear to them. It was not their concern, and it would never be" (25). Lamming underscores the ominous, disciplinary force of narrative in his treatment of Mr. Creighton's party: the lustful soldier's response to his naive partner's anxiety about getting pregnant is a transparently hollow narrative of patriotic duty—"England expects every man to know his duty" (177)— while the landlord's narrative is a thinly veiled threat that if "the natives" do not behave, the land will be sold to someone much less inclined to humor them. Thus Lamming evidently believes that meaning is of urgent concern, and that simply presenting a "clear and coherent" tale, one whose apparent import is instantly assimilable, is a far from exemplary way of delivering it.[15] In distinguishing himself from the preponderance of realist authors emerging into prominence in 1950s London, Lamming was signaling not only his own difference but also the importance of a different (ostensibly more difficult) discourse.

In contemporary reviewers' resistance to Lamming's complexity, another, more racially directed discourse is detectable, one which expands the utility of literary difficulty to an immigrant artist such as Lamming. Apparently underlying many of the critiques of Lamming as a type of failed modernist is the supposition that he is better suited to writing intuitively and "more naturally." The most explicit statement of this view occurs in the *Times Literary Supplement*'s 1955 review article "Caribbean Voices." After describing how Edgar Mittelholzer's work attempts to remedy what the unnamed reviewer takes for granted as the widespread West Indian inability to think outside of the immediate moment, the article introduces Lamming with a distinctly arch appraisal: "The discontinuity of consciousness which Mr. Mittelholzer attempts to eradicate is accepted by Mr. George Lamming, apparently, as normal to the human condition" (38). The import of such an assessment is not merely to suggest that Lamming, the naive native, has yet to grasp the sophistication of his European brethren—foolishly mistaking his own culture's condition (of ignorance) for a universal one—but also to reduce Lamming's writing process to a largely unconscious representation of his own confusion. The article reiterates this view throughout, asserting, for example, its author's difficulty in establishing whether *In the Castle of My Skin* is about the childhood of one boy or about that of a group of boys: "It is also difficult to see how conscious the author was of what he was doing. The reasons for the shift from the first to the third person cannot be perceived by the intellect. It would be hard to justify by analysis" (39).[16] The

---

15. The counterdiscursive nature of postcolonialism is hardly a revelation, but the more specific focus here is that Lamming, like many modernist authors before him, employs formal elements to underscore the ideological persuasiveness of narrative.

16. Of course, for many critics, Lamming included, this blending of the narration between first and third person, between a singular subject and a more plural, village-oriented one, articulates via formal qualities precisely the hesitation and struggle between individual and community on which the book's content focuses.

emphasis on "intellect" and "analysis" reveals an investment in a long familiar discourse about non-European irrationality, and the review continues in a similar vein, postulating that "Lamming's effects are achieved intuitively" and concluding that "in far too many cases the author becomes self-consciously an 'experimental writer' whose effects are much less original than those he achieved unconsciously when he was not trying" (39). Before going on to castigate Samuel Selvon for the "same muddied intellectualism," the reviewer remarks that Lamming has not quite developed out of his "natural brilliance" into, it is implied, a more controlled, civilized writer.[17] Even as sensitive a critic as V. S. Pritchett, although he clearly if somewhat paradoxically distinguishes Lamming from the West Indian people he portrays, describes the context of *In the Castle of My Skin* in similarly blithe terms: "We are in the heart of a coloured or half-coloured community, sharing its sudden, unreasonable passions . . . its naive illusions about the world outside" (466). One reviewer of *The Pleasures of Exile* complains of Lamming: "He is no theoretician: his spasmodic attempts to mix Haiti, Hakluyt, *The Tempest*, and Portland Place into a critical synthesis on the British West Indian's position only make lumpy literary porridge. He is best when he just talks on about London and the Caribbean" ("Place in the Sun" 13). Another suggests that Lamming has yet to surmount the inherent difficulty that, in the Caribbean, the "laws of cause and effect are held in abeyance" (Calder-Marshall, "Youth").

Such ethnocultural suppositions, expressed as issues of aesthetic critique, provide another rationale for Lamming's insistence on difficulty. Arthur Calder-Marshall notes Lamming's personal suspicion of "just documentary" writing in the Caribbean context (*Caribbean*

---

17. The suggestion of untutored, undeveloped primitivism, though couched within the terms of literary development, is woefully familiar in colonial contexts. Even Lamming's later works get labeled with the same qualities of "immaturity." This discourse of development had familiar manifestations in a political context as well, with claims advanced even in the 1960s that British colonies were not yet ready or mature enough for independence. Said's citation of Karl Marx in his first epigraph to *Orientalism*—"They cannot represent themselves; they must be represented" (xiii)—captures the essence of this imperial logic, which the work of both Said and Lamming always seeks to question.

Voices), and in *The Pleasures of Exile* Lamming himself makes the connection between a sophisticated use of language and a need to fight the degrading assumptions fostered by the discourses of colonialism. Placing the issue into his characteristic Prospero-Caliban trope, Lamming argues that Caliban must order (command) Prospero's attention by ordering (narrating) a new form of history, with the issue of language firmly at the center of the effort: "we shall never explode Prospero's old myth until we christen Language afresh; until we show Language as the product of human endeavor; until we make available to all the result of certain enterprises undertaken by men who are still regarded as the unfortunate descendants of languageless and deformed slaves" (119).[18] In another essay in this collection, Lamming praises German scholars who had been taking an interest in West Indian literature for carefully paying attention to what Caribbean writers have to say: "what really matters here is that they are serious readers and the nature of their interest is a good basis for dialogue" (29). In such a light, Lamming's overtly constructivist approach to literature can be seen as a rejection of any notions of primitive genius or unthinking native intuition, a pointed invitation to consider Caribbean people as intelligent, conscious shapers of language, and hence as thinking beings in their own right.[19]

This perception of non-Europeans as primitive, immature, or otherwise not up to Western standards of ratiocination finds its academic apotheosis in the practice of anthropology. Although Jed Esty is persuasive in arguing that as early as the thirties, with the steadily more evident decline of the British Empire, the English began turning the anthropological lens inward onto their own perceived

---

18. This modernist call to make language new is particularly straightforward and urgent in the case of the Anglophone Caribbean: English was almost unavoidably the mother tongue, and thus the Caribbean subject had no other language in which to take nurturing, anti-English refuge. A similar situation obtains for most immigrant authors. Lamming, as well as many contemporary postcolonial critics, welcomes this circumstance as a liberating limit to the lure of nativism, seeing his linguistic inheritance as a powerful emblem of the inherent sense of exile that lies at the foundation of the modern (or postmodern) condition.

19. This sentiment recalls Lamming's dismissal of Kingsley Amis's criticism as emanating from "the type of mind [that] cannot register the West Indian writer as a subject for intelligent and thoughtful consideration" (*Pleasures* 29). Many contemporaries of Amis might plausibly object that such inconsideration extended well beyond the boundaries of the category "West Indian."

national culture, his emphasis on emergent British nativism should not obscure the fact that the outward gaze at the "others"—usually objectified and judged lacking—retains a major hold on the British cultural imagination in the postwar years.[20] The special autumn edition of the *Times Literary Supplement* of 1962—"A Language in Common," devoted to the writing in English of the non-English, including Scottish and Welsh writers—provides a glimpse of how impermeable these imperial social and cultural categories remained. The review of Caribbean writers, "The Caribbean Mixture," begins with a disquisition on the intransigent resistance of cultures to fusion, attributing it to an inherent, disinterested, universal law that when two cultures (rendered equivalently as "races" in the article) are juxtaposed, one, apparently by happenstance, "usually adopts the habits of a master race and imposes its cultural pattern on the other." The anonymous reviewer, positing this chance capitulation of one culture to another, then asserts that such a relationship may at first induce diffidence on the part of the subject culture but later allows for a sort of minor culture—the example, of course, is West Indian literature—to flourish. The article then connects this minor culture to other objects of anthropological interest: "The emergence of self-assured West Indian writers can thus be related to . . . the continually expanding interest in folk-lore, to the Scottish Renaissance and to that tale of Myles na Gopaleen's where the American recording engineer tapes the grunting of pigs under the impression that it is an authentic Irish story."[21] The far from elevated company in which

20. Indeed, although it is largely a matter of emphasis, it could be argued that such a concentrated reconsolidation of English identity as Esty demonstrates both presupposes and reinforces an even firmer (though perhaps more widely applicable, and hence more diffuse) conception of what is considered "not-English." Both Ian Baucom and Simon Gikandi, as Esty notes, provide compelling witness to the necessary reimaginings of Englishness accompanying the migration of former colonial subjects to metropolitan England.

21. The first item in the series, oddly, is *The Waste Land*, which the author apparently likewise sees as an object of mainly anthropological interest, and like the others, a dire expression of the breakdown of the rules of language, which he attributes to the public's desire for "verbal excitement that springs from the abrogation of grammatical rules and syntactic laws" ("Caribbean Mixture" 578). Michael North's *The Dialect of Modernism* describes precisely this sense of linguistic crisis as an operative and influential locus of modernist creation. The sense in the review is of West Indian writing as degenerate, just like the writings of the modernists.

West Indian literature is grouped—seemingly as an amusing anthropological curiosity—is underscored at the end of the article, whose conclusion unreservedly states that no West Indian writer, "viewed from the highest standards, has yet contributed much to the English language." The final sentences of the review find solace for this artistic failure in the purely anthropological function of West Indian literature: "they have given us insights which would otherwise have been denied us into the kinds of life that are lived in the tropics and—what has not been mentioned before because it is so obvious—many wonderful glimpses of the scenery that can be found there." The pronoun usage clearly delineates the contours of the chosen community, as Caribbean writing, outside the pale in several senses, is reduced to the level of a tourist's narrowly ethnographic glimpse of the exotic.[22]

Thus if from a producer-centered view Lamming's constructivist highlighting of the Caribbean artist aims to counter claims of West Indian simplicity, a more reception-oriented vantage can espy in Lamming's attempts to disrupt narrative a mechanism designed to short-circuit any easy attempt by readers to process the descriptions of Caribbean characters and situations in an objectifying, anthropological way. Lamming's technical experimentation functions as a strategy to resist consumption of his novels as, in the phrase singled out in Jeremy MacClancy's discussion of anthropology in early twentieth-century Britain, "the latest form of evening entertainment" (78). In discussing the importance of his generation of West Indian writers, Lamming notes the shortcomings of previous efforts to depict Caribbean society, explicitly connecting anthropology with what he characterizes as realistic representation that is merely rudimentary: "We have had the social and economic treatises. The anthropologists have done some exercises there. We have had Government White papers as well as the Black diaries of Governor's wives. But these worked like old-fashioned cameras, catching what they can—which wasn't very much—as best they

---

22. C. L. R. James wrote a letter to the editor that appears in the September 28, 1962 *TLS*, asserting that West Indian novels provide far more than simple insights into Caribbean life and placing the article's unnamed author in the tradition of James Froude, a somewhat notorious English apologist for empire and slavery in the Caribbean.

could" (*Pleasures* 38). The old-fashioned, mechanical apparatus of anthropological realism, for Lamming, must make way for a different, more sophisticated rendering by the West Indian novelist. Lamming remarks on the deleterious effects of such distanced observation in *The Emigrants* in a statement by Tornado, one of the more heroic and politicized of the eponymous characters, in response to the suggestion that the British-Caribbean relationship is one of unaffectionate parent to child. Tornado does not quite agree with this metaphor, identifying the problem as a lack of knowledge, empathy, and egalitarian awareness and respect: "Seems to me . . . the people here see these things from their side. They know that England got colonies an' all that, an' they hear 'bout the people in these far away places as though it was all a story in a book" (186). A removed, distracted perception of an urgently felt and lived human existence is what Tornado sees as most criminal in the English. He goes on to suggest that because of this betrayal, West Indians would "be nastier to the English than anyone" if the opportunity should arise. In a personal anecdote, Lamming underscores the casual objectification implicit in the English relationship with colonial subjects: he describes a cordial conversation with a Chelsea pensioner that ends with the older man's parting words: "Oh by the way, there is something I wanted to ask you. Do you *belong* to us or the French?" ("Coldest Spring" 7).[23] Lamming notes the extraordinary naturalness of the man's demeanor while asking his question and expresses amazement at how casually he "had turned the person to whom he was speaking into an object, into one of his possessions" (7).

Lamming depicts the horrifying effects of such a dispassionate, disinterested approach to "others" toward the end of *The Emigrants*. Dickson, thinking he has been chosen by his white landlady for seduction on the basis of education—"the common language of a common civilization," as Dickson expresses it—discovers that both

---

23. Lamming finds a similar lack of engagement or consideration in "the English critic's leisurely objectivity in assessing a colonial literature" (*Pleasures* 30). This formulation conveys Lamming's disdain for such criticism's inability to recognize the actually existing, human context from which the colonial authors it discusses write and also suggests the socioeconomic basis for such critics' privileged presumption of disinterestedness.

she and her sister want only to observe him naked, as a foreign thing: "The women were consumed with curiosity. They devoured his body with their eyes. It disintegrated and dissolved in their stare, gradually regaining its life through the reflection in the mirror" (256). The consequences of this anthropological consuming of his objectified body are disintegration, dissolution—indeed, he goes mad—and a complete demolition of himself as a person; the landlady's mirror—her own racist representations—takes control, providing the only remaining form of his body's existence and giving the lie to Dickson's notions of a civilized commonality. The scene is overtly experimental in form, juxtaposing Dickson's increasingly ragged and disjointed thoughts with a third-person narration, bringing home the stark difference between a (supposedly) objective view, associated with the Englishwomen, and the hopes, fantasies, and eventually insane disappointment of the human being who is caught in it.

In the later novel *Season of Adventure* (1960), Lamming again casts doubt on the capacity of an analytic, anthropological approach to do justice to its subject. This novel—his fourth, and by far his most realistic and least experimental—is famously interrupted near its end by an "Author's Note," a direct intrusion into the third-person narration by the authorial voice. The essential thrust of the section is the ultimate unknowability of Powell, the failure of analytic (and poetic) interpretation to capture his motivations and thoughts. While acknowledging the provisional worth of any such attempts, the author's note suggests that something nearer and more involved is needed to recover Powell's truth, which turns out to be nothing less than an acceptance of responsibility for the character's conduct.[24] Only with such an intimate, deeply felt understanding of Powell's humanity—something anthropology apparently cannot offer—can an appropriate conclusion be reached. Immediately following the author's note is another passage declaring the illegitimacy of a presumed objective view distanced from the popular understanding: such a view "can only prove, select and prove the details of an order

---

24. In the end, of course, the author takes personal responsibility for Powell's murderous actions, with intimations of a Sartrean ethical stance of unconditional responsibility for the other.

which it has assumed; a method of discovery that works in collusion with the very world of things it sets out to discover" (333). The use of "things" underscores the inadequacy of the scientific method for dealing with people, while "collusion" ominously points to its incapacity to accomplish what the author names as his most critical task—to fight "against the Lie as it distorts the image of [his] neighbor in his enemy's eyes" (330). In the end, the author's note implies that in order to recover the truth, readers cannot simply abstract Powell into either an illustration of analytic theory or a mere character in a tale: it forcibly removes readers from any complete investment in the ethnographic realism of the narration and suggests the necessity of a deeper commitment, beyond anthropology, as it were, to an idea of Powell's ineffable humanness. Though the *TLS* reviewer may find Lamming's "use of techniques like changing narrators in mid-narrative, and of tricks with space and time . . . pretentious and ineffectual" ("Caribbean Mixture" 578), these "tricks" preclude any sheer apprehension of his novels as the wondrous reportage of a particularly observant and literate native informant.

Oddly, many of Lamming's more recent critics seem to be as resistant as his earliest reviewers to the difficulties of his technique and its implicit affiliation with modernist practice. The most outspoken of them, A. J. Simoes da Silva, takes Lamming to task for an allegedly pessimistic, overly intellectual attitude. Like the earliest reviewers, who demanded a more natural, intuitively vibrant literature from West Indian authors, Simoes da Silva criticizes Lamming for his "intellectualized" denial of "Caribbean vitality" (7) and considers Lamming's difficulty a symptom of unproductive political hesitancy. Echoing contemporary reviews of Lamming's last novel, Simoes da Silva suggests that *Water with Berries* (1971) is rightfully perceived as "pretentious" (158) and generally contends that the difficulty of interpreting Lamming's texts connotes their ultimate ambivalence, for Simoes da Silva an unfortunate sign of artistic and political failure. Supriya Nair, while not overtly condemning Lamming's difficulty, has deep reservations about its political implications, in that his "work is too 'hard' for students within the institutional sites," let alone for the peasants whose cause he wishes to champion (21). Alternatively, many critics simply elide the difficulty of Lamming's books for political ends, either by focusing almost exclusively on symbolism, narrative, and character, as Sandra Pouchet Paquet's foundational study of Lamming's oeuvre generally does, or by extracting clear-cut nationalist messages from discrete segments of his books, as Neil ten Kortenaar does in his analysis of *In the Castle of My Skin*.[25] The only book truly to take up such issues is Simon Gikandi's *Writing in Limbo: Modernism and Caribbean Literature*. Gikandi's book is predicated on the understanding that "Caribbean writers cannot adopt the history and culture of European modernism ... but neither can they escape from it because it has overdetermined Caribbean cultures in many ways" (3), and his chapters on Lamming give recognition to the contestatory and self-conscious energies that Lamming's difficulty engenders.[26] Although he does not engage historically with the meaning of literary modernism (which, in fact, was neither hegemonic nor even named, let alone theorized as a coherent artistic movement, at the time of the Windrush generation's emergence), Gikandi convincingly delineates the dense, formal counterdiscursive strategies of Lamming's early prose. His readings of Lamming firmly connect the novels' experimentation with anticolonial critique and generally acknowledge Lamming's insistence on a form of modernist irony as an essential basis for any productive, progressive Caribbean nationalism.

Gikandi notes in his conclusion his continuing surprise at the "strong critical resistance to modernism" in Caribbean literary studies (252). He attributes this resistance, in its simplest incarnations, to two factors: a "narrow identification or definition of modernism in terms of European 'high' modernism," and the inability of incessant modernist self-questioning "to fit neatly into a nationalist discourse that was trying to effect a clean break from its antecedents" (252–53). Gikandi's points outline some of the major struggles over

---

25. Ten Kortenaar's basic claim that Trumper's espousal of Black Power is the final word of Lamming's first novel willfully overlooks the narrator's clear discomfort with Trumper's certainty, the later inclusion of Pa's voice, and the narrator's ambiguous departure from the island at the end of the book. Indeed, Lamming himself warns against absolutist readings like this in his introduction to the 1983 edition (xlv).

26. Throughout the book, Gikandi's notion of modernism is sometimes conflated with the quite different, frequently antagonistic concept of modernity, leading him to oscillate between championing modernism's critical, disruptive techniques and bemoaning the crushing burden of economic rationality and race/gender/class divisions it supposedly inaugurated in the Caribbean.

orthodoxy and identity that bedevil almost all "ethnic" literatures, whether migrant, immigrant, exilic, or diasporic in their self-classification: these struggles suggest a potentially debilitating anxiety over cultural purity—a fear of "contamination" by European culture that mirrors in some sense the colonizers' own panic when faced with native and slave populations—and a nervous policing of the borders of political propriety that places tightly defined strictures on what is considered authentic and representative.[27] It is here that a geographically recontextualized examination of Lamming's difficulty can be instructive. Lamming, like nearly all the Windrush writers, is profoundly nationalist in his cultural sentiments, seeing his generation's literary figures as "the first builders of what will become a tradition in West Indian imaginative writing: a tradition which will be taken for granted or for the purpose of critical analysis by West Indians of a later generation" (*Pleasures* 38). In terms of education, language, and culture, however, Lamming is intellectually unable to deny his British heritage, claiming himself, in the familiar *Tempest* trope, not only as a descendant of Caliban but also as "a direct descendant of Prospero worshipping in the same temple of endeavor, using his legacy of language" (*Pleasures* 15). Lamming is far from being a quiet, obedient worshipper, but he acknowledges the shared field of activity and the inheritance of critical, cultural, and linguistic terms by which he is enabled to participate in it. In postcolonial criticism concentrating on the situation in the colonial homeland, such an acknowledgment is not frequently or easily made; placing Lamming's work into its metropolitan context allows more space for emphasizing how his novels foreground the practical impossibility of claims for pure cultural absolutism or an unproblematically static, rooted cultural identity, all while still strongly asserting claims of a personal and aesthetic sovereignty.[28]

---

27. In Lamming's case, this dynamic leads to a sense that the native-coded antimodernism of 1950s England has been transposed into a more contemporary setting with the parties reversed: despite the differing ethnicities and locations of the audiences, Lamming's neomodernism is still often read and condemned as "other" or "foreign."

28. Ato Quayson uses Biodun Jeyifo's categories of postcoloniality—nationalist, authenticity-oriented "normative" postcoloniality and cosmopolitan "interstitial or liminal" postcoloniality—to discuss these varying locational emphases within postcolonial

Thus, taking into account the (necessarily incomplete) view of Lamming's work in terms of its British inheritance can serve to highlight his difficult technique as a tactical negotiation of the politics of literary form. Placed in the underexamined context of contemporaneous British reception, the difficulty of Lamming's novels can be perceived as a strategy to navigate the complex literary and social field of a dominating culture in the process of expressing a contestatory political valence. In such a light, Lamming's fiction exemplifies Homi Bhabha's formulation of "postcolonial literature" as writing that is necessarily constrained by imperial and metropolitan influence yet nevertheless capable of illustrating, to productive effect, "how easily the boundary that secures the cohesive limits of the Western nation may imperceptibly turn into a contentious *internal* liminality providing a place from which to speak both of, and as, the minority, the exilic, the marginal and the emergent" (149).[29] Maintaining a certain distinction from the most popular literary practices of the day, Lamming's novels attempt to protect against an often unwitting exoticism that carries such distinction to adverse extremes, plotting a careful course between Peter Hulme's poles of assimilation and exoticism while advancing nuanced claims of West Indian cultural, intellectual, and political autonomy.

A focus on the local British reception of Lamming's work does entail the risks of both a reduplication of the colonial practices that locate value only in the metropolitan center and a stubborn maintenance of the rigid colonizer-colonized binarism that reads

---

criticism. Quayson notes that the latter, more metropolitan focus allows anticolonial writers to "simultaneously attack concepts and ideas within their local cultures that serve to reproduce colonial frames of reference and practices in the guise of nationalist sentiment" (78–79). Quayson accepts the legitimacy of both categories, stressing that the main difference lies in the location from which the works are *read*.

   29. There are, of course, crucial questions to be asked about how such internal liminality might be subject to co-optation, assimilation, or a politically suspect multicultural tokenism: Lamming himself was suspicious of the inclusion of "other voices" in British literature, noting the acceptance of the "new West Indian novel" in England as "deserving if somewhat dubious" (*Caribbean Voices*). Nevertheless, Bhabha's formulation has the advantage of theorizing a resistant cultural space appropriate for studying immigrant writers which can productively steer clear of straightforward appeals to romantic, nativist narratives of "home."

the actions of colonial subjects *simply* as scripted reactions to colonial paradigms and demands. However, the type of postcolonial critique that remains resolutely rooted solely in the concerns of the homeland is equally incomplete, particularly given the concentrations of economic and cultural power characteristic of metropolitan sites.[30] Indeed, an "immigrant reading" of George Lamming—reading his novels in a much different place than the Caribbean setting traditionally pursued within postcolonial literary studies—effects a sort of institutional defamiliarization which would seem to be precisely the response invited by a writer so concerned with breaking up habitual patterns of thought in order to allow for a newly perceived view of a world long considered familiar.[31] From such an uncustomary critical vantage, the difficulty of George Lamming can be viewed as a traditionally modernist strategy cunningly adapted into a politically salient immigrant technique. Like the interruptive techniques of James Joyce and Virginia Woolf, Lamming's writing style works within the prevailing British cultural boundaries while aiming to prevent readers from uncritically absorbing his books. With such a style, Lamming encourages his readers not to proceed without pausing to consider the notion of their "civilization" in light of the historical, human source of the product in their possession.

Brooklyn College
City University of New York

---

30. Pascale Casanova's *The World Republic of Letters* makes a compelling case for locating the most powerful forces of literary consecration and canonization worldwide in the metropolitan capitals of culture in the North, specifically Paris, London, and New York. This view has the advantage of bringing out the striking parallels among all of those whom she calls "dominated" (in a cultural sense) writers—including those considered immigrant and postcolonial writers—and providing an analysis of the strategies necessary for them to become accepted outside of their own regional or national constituencies.

31. While this positioning as "antagonistic to existing institutions of representation" (107) is what defines the process of decolonization for Lisa Lowe, the drive to "make it new," to disrupt traditional mechanisms of perception and interpretation, is of course a defining characteristic of modernism as well, suggesting important similarities not only between immigrant literature and postcolonial literature, as Lowe demonstrates, but also between those types of literature and what is frequently viewed as their antithesis, high modernism.

WORKS CITED

Amis, Kingsley. "Fresh Winds from the West." *Spectator* 2 May 1958: 565–66.

Bader, Rudolph. "George Lamming." *International Literature in English: Essays on the Major Writers*. Ed. Robert L. Ross. New York: Garland, 1991. 143–52.

Baucom, Ian. *Out of Place: Englishness, Empire, and the Locations of Identity*. Princeton, NJ: Princeton UP, 1999.

Bhabha, Homi K. *The Location of Culture*. New York: Routledge, 1994.

Boehmer, Elleke. *Colonial and Postcolonial Literature: Migrant Metaphors*. Oxford: Oxford UP, 2005.

Booth, Howard J., and Nigel Rigby, eds. *Modernism and Empire*. Manchester: Manchester UP, 2000.

Calder-Marshall, Arthur. Rev. of *In the Castle of My Skin*, by George Lamming. *Caribbean Voices*. BBC World Service. London. 22 Mar. 1953. Transcript from BBC Written Archives Center.

———. "Youth in Barbados." Rev. of *In the Castle of My Skin*, by George Lamming. *Times Literary Supplement* 27 Mar. 1953: 206.

"The Caribbean Mixture, Variations and Fusions in Race and Style." *Times Literary Supplement* 10 Aug. 1962: 578.

"Caribbean Voices." *Times Literary Supplement* 5 Aug. 1955: xvi–xvii.

Casanova, Pascale. *The World Republic of Letters*. Trans. M. B. DeBevoise. Cambridge, MA: Harvard UP, 2004.

Cheng, Vincent J. *Joyce, Race, and Empire*. Cambridge: Cambridge UP, 1995.

———. "Of Canons, Colonies, and Critics: The Ethics and Politics of Postcolonial Joyce Studies." *RE: Joyce: Text, Culture, Politics*. Ed. John Brannigan, Geoff Ward, and Julian Wolfreys. London: Macmillan, 1998.

Diepeveen, Leonard. *The Difficulties of Modernism*. New York: Routledge, 2003.

Duffy, Enda. *The Subaltern Ulysses*. Minneapolis: U of Minnesota P, 1994.

Esty, Jed. *A Shrinking Island: Modernism and National Culture in England*. Princeton, NJ: Princeton UP, 2004.

Eysteinsson, Astradur. *The Concept of Modernism*. Ithaca, NY: Cornell UP, 1990.

Gikandi, Simon. *Writing in Limbo: Modernism and Caribbean Literature*. Ithaca, NY: Cornell UP, 1992.

Hulme, Peter. "The Profit of Language: George Lamming and the Postcolonial Novel." *Recasting the World: Writing after Colonialism*. Ed. Jonathan White. Baltimore, MD: Johns Hopkins UP, 1993. 120–36.

"In Search of a Future." Rev. of *The Emigrants*, by George Lamming. *Times Literary Supplement* 8 Oct. 1954: 637.

James, C. L. R. Letter. *Times Literary Supplement* 28 Sept. 1962: 766.

Jennings, Elizabeth. "The Better Break." Rev. of *The Emigrants*, by George Lamming. *Spectator* 1 Oct.1954: 411–12.

Joyce, James. *A Portrait of the Artist as a Young Man*. 1916. New York: Viking-Penguin, 1977.

Kortenaar, Neil ten. "George Lamming's *In the Castle of My Skin*: Finding Promise in the Land." *ARIEL: A Review of International English Literature* 22.2 (1991): 43–53.

Lamming, George. *Caribbean Voices*. BBC World Service. London. 6 Jul. 1958. Transcript from BBC Written Archives Center.

———. "The Coldest Spring in Fifty Years: Thoughts on Sam Selvon and London." *Kunapipi* 20 (1998): 4–10.

———. *Conversations; George Lamming: Essays, Addresses, and Interviews, 1953–1990*. Ed. Richard Drayton and Andaiye. London: Karia, 1992.

———. *The Emigrants*. 1954. London: Allison & Busby, 1980.

———. *In the Castle of My Skin*. 1953. Ann Arbor: U of Michigan P, 2001.

———. Interview. Conducted by Ian Munro and Reinhard Sander. *Kas-kas; Interviews with Three Caribbean Writers in Texas: George Lamming, C. L. R. James, Wilson Harris*. Austin: African and Afro-American Research Institute, U of Texas at Austin, 1972.

———. *The Pleasures of Exile*. 1960. Ann Arbor: U of Michigan P, 1995.

———. *Season of Adventure*. 1960. London: Allison & Busby, 1979.

———. "The Sovereignty of the Imagination: An Interview with George Lamming." Conducted by David Scott. *Small Axe* 12 (2002): 72–200.

Lazarus, Neil. "Modernism and Modernity: T. W. Adorno and Contemporary White South African Literature." *Cultural Critique* 5 (1986–87): 131–55.

———. "The Politics of Postcolonial Modernism." *Postcolonial Studies and Beyond*. Ed. Ania Loomba et al. Durham, NC: Duke UP, 2005. 423–28.

Lowe, Lisa. *Immigrant Acts: On Asian American Cultural Politics*. Durham, NC: Duke UP, 1996.

MacClancy, Jeremy. "The Latest Form of Evening Entertainment." *A Concise Companion to Modernism*. Ed. David Bradshaw. Oxford: Blackwell, 2003. 75–94.

Morrison, Blake. *The Movement: English Poetry and Fiction of the 1950s*. Oxford: Oxford UP, 1980.

Muir, Edwin. "Indirections." Rev. of *The Emigrants*, by George Lamming. *London Observer* 19 Sept. 1954: 13.

Naipaul, V. S. "New Novels." Rev. of *Of Age and Innocence*, by George Lamming. *New Statesman* 6 Dec. 1958: 826–27.

Nair, Supriya. *Caliban's Curse: George Lamming and the Revisioning of History*. Ann Arbor: U of Michigan P, 1996.

"New Fiction." Rev. of *Of Age and Innocence*, by George Lamming. *London Times* 13 Nov. 1958: 15.

North, Michael. *The Dialect of Modernism: Race, Language, and Twentieth-Century Literature*. New York: Oxford UP, 1994.

Paquet, Sandra Pouchet. *The Novels of George Lamming*. London: Heinemann, 1982.

Perelman, Bob. *The Trouble with Genius: Reading Pound, Joyce, Stein, and Zukofsky*. Berkeley: U of California P, 1994.

Phillips, Mike, and Trevor Phillips. *Windrush: The Irresistible Rise of Multi-Racial Britain*. London: HarperCollins, 1998.

"A Place in the Sun." Rev. of *The Pleasures of Exile*, by George Lamming. *London Times* 28 Jul. 1960: 13.

Pritchett, V. S. "A Barbados Village." Rev. of *In the Castle of My Skin*, by George Lamming. *New Statesman* 18 Apr. 1953: 460.

Quayson, Ato. *Postcolonialism: Theory, Practice, or Process?* Cambridge: Polity, 2000.

Rabinovitz, Rubin. *The Reaction against Experiment in the English Novel, 1950–1960*. New York: Columbia UP, 1967.

Ramchand, Kenneth. *The West Indian Novel and Its Background*. London: Heinemann, 1983.

Said, Edward. *Orientalism*. 1978. New York: Vintage, 1994.

Simoes da Silva, A. J. *The Luxury of Nationalist Despair: George Lamming's Fiction as Decolonizing Project*. Amsterdam: Rodopi, 2000.

Sinfield, Alan. *Literature, Politics, and Culture in Postwar Britain*. Berkeley: U of California P, 1989.

Slemon, Stephen. "Modernism's Last Post." *ARIEL: A Review of International English Literature* 20.4 (1989): 3–17.

Steiner, George. "On Difficulty." *On Difficulty and Other Essays*. Oxford: Oxford UP, 1978. 18–47.

Stevenson, Randall. *The British Novel since the Thirties: An Introduction*. Athens: U of Georgia P, 1986.

Swan, Michael. Rev. of *In the Castle of My Skin*, by George Lamming. *London Magazine* 1.6 (1954): 92–98.

Swanzy, Henry. *Caribbean Voices*. BBC World Service. London. 4 Jan. 1948. Transcript from BBC Written Archives Center.

"Time and Change." Rev. of *Of Age and Innocence*, by George Lamming. *Times Literary Supplement* 21 Nov. 1958: 669.

Wyndham, Francis. "Out of the Ordinary: New Fiction." Rev. of *Season of Adventure*, by George Lamming. *London Observer* 23 Oct. 1960: 22.

ALISTAIR CORMACK

Migration and the Politics of Narrative Form: Realism and the Postcolonial Subject in *Brick Lane*

M onica Ali's 2003 novel of Bangladeshi immigrants in London, *Brick Lane*, has been a huge success on both sides of the Atlantic. Because it is a realist narrative with a postcolonial story, it offers an excellent opportunity to examine the relationship between the formal strategies of mimetic fiction and the historical contexts of multiculturalism and immigration.[1] In the chapter "Multicultural Personae" in *The Cambridge Introduction to Modern British Fiction, 1950-2000*, Dominic Head has investigated "the hybridized cultural forms that might be produced in an evolving, and so *genuinely*, multicultural Britain" (156). The novels he looks at have much in common in terms of subject

I would like to acknowledge the help of Sebastian Groes—with whom I have had many conversations about London, postcolonialism, and realism—in developing this essay.

    1. The term "realism" is one that cannot be used naively; it bears the burden of centuries of critical debate. What I mean should become clear as the essay progresses. For now it is enough to say that I follow Georg Lukács's formal explanation of the term. As Lukács argues in "The Ideology of Modernism," realist fiction involves selective criteria—a winnowing down of the "bad infinity" of "abstract potentiality"—and thus a linear and developmental account of history (23–24). The stable, coherent, and knowable world of the realist text is generated by carefully controlling narrative focus and deliberately employing traditional novelistic discourse. In this account, realism does not mean the slavishly accurate portrayal of a given historical moment. Following Victor Sage's commentary on Aristotle, I use "realism" to mean a poetics of mimesis, not a mimetic fallacy (27). In "Against Georg Lukács," Bertolt Brecht rightly accuses Lukács of "formalism": realism is not one form (the nineteenth-century novel) but whatever mode most suits the historical reality of the time (70). Nonetheless, Lukács's interpretation, I believe, helps us to understand Ali's novel.

Contemporary Literature XLVII, 4   0010-7484; E-ISSN 1548-9949/06/0004-0695
© 2006 by the Board of Regents of the University of Wisconsin System

matter with *Brick Lane*; it is thus interesting that he addresses the question of the troubled relationship of postcolonialism and realism in a subsection titled "Ethnic Identity and Literary Form." He argues:

> [A] productive cultural hybridity is commonly (and erroneously) perceived to go hand-in-glove with overtly experimental forms. In such a view, you either have a startlingly innovative style *and* rapturous presentation of multicultural energies, or you have neither. Rushdie's exuberant magic realism is thus sometimes seen to exemplify the kind of formal reinvigoration of the novel in Britain that the postcolonial era makes possible. . . . However, such an easy equation between experiment and cultural hybridity can imply a simple opposition between experiment and tradition that is inappropriate, with traditional realism coming to embody a reactionary conservatism.
>
> (172)

Head's point is that many novels that can be described as traditional— that is, characterized by linear narratives (often focused on individual growth), the cultivation of linguistic transparency, and an invitation to the reader to "identify" with the characters—have examined the experience of multicultural Britain in an innovative fashion. Thus, he feels, it is wrong-headed to assume that realism can be equated with a broad cultural conservatism. Head's argument, however, is essentially content-led: for him, the radical nature of postcolonial subject matter is transmitted to the reader irrespective of the formal strategies employed by the writer. While I agree that there is no necessary connection between cultural hybridity and experimental form, I shall argue here that cultural hybridity has a formal as well as a thematic register; to depict Britain's new hybrid society through realism is not the same as to depict it through other representational modes. In the case of *Brick Lane*, the exchange between form and content seems to work in two directions. On one hand, realism ceases to be traditional, because it is called upon to depict this new social juncture; the form's limits become visible, as do the presumptions by which it works. On the other, and perhaps more importantly, what I will term the "doubleness" of hybrid cultural and psychological structures is flattened when it is represented in a form that stresses linear development toward self-awareness. This is particularly played out in the realm of translation, both in its literal sense (the way English is used to render Bengali) and as metaphor (the question of whether an identity forged in one culture can become knowable and exert its agency in another). This second sense leads to the interesting way in which the novel's narrative voice is unable fully to map the consciousness of the central character, Nazneen. It is at this point that some of the political effects of using realism as a form in a postcolonial context emerge. Realism may not be synonymous with cultural conservatism, but it does seem to bar a more radical conception of subjectivity—a conception that is crucial for postcolonial critiques of epistemology.

To understand entirely Head's argument, and indeed what he leaves out, we need briefly to sketch a critical genealogy. Head's understanding of the novel form stems in part from the project begun by Andrzej Gąsiorek in *Post-War British Fiction: Realism and After* (1995) to refine the definition of realism in the wake of the attack mounted on it by British poststructuralism as embodied in Colin MacCabe's *James Joyce and the Revolution of the Word* (1979) and Catherine Belsey's *Critical Practice* (1980). Head transposes this debate to the one regarding postcolonial literatures, attacking an imagined—and by no means unimaginable—scholar who celebrates magical realism at classical realism's expense. Interestingly, he does not *reject* utopian readings of magical realism; he merely suggests that such utopian readings can be made of texts in any mode. For many, however, it is precisely the novel form that is at stake. Philip Engblom, summarizing Fawzia Afzal-Khan and Mark Edmundson, suggests that Salman Rushdie's *Midnight's Children* represents a "new postmodernism" (Edmundson 65; qtd. in Engblom 295). This form, Engblom argues, opens space "for the undiluted speech of a multitude of voices. Room is created for dialogue, shrill as it sometimes becomes, between innumerable, irreducible claims, visions, and ideologies with no ultimate authority held in reserve by any of them that guarantee the outcome" (295). This sort of hybridity becomes a postcolonial attack on the "strategies of containment" inherent to the realist novel (Afzal-Khan 137; qtd. in Engblom 295). Such a reading, as we shall see, is legitimated by Rushdie's own comments about the novel in general and his own output in particular.

This celebration of Rushdie's formal innovation leads us to another problem. Engblom's characteristic application of Mikhail Bakhtin to postcolonial literature is open to the critique of applying

Western postmodernism to postcolonial forms; by making Rushdie an example of a general "dialogism" in literature, the specific *Indian* contexts of his work are somewhat erased. The danger here is that the particular history of postcolonial states and subjects becomes subsumed beneath a set of concerns that arise within Western capitalism but are thought to be universal. Head clearly has postmodernist modes of writing and reading in mind when discussing "ethnic identity and literary form."[2] However, he does not address the key debate about the relation between the international discourse of postmodernism and the specific, regional, and thus more politicized realm of postcolonialism.

As Kumkum Sangari's essay "The Politics of the Possible" makes obvious, the choice of nonmimetic modes—those novelistic forms that refuse verisimilitude, linear progress, and a coherent textual surface—by the postcolonial author is of profound importance, as are the ways in which these modes are read.[3] Analyzing the "nonmimetic modes, emerging from countries that have been subject to colonial regimes" (1), she compares Gabriel García Márquez to Rushdie, finding the latter a touch less felicitous, but arguing that the work of neither should be too hastily assumed to have been produced by the postmodern condition. García Márquez's work "has the capacity both to register and to engage critically with the present and to generate a new way of seeing" (5). In particular, she commends the way "marvellous realism" has its source in collectivity and the social construction of meanings (5). Neither narrative voices nor the narrators themselves are "individuated in the bourgeois sense of being authored/authorized by a singular subjectivity or a single perspective" (9). In her essay, *Midnight's Children* appears as an interesting conflation of indigenous epic forms and modernism. Western forms

2. "Postmodernism" means, as KumKum Sangari puts it, "the specific preoccupations and 'sensibility' of both contemporary fiction and of poststructuralist critical discourse" (1). The reading of Bakhtin that leads to the favorable accounts of Rushdie referred to above is part of this "sensibility." The reading can be traced to Julia Kristeva's influential essay "Word, Dialogue, Novel." It was out of this encounter with Bakhtin that Kristeva developed the canonically postmodern concept of "intertextuality."

3. See also in this context Aijaz Ahmad's *In Theory: Classes, Nations, Literatures*. Ahmad argues against the tendency in postcolonial criticism to adopt poststructuralism as an account of non-Western subjectivity. He is particularly suspicious of Homi K. Bhabha's and Salman Rushdie's enthusiasm for metropolitan spaces and, indeed, metropolitan audiences.

are employed by Rushdie, and this causes problems in the Indian context: while the epic and the folktale do not "always constitute the real and the not-real as binary opposit[es]," for modernism, "realism is the implied or habitual mode of perception that has to be countered or subverted" (20). Thus the "totalizing and meandering potential of [Rushdie's] chosen form cohabits uneasily with a modernist epistemology of the fragment, the specific perspectivism of a bourgeois subject" (23). Finally, this means that Rushdie renders himself available to a reading that assimilates him entirely to "the postmodern marketplace" (23). The indigenous context of *Midnight's Children* can be glossed over more easily than is the case with García Márquez because Rushdie's aesthetic project relies in part on reified and individuated procedures of narration. Perhaps the Bakhtinian readings referred to above, which seem utopian in one view, can seem like a rather glib relativism in another; the loss of an ability to distinguish between the truth-claims of different discourses can be understood more as a capitulation to the logic of the market than a liberation from authority. Sangari's nonmimetic modes are the result of and the response to the specific hybridized history of colonial spaces. Such hybridization is always susceptible to reclassification as a symptom of the dissolution of the bourgeois subject and the crises of representation and knowledge in the postmodern era. In particular, Sangari views the dual nature of Rushdie's narrative as precarious:

> [N]either parodic rejection nor large-hearted assimilation is a sufficient confrontation of the formation of the Indian middle-class subjects; the axes of their hybridization, both through a history of precolonial syncretism and through colonial transactions, are not identical with the paradigmatic "literary" formation of either a coherent bourgeois self grounded in realist ontology, or a self-fracturing "high" bourgeois suffused with alienation. In sum, degrees and forms of embourgeoisement are at issue.
>
> (22)

I find this passage instructive and will develop some guiding principles from it in what follows. One is that form encodes important ideas about the construction of subjectivity. Another is that a key question to be addressed is the extent to which the formal properties of a text relate to "forms of embourgoisement." That is to say, how do realism or experimentalism, in Head's terms, relate to coherent or fractured bourgeois identities, and to what extent do they relate to the sort of non-Western cultural resources characterized by Sangari as "precolonial syncretism"? Finally, it is important to notice that while Sangari resists the simple mapping of Western forms on non-Western texts, she remains sensitive to the moments when such mapping is appropriate. Rushdie *is* in part a Western modernist. This recognition will be important in trying to trace the meaning of Ali's realism.

Head's insistence on "an ethical criticism, sensitive to its object as other" and attendant rejection of what he calls the "realist/experimental dichotomy" (259) is an attack on the formalism of the postmodernist aesthetic. There is a danger that in this conception of the debate, form becomes a mere appurtenance, an obstacle the reader/ critic must overcome to engage with the central ethical content. In order to investigate the implications of Head's position, I would like to offer two interpretations of *Brick Lane*. The first will attend to its ethics in terms of the construction of identity. I will look here at how the plot investigates ideas about migrancy, using some ideas from Homi K. Bhabha. I then want to investigate whether our perceptions are altered if we take as our starting place the meanings of the novel form. I want to see if reading *through* the form—in this case a version of classical realism, rather than Rushdie's nonmimetic magical realism—offers an alternative perspective on the questions of identity that I'll focus on in the first interpretation.

Brick Lane and the Ethics of Migrant Identity

Brick Lane, in a variety of ways, stages debates about the nature of immigrant subjectivity. The novel is particularly of interest as an examination of the double bind that female migrants face, treated as alien by their host nation and as commodities by the men in their own communities. The paradoxes of migration are dramatized in the various characters, but especially through the central character Nazneen's relationships with her husband Chanu and her lover Karim. The novel begins with the story of "How You Were Left to Your Fate"—the tale of Nazneen's birth in Bangladesh in 1967. Despite her child's illness, Nazneen's mother decides against taking the baby to a hospital in a city, arguing: "[W]e must not stand in the way of Fate. Whatever happens, I accept it. And my child must not waste any energy fighting against Fate. That way, she will be stronger" (9). It is important to note that this event is already at one remove from the diegetic space of the novel; indeed, it is not an event as such but is already a narration:

> As Nazneen grew she heard many times this story.... It was because of her mother's wise decision that Nazneen lived to become the wide-faced, watchful girl that she was. Fighting against one's Fate can weaken the blood. Sometimes, or perhaps most times, it can be fatal. Not once did Nazneen question the logic of the story.... What could not be changed must be borne. And since nothing could be changed, everything had to be borne. This principle ruled her life.
>
> (10–11)

The construction of Nazneen's identity is analogous to the double narrative of pedagogy and performance that Homi K. Bhabha argues is at the heart of the construction of the "people" of a nation. The first element of the narrative is external and official: "the people are the historical 'objects' of a nationalist pedagogy, giving the discourse an authority that is based on the pre-given or constituted historical origin or event" (297). As in the case of a nation, Nazneen's origin is situated in a distant past. A factor that further comments on Bhabha's ideas is that this moment is characterized by pure fatalism, the story being renarrated until it becomes the fundamental "principle" that rules Nazneen's life. She is the object of this discourse, central yet entirely exterior to its enunciation. The nature of her passage to England is also reflected in this story: she is the object of a transaction between men—her father and her husband—and does not allow herself even to wish for a different life (13).

Bhabha identifies how national and personal identity point in another direction as well: "[T]he people are also the 'subjects' of a process of signification that must erase any prior or originary presence of the nation-people.... The scraps, patches and rags of daily life must be repeatedly turned into signs of a national culture" (297). Nazneen's behavior is policed by the pedagogic narration of her origin. Yet displaced from the village life whence it sprung and landed in urban London, the story that locates her source in fatalism becomes less able to maintain its organicism and project a coherent identity for her. In a bold moment of prolepsis, the passage quoted above from the opening pages of *Brick Lane* ends by reviewing the whole story, so we are forced to encounter with Nazneen the performance of her identity in the contradictory world of lived experience:

> So that when, at the age of thirty-four, after she had been given three children and had one taken away, when she had a futile husband and had been fated a young and demanding lover, when for the first time she could not wait for the future to be revealed but had to make it for herself, she was as startled by her own agency as an infant who waves a clenched fist and strikes itself upon the eye.
>
> (11)

Even this early in the novel, only moments after her foundation has been described, we see that the scraps of her life cannot be shaped by the neat linearities of the pedagogic. Instead, a new and shocking story must be allowed to come into being. Her status and circumstances force Nazneen to construct her identity through the dialogue between the narration of her origin and the reality of the history through which she lives.

The tension between the pedagogic and the performative underlies the problems and anxieties of Nazneen's husband Chanu, another first-generation immigrant. He constructs a mythic Bangladesh to compensate for his failure to succeed in English culture. It is his opinion that the Bengali poet Rabindranath Tagore is "the true father of [the] nation" (147), and he demands that his deracinated daughters learn to recite Tagore's poem "Golden Bengal," in order to understand fully their roots. Twin to this notion of a pedagogic national culture is his obsessive rehearsal of Bangladesh's past:

> In the sixteenth century, Bengal was called the Paradise of Nations. These are our roots. Do they teach these things in the school here? Does Shahana know about the Paradise of Nations? All she knows about is flood and famine. Whole bloody country is just a bloody basket case to her.
>
> (151)

He consistently expresses a desire to return, not prepared to admit the discrepancy between his fantasies, built on an institutionalized version of Bangladeshi identity, and what the Western reader takes to be the realities of contemporary Bangladesh revealed in the letters from Nazneen's sister Hasina.

The dilemma of identifying with an unreal home and living in a new society perceived as alien is staged in the confrontation between Chanu and Mrs. Azad, the Anglicized wife of Chanu's "friend" Dr. Azad. Chanu outlines his version of the "immigrant tragedy":

> I'm talking about the clash between Western values and our own. I'm talking about the struggle to assimilate and the need to preserve one's identity and heritage. I'm talking about children who don't know what their identity is. I'm talking about the feelings of alienation engendered by a society where racism is prevalent. I'm talking about the terrific struggle to preserve one's sanity while striving to achieve the best for one's family.
>
> (92)

Chanu is almost always depicted as quixotic; here, however, he is allowed to articulate his attitude with considerable coherence. Nevertheless, the speech is at heart unconvincing, because the reader knows that his "identity" is far more compromised than the passage would imply. Earlier in the scene he has ventured, "It's not only immigrants. Shakespeare wrote about it" (92). Rather than personifying the clash of cultures and a dignified attempt to maintain an authentic connection to his home, Chanu is an embattled figure who desperately lurches between an outmoded aspirational Englishness embodied in a Leavisite account of literary culture and a version of himself as an "educated man" who has stooped to the condition of moneymaker in order to return to an unsullied home. He repeatedly refuses to confront the realities of his situation in favor of a fantasy built on pedagogic notions of both Bangladesh and England. The reader feels that the argument is a more accurate depiction of Nazneen's struggles than Chanu's.

Mrs. Azad rejects his arguments as "crap," insisting on the "fact" of their consciously willed presence in England (92–93). Her daughter's assimilation to "Western values" is inevitable and, indeed, to be welcomed. She contrasts the proscribed life she is forced to lead when in Bangladesh—and, pointedly regarding Nazneen, those led by women who "spend ten, twenty years here and they sit in the kitchen grinding spices all day and learn only two or three words of English"—with her own in London, where she feels free to choose between Western and Bangladeshi culture (93). As with Chanu, the text somewhat subverts Mrs. Azad, in this case by making her physically repulsive. The narrator lingers over her "opulent backside" and "large brown thighs" and implies disgust that she adjusts "her underwear with a thumb" (88) and belches "with quiet satisfaction" after consuming beer (89). The narration is closely focalized through Nazneen—a point to which I shall return—so we in part read her disapproval, but here the reader seems pushed toward an understanding of "assimilation" as a loss of physical decorum.

In terms of the morality of the novel, Chanu and Mrs. Azad stand accused of orienting themselves by cultures perceived as static and monolithic. They maintain what Bhabha would describe as a notion of cultural "diversity" (312–13)—that is, a metaphysical belief in conflicting and competing cultural essences to which one may remain loyal or, alternatively, to which one may assimilate. Bhabha opposes this concept to one of cultural "difference" in which the signs of affiliation are constructed differentially, with no underlying truth that can put an end to their infinite semiosis.

Perhaps the most interesting place in which the dialogue between the pedagogic and performative is enacted is in the relationship between the lovers Nazneen and Karim. One of the first things we learn about Karim is that he stammers in Bengali but expresses himself confidently in English (173–74). Nazneen is transfixed by the confident way he orients himself in the world: "And he was sure of himself. He took a strong stance. Sometimes his right leg worked to a random beat. He wore white trainers [sneakers] and a thin gold chain around his neck" (173). His certainty, dress, and language are signs that he belongs in the Western world—a characteristic to which Nazneen feels strongly attracted. After they have become lovers, we discover her thinking "of what he had that she and Hasina and Chanu sought but could not find. The thing that he had inhabited so easily. A place in the world" (218). The reader begins to understand that Karim is the first person Nazneen has met who seems to "fit in" with his location. Even his extreme religious orthodoxy is denuded of its originary meanings and rendered a performative hybrid. He receives "Salaat alerts" on his mobile phone, and when he begins to pray, Nazneen finds the experience erotic. She cannot stop herself from the forbidden act of praying with him; she hears "blood pound in her heart" and enjoys, when he bows, "how well he moved." The narrator finally comments, "It was he who moved, but she who felt dizzy" (193). His masculinity is allied in her mind to his hybrid identity: his comfort, confidence, and sexuality are, at first, a seamless whole. He also represents an alternative, perhaps more Western way for the genders to interact. While Chanu never listens to her, Karim often "made her feel as if she had said a weighty piece, as if she had stated a new truth" (216). He offers a means for her to gain entry to the space in which she lives and a glimpse of the world outside the pedagogic construction of cultural and individual identity.

For his part, Karim's attraction to Nazneen is generated by the inverse sentiments. He explains:

> There's your westernized girl, wears what she likes, all the make-up going on, short skirts and that soon as she's out of her father's sight. She's into going out, getting good jobs, having a laugh. Then there's your religious girl, wears the scarf or even the burkha. You'd think, right, they'd be good wife material. But they ain't. Because all they want to do is *argue*. And they always think they know best because they've been off to all these summer camps for Muslim sisters.
>
> (319–20)

When Nazneen asks, "What about me?" Karim replies: "Ah, you. *You* are the real thing" (320). The authenticity that he perceives in Nazneen's identity is bound by culture *and* gender. Unlike the Westernized girls who presumably pose a threat to his sense of ownership, Nazneen does not display her sexuality to anyone but him. Nor does she question his rather confused understanding of religion and politics but instead listens to and registers his monologues. Indeed, when we look back to the points at which Nazneen feels Karim pay attention to her, we notice that she is merely adding phatic markers to the conversation: it is his own voice that he listens to and approves of. She also represents an untroubling Bangladeshi identity. After she has heard this speech from Karim, Nazneen recalls Chanu's words: "*An unspoilt girl. From the village. All things considered I am satisfied*" (320). For Karim—a young man just as much at sea in the complexities of culture and belonging as his lover—Nazneen represents the imaginary stability of homeland and a receptive femininity to bolster his sense of self. She is linked to his attempts to find an authentic identity through politics. His rather ineffectual faction, the "Bengal Tigers," represents a conflation of nationalist and fundamentalist certainties. The full implications of his view of Nazneen can be seen in their early encounters. When they meet, he comments, "That sari.... My mother had one" (175). When he invites her to a meeting of the Bengal Tigers, it is because "we don't have any older women" (193). The death of Karim's mother is linked in his mind to his separation from an authentic Muslim community. Nazneen represents a maternal preoedipal space in which Karim is not threatened by the realities of multiplicity and difference with which life in London confronts him.

The novel develops through three main plotlines: the affair with Karim, the potential return to Bangladesh planned by Chanu, and the extraction of the debt incurred by Chanu to buy a computer— and perhaps more importantly a sewing machine—by the villainous Mrs. Islam. The denouement of all three stories involves Nazneen straightening out problems through her own agency, in part liberated by her sister's revelation that their saintlike and fatalist mother committed suicide to escape her marriage. Nazneen's confrontation with Karim is perhaps the most important. Chanu is to be dispatched to Dhaka on his own, Mrs. Islam has been faced down, and now the plot seems to point toward a marriage between the lovers. However, the narrator notes that Nazneen has managed to see Karim's love for what it is: "A Bengali wife. A Bengali mother. An idea of home. An idea of himself that he found in her" (380). Furthermore, she is forced to understand that *he* is not what *she* thought. It turns out that he does stutter in both languages after all; her English was simply not good enough to recognize the fact. Karim has been a catalyst, forcing her into an existentialist realization of her bad faith, but he offers her no space for her own identity. To fall in with him would be to reject one form of pedagogy and to accept another. Instead, Nazneen embraces a performance of her identity without the stable compass points that her national and religious backgrounds have created, and without merely assimilating in the mold of Mrs. Azad. She ends the novel within a self-authoring female community, about to go skating with her daughters and her honest friend Razia. Nazneen has confronted her oppression within the discourses of gender, race, and religion and won for herself an independent space.

Brick Lane and Translation

What I have offered above would appear to be the preferred reading, in that it follows the novel's trajectory toward a sense of liberation. It is interesting that it is so similar to many readings offered of *The Satanic Verses*, at least in its depiction of the nature of migrancy. Ian Baucom, for instance, writes, "if [Rushdie] generally renders migrancy visible as the delirium of the multiple, he also represents it as the refusal of multiplicity, as the desire for unity, the longing to inhabit a known and bounded space and to be possessed by a sole and unitary narrative" (201). Indeed, with second-generation daughters referring to their parents' home as "Bungleditch" (*Satanic Verses* 259), with an East End riot bringing the novel to a close, and for numerous other reasons, *The Satanic Verses* and *Brick Lane* could be said to be closely related. I would argue, however, that the books are enormously different. Bearing Dominic Head's argument in mind, this is more surprising and important than it might seem.

The idea of translation has become a key way of conceptualizing hybridity in postcolonial discourse, and through it I can suggest certain problems with the reading of *Brick Lane* offered above. As Baucom argues, referring to the speech of the radical Dr. Uhuru Simba, translation is central to the idea of redemption and renewal in *The Satanic Verses* (215). It is through "fusions, translations, conjoinings," the novel posits, that "newness comes into the world" (*Satanic Verses* 8). Gibreel Farishta envisages a "tropicalization" of London that translates it. It is in this way that change can occur—as Baucom puts it, "not as an utter beginning or the manifestation of some pure element never seen before, but as a novel conjoining of what already exists, as transfusion, as the hybridization of the here and the elsewhere" (212). As was the case with *Midnight's Children*, this idea points at once to a specific colonial history and a more generalized postmodern version of subjectivity. Gibreel Farishta is "cracking up" as a result of postmodern dispersal (he is lost in the global village), but what he becomes is the precolonial multitude. The idea of "content" in this account is utterly transformed by the "form" of translation; London becomes new and other. It seems likely that it is precisely these ideas that prompted Bhabha's adaptation in "DissemiNation" of Walter Benjamin's meditation on the role of the translator. Bhabha argues:

> The "foreignness" of language is the nucleus of the untranslatable that goes beyond the transparency of subject matter. *The transfer of meaning can never be total between differential systems of meaning.* ... Benjamin's argument can be elaborated for a theory of cultural difference. It is only by engaging with what he calls the "purer linguistic air" ... that the reality-effect of content can be overpowered which then makes all cultural languages "foreign" to themselves. And it is from this foreign perspective that it becomes possible to inscribe the specific locality of cultural systems— their incommensurable differences—and through that apprehension of difference, to perform the act of cultural translation. In the act of translation the "given" content becomes alien and estranged; and that, in its turn, leaves the language of translation *Aufgabe*, always confronted by its double, the untranslatable—alien and foreign.
>
> (Bhabha 314–15; emphasis added)

One thing that this passage makes clear is that to use Bhabha to read content, as I attempted to do earlier, is highly problematic. Hybridity is a notion that, like translation, challenges the "reality-effect of content," whether understood as ethics or as a narrative of identity. Content cannot be borne across intact. The signifying systems that one culture uses to understand itself cannot be rendered transparently in a new language; material that cannot be assimilated is jettisoned, material that represents the productive new world of the hybrid. Bhabha suggests that the notion of translation threatens what we might call, referring back to Afzal-Khan, the "strategies of containment" of the realist form. If it does not attempt to camouflage its tendencies, translation blows open what Bakhtin calls the "centralizing and unifying influence of the artistic and ideological norm" (144) by showing the incommensurability of different systems of meaning.

Brick Lane could be said to be a novel that *centers* on the notion of translation—the bearing across of words, identities, and cultures— but I would argue that it works here in a very different way from the one envisaged by Bhabha. A key moment at which we see this occur is when Nazneen watches ice skating on television:

> Chanu liked to keep [the television] glowing in the evenings, like a fire in the corner of the room. ... A man in a very tight suit (so tight it made his

private parts stand out on display) and a woman in a skirt that did not even cover her bottom gripped each other as an invisible force hurtled them across an oval arena. The people in the audience clapped their hands together and then stopped. By some magic they all stopped at exactly the same time. The couple broke apart. They fled from each other and no sooner had they fled than they sought each other out. Every move they made was urgent, intense, a declaration.... [The woman] stopped dead and flung her arms above her head with a look so triumphant that you knew she had conquered everything: her body, the laws of nature, and the heart of the tight-suited man who slid over on his knees, vowing to lay down his life for her.

(27–28)

The passage describes Nazneen's failure to translate the culture she sees, although the narrating voice is able to bridge the gaps she cannot. James Wood depicts this passage as an example of "estrangement" (30). One must be careful, however, about what it is we see with new eyes. It seems to me that it is less the ice skating and more Nazneen's naive subject position that we are forced to confront. The passage works by means of the close focalization of the narrative voice through her, while it simultaneously maintains a distance and objectivity; the Western world is seen through the eyes of someone whose frame of reference is radically different, but this event is rendered by a voice that is not so unsophisticated. The television is already like a fireplace, pointing out the divergence of this world from Nazneen's home, and what is pictured on it seems absurdly alien to her, but perhaps not to the reader. The clothes are revealing, and the skaters' movements and the responses of the crowd appear magical. The female figure represents everything that Nazneen is not: she dominates nature, the opposite sex, and her own body. These sensations are not experienced directly by the reader. Were we, indeed, to experience Nazneen's stream of consciousness without the mediation of the narrator, we surely would be faced with something genuinely strange and quasi-modernist—a representation utterly without context. Instead, the experience has already been recuperated into a comprehensible realist frame by the narrative voice.[4]

4. To anyone brought up in Britain in the eighties, it is clear that Nazneen is watching Jayne Torvill and Christopher Dean's gold-medal-winning ice dance based on Maurice Ravel's *Bolero*. Thus for a large portion of Ali's readership, the scene is not simply comprehensible but *familiar*, because it has already been widely disseminated.

What we are presented with is clarified by what follows. Nazneen asks, "What is this called?" and Chanu answers, "Ice skating." Nazneen is unable to repeat the word. One of those peculiar readerly moments occurs when one has to stop and try to work out what is going on. Apart from the words "ice skating," the remainder of the conversation, were it to be rendered "mimetically," would be in Bengali—the text flits from one language to the other with no marker. We have been reading Nazneen speaking perfectly good English up to this point; her mispronunciation ("Ice e-skating") makes sense only if the reader accepts that here two languages are being represented through one. What becomes clear is that the effect of realism is generated by an act of control that *translates* all experiences and indeed words into an English register; the appearance of mimesis is generated through an elementary refusal to depict things as they might in fact be. Translation as productive impossibility has been replaced by an unproblematic rendering of one culture's signifying systems in another's. Rather than encounter a mode of representation that is fragmentary or provisional, we find a voice that confidently synthesizes different experiences to one identifiable reality.

Salman Rushdie's much-quoted essay "Imaginary Homelands" offers a way into this debate:

> Many have argued about the appropriateness of [English] to Indian themes. And I hope all of us share the view that we can't simply use the language in the way the British did; that it needs remaking for our own purposes. Those of us who do use English do so in spite of our ambiguity towards it, or perhaps because we can find in that linguistic struggle a reflection of other struggles taking place in the real world, struggles between the cultures within ourselves and the influences at work upon our societies. To conquer English may be to complete the process of making ourselves free.
>
> (17)

In *Brick Lane*, English does not appear to be remade but rather is used intact, as a novelistic lingua franca, and it is this that generates the effect of realism. There is an unavoidable irony in depicting Nazneen's struggle with English entirely within that language. The focalization becomes a complicated multiple mediation. The narrator reviews the story, as we have seen, from a vantage point after the events have occurred, with an understanding far in advance of Nazneen, but with access to her thoughts. These are rendered in English with a bat squeak of mockery. The novel certainly confronts the "struggles between the cultures" in immigrant identity, but in terms of the language and form of the novel, those struggles seem to be over. There is a tension here that we must register. I have attempted to trace an account of what can be termed the content of the novel and to understand it as a means of describing the doubleness involved in the construction of identity. However, the formal construction of the novel follows a trajectory away from doubleness. What I am offering here is not a criticism of Monica Ali or a suggestion that the novel is somehow "inauthentic." I *am* arguing that there is a rhetoric to be detected in form; in this case, we find ourselves aware of the problem of translation—in the literal linguistic sense as well as in its broader cultural implications—and, through this problem, aware of the exclusions that realism entails. If, for Dominic Head, novels like *Brick Lane* and *The Satanic Verses* might in some senses perform the same function of depicting postcolonial history, I want to point out that there are differences having to do with their portrayals of the nature of hybridity.

At the end of the novel, Nazneen is taken, blindfolded, to an ice rink. The scene and the tone in which it is depicted are somewhat at odds:

> A woman swooped by on one leg. No sequins, no short skirt, She wore jeans. She raced on, on two legs.... To get on the ice physically—it hardly seemed to matter. In her mind she was already there.
> She said, "But you can't skate in a sari."
> Razia was already lacing her boots. "This is England," she said. "You can do whatever you like."

(413)

The first observation to make is that, in terms of the trajectory of the plot, Razia's words must be taken more or less literally. The mobility and sexual freedom promised by the skaters early in the novel are now available to Nazneen. That this scene represents something more ideological than physical, and that it has been achieved through the plots previously mentioned, is indicated by the fact that Nazneen is "already there" in her mind. In England one *can* "skate in a sari." This is a sign of her hybrid identity and the capacity of English forms of writing and political organization to include the other. We can read *Brick Lane* as the story of a character growing into the form in which she is rendered. The effect of the first skating scene is generated by the distance of the narrative voice from the consciousness it depicts. Realism is not merely about mimesis—it is also about movement, historical progress, the Aristotelian telos. This evolution is in terms of individual development or *Bildung*, a development that is characterized as a change from being the passive object of historical forces to being in a position of control. This is exactly the trajectory we follow in the case of Nazneen. She arrives in England imprisoned by her quixotic husband and her Islamic fatalism. By disposing of Chanu, rather sensitively, and confronting Mrs. Islam, she overcomes her submissiveness and becomes the forger of her own identity. The dwindling distance between character and narrator is most clear when Nazneen is most assertive. If she subtly exploits her modesty in her defeat of Mrs. Islam, simply stating that the debt has been paid and offering her arm to be broken, when rejecting Karim, she frankly states her decision: "I don't want to marry you" (377). We have already noted that the narrator registers Nazneen's realization that Karim has invented her—"A Bengali wife. A Bengali mother. An idea of home. An idea of himself that he found in her" (380)—and are familiar with this enlightened voice describing her thoughts in a register that cannot be Nazneen's own. What is interesting here is that for the first time Nazneen herself adopts precisely this language. As she puts it: "I wasn't me, and you weren't you. From the very beginning we didn't see things. What we did—we made each other up" (380). Although this conversation takes place in Bengali, the idiom seems to belong entirely to the English language. Formally and thematically, this represents Nazneen's growth into a Western bourgeois subject, with all the political rewards and penalties that implies.

Here we must return to Razia's words, which end the novel. Surely only the most naive readers are borne along by the plot to such a degree that when they read "This is England. . . . You can do whatever you like" they fail to perceive a terrible irony. As a summary of the England we have been presented with, the statement has an appallingly false ring. In the postcolonial context of *Brick Lane*—

and particularly in the aftermath of the September 11 attacks—these words point to the limits of the developmental narrative implicit in realism. Freedom is certainly not guaranteed to Nazneen. Her rejections of fatalism and Karim represent liberation but also a move away from any potential political collectivity in which she might be able to recognize herself. The meetings of the Bengal Tigers represent at least some attempt to construct the political meanings of Islamic identity through discussion. A true freedom that recognizes the entirety of Nazneen's subjectivity would have to be conceived in the public realm as well as in the cloistered world of family and friendship. Instead, Nazneen becomes the owner, in a small way, of the means of production—she starts a clothing company with Razia— and a competitive individual in a market economy. She has become a new manifestation of the sovereign bourgeois subject who could, should she so desire, write a realist novel.[5]

Brick Lane and the Limits of Realism

I now want to look back through *Brick Lane* and register the moments when the formal constraints of realism cause particular tensions— the moments at which collective and socially constructed meanings might be seen to persist within the individualized narrative frame. Even if, by the end, Nazneen could write a realist novel, she does not. Instead, a ghostly narrator is used whose apparently confident tech-

---

5. Jane Hiddleston has argued that *Brick Lane*'s realism is in question, in the sense that the novel cannot reveal the truth of the community it seeks to represent and is aware of its own limitations as a fictional construct. I agree broadly with this understanding and applaud Hiddleston's attentiveness to the question of how the novel self-consciously employs stereotypes—although I would argue that she somewhat overstates its parodic/dialogic quality. In the case of this essay, I am interested in the conventions of reading implied by the text. *Brick Lane* offers a reading experience in which an authoritative view of the world is recuperable. That is to say, while the world represented may not be historically *real*, the diegetic space in which the narrative takes place is deliberately coherent. While neither *The Satanic Verses* nor *Brick Lane* contains authoritative documentary experiences of Bangladeshis in London, they are clearly formally very different. *Brick Lane* employs the discourse of literary realism. My rather different focus leads me to an alternative conception of the novel's self-consciousness. To me, the distance between Nazneen and the narrator has more to do with the generic constraints of realism than with Ali's position inside and outside the Bangladeshi immigrant community.

niques of translation cannot bridge the gap between the different cultural worlds to which Nazneen has belonged. The structures of realism are subtly changed in this transaction.

In a passage that anticipates Bhabha's ideas about the performative and points toward the problems of the novel form with which we are dealing, Rushdie writes:

> John Fowles begins *Daniel Martin* with the words: "Whole sight: or all the rest is desolation." But human beings do not perceive things whole; we are not gods but wounded creatures, cracked lenses, capable only of fractured perceptions. Partial beings, in all senses of that phrase. Meaning is a shaky edifice we build out of scraps, dogmas, childhood injuries, newspaper articles, chance remarks, old films, small victories, people hated, people loved; perhaps it is because our sense of what is the case is constructed from such inadequate materials that we defend it so fiercely, even to the death. . . . Writers are no longer sages dispensing the wisdom of the centuries. And those of us who have been forced by cultural displacement to accept the provisional nature of all truths, all certainties, have perhaps had modernism forced upon us. We can't lay claim to Olympus, and are thus released to describe our worlds in the way in which all of us, whether writers or not, perceive it from day to day.
>
> ("Imaginary Homelands" 13)

Rushdie argues here that cultural displacement gives rise to modernism—that constructions of reality, once you have been forced to experience more than one, become suspect or provisional, and thus realism in terms of verisimilitude becomes impossible. In a sense, *Brick Lane* takes a very different view. Precisely the experience of cultural jarring described by Rushdie occurs to Nazneen in the first skating scene, but the text remains reliably recuperable to a single world of meaning. Reality, the novel seems to argue, is one thing; we must simply come to understand it. English realism is thus the definitive form of representation. Nevertheless, there is some material that the English narrative voice cannot synthesize and control that thus remains outside the limits of realism—or at least is decidedly recalcitrant. Stories and images that come from a different world of meanings than the realist novel do appear in *Brick Lane*.

One could certainly describe the main plot as claustrophobic, and this sense is surely doubled by the narrator's voice. It is thus with some relief that we journey away from both into the world of Nazneen's sister Hasina's letters. Her story mirrors Nazneen's; both are searches, within historically oppressive conditions, for female independence. Hasina has remained in Bangladesh but made a love marriage—one could almost say that she has made the mistake Nazneen avoided when she refused Karim—abandoned it, been a garment worker in a sweatshop, fallen into near prostitution, and finally been taken in as a servant by a wealthy family. This world is beyond the reach of the voice that represents Nazneen's thoughts and experiences in London, so the letters that tell this story are presented unmediated by any metalanguage. However, this narrative strategy causes the problem of translation for the reader to become more difficult to work through than anywhere else in the novel. Without any account by the narrator, it is hard to know exactly what we are reading—whether the letters represent inept attempts at English or are a free translation from illiterate Bengali. If the first is the case, then we are confronted with an interesting anomalous voice in the text. The very distance between cultures is crucially shown by Hasina's mutilated attempts to render her experiences in the foreign tongue and Bangladesh's resistance to representation accentuated. If, as seems more likely, the latter is true, then we stay in a world edited or arranged by the narrator. The realist frame remains, warped but finally intact, and Hasina is ultimately silenced.

Additionally, there are other moments in which the shadows of other forms of representation than the realist are felt. After she has started the affair with Karim, Nazneen is confronted by a number of apparitions. First, while walking down Brick Lane, she envisions all the recording angels that surround each individual: "She walked with her face turned down to her feet and she felt her head pushing through a density of wings" (210). Later, she is visited by her dead mother, referred to as Amma, whose message in death, as in life, is that of fatalism: "I will tell you how to pass the test.... You just have to endure" (267). One of the most painful moments in the novel is the death of Nazneen's infant son Raqib. Just before it is revealed that Amma's death was a suicide, she returns to blame Raqib's death on Nazneen: rather than leave him to his fate, Nazneen intervened, taking him to a hospital. Magical realism should represent the unmediated survival of sacred and, more importantly, communal forms of storytelling in the confines of the bourgeois form of the novel; however, that is not the case here. The first visit of Nazneen's mother is explained by the fever that follows it; the latter is merely a bad dream. The angels on Brick Lane are simply phantoms produced by Nazneen's guilty conscience. In each case a textual explanation is offered through which a realist reading is recuperable. As with Hasina's letters, we feel the surface of realism being stretched but not actually breaking.

Perhaps the most interesting example of this tendency in the novel is the account of the possession, by a jinn, of Nazneen's mother. The story is preceded by the tale of Nazneen's aunt's good jinn, who dispensed advice, through her, to the village. Amma is scornful of the aunt, Mumtaz, but has her own jinn. When possessed, she does not wash, smells "like a goat," and attacks her husband (332). A fakir exorcises the demon, casting the spirit out of Amma and into a servant boy. There ensues a tussle, initially controlled by the fakir, who puts the boy in a headlock that turns his face "an impressive shade of purple" (334). However, when the tables are turned and the boy has the fakir by the beard, the latter shouts "He's faking!" (335). Eventually the two are separated, but the precise status of what has gone on is debated. The fakir is reluctant to let the boy get away with attacking him, but if he insists that the boy is faking possession, then he must admit that the exorcism is a failure. A compromise is reached whereby the headlock is reengaged and the exorcism completed. The story ends on a decided note of irony: "The fakir was most thorough. Everyone agreed he threw himself into the job with great energy" (336).

By the tone we can be entirely sure of the narrator's view of the exorcism. The world of spirits, religion, and village folklife is primitive and comic. Nazneen is less certain, however. She believed in her mother's delivery from the jinn at the time, and at the point of narration, there is still a residue of acceptance: "she began to wonder what had really happened that day, and why it was that Amma believed only in bad jinn and not in good." An enlightened psychologizing reading is strongly suggested: Amma used the bad jinn to allow her to vent her frustration with her husband; without this outlet, she commits suicide. However, the status of what has occurred is by no means easily explained. The boy's language when "possessed," his strength in attacking the fakir, and his subsequent foaming at the mouth are not entirely accounted for, despite the narrator's describing them as a "strategy" (336). We have finally to decide that despite the attempts by the narratorial voice to synthesize this event into its realist register, the material does not quite work: some mode of storytelling that is outside the discourse of the bourgeois novel persists.

Brick Lane and the Novel

Kumkum Sangari makes a convincing argument in relation to García Márquez:

> The power of [his] narratives lies in the insistent pressure of *freedom* as the *absent horizon*—which is neither predictable nor inevitable. The way marvellous realism figures collectivity and takes metaphor to excess indicates a reality that exceeds the space allotted to it by its own history. The excess of meaning bursting out of its present time into an imaginable (or probable) time exerts immense pressure in his narratives.
>
> (18)

García Márquez's form makes an argument about the problems of postcolonial history and identity. It encodes their specific collective and hybrid nature and points toward an absent freedom—akin to the "newness" Baucom sees in Rushdie's versions of translation. The use of realism in *Brick Lane* points toward a different, traditional Western Enlightenment argument about freedom. One may overcome the problems of postcolonial identity, the novel seems to argue, through transcending history and achieving self-authorship. *Brick Lane* does not agree with Sangari that the postcolonial subject can never be "identical with ... a coherent bourgeois self grounded in a realist ontology" (22). However, the process by which this secure ground is won visibly closes off precisely the collectivity that Sangari celebrates in García Márquez. To return to our most important site of comparison, if what we encounter in *The Satanic Verses* is a subjectivity seen in constant movement—both as the result of a prebourgeois collectivity and an haute-bourgeois fragmentation— what is interesting about *Brick Lane* is that it seems to argue for a more stable and linear version of subjectivity. Whereas *The Satanic Verses* might seem to ally the negative results of a history of colonialism with Western reason, *Brick Lane*—at least to some extent—argues that Western reason is the answer to the problem, not its cause. More, not less, enlightenment in the bourgeois tradition is required.

To return to my starting place, I want to assert that, although it is not conservative in the range of material it can depict, realism's drive toward transparency and its linear conception of development inevitably mean that it will tend to endorse a notion of subjectivity at odds with more radical notions of hybridity. Realism may be capable of representing an ethnically diverse Britain, but it can do so only by an act of untroubled translation, the effect of which is to diminish the jarring differences between cultures; the immigrant subject does not have to choose between competing accounts of the same world but must negotiate inhabiting incommensurable worlds.

It is also important to emphasize the specificity of texts like *Brick Lane* and to note how forms change in different circumstances. If there is a simple maneuver to ally all marvelous realism to postmodernism, then an analogous act can be wrought on postcolonial realism. An interesting example is the review of *Brick Lane* offered by James Wood:

> Plenty of readers, critics, and academics have been grateful for the augmentation of material, the opening of "colorful" worlds, not to mention the at times radical literary techniques, that ... [immigrant] life has brought to fiction. ... What is not so often said is that this new material has another and perhaps more momentous service to perform, which is to return fiction to its nineteenth-century gravity. This it does by re-importing into the Western novel traditional societies, with their ties of marriage, burdens of religion, obligations of civic duty, and pressures of propriety—and thereby restoring to the novel form some of the old oppressions that it was created to comprehend and to resist and in some measure to escape.
>
> (29)

What Wood says here might seem fairly similar to what I have argued: he is noting that *Brick Lane* pushes the novel's concerns away from new formulations of the role of the subject. However, the rather unfortunate application of the language of import and trade in this passage reveals the problems of this position: the cost is underdevelopment, the benefit, good old-fashioned novels. To

regard Bangladesh as a society that offers "nineteenth-century gravity" is to misunderstand postcolonial history; just as we should
resist making magic realism a subset of late twentieth-century postmodern fragmentation, we must be careful not to identify a
postcolonial realism with the concerns of another period of the
West's history. The taboos that Nazneen faces are part of the specific
set of conditions that arise in the context of an ethnically diverse
England. If *Brick Lane* has much in common with, for instance,
Villette—a heroine in an unfamiliar land trying to work out who, if
anyone, might be the hero and eventually asserting herself in her
own space—this similarity should not be understood as a happy
return of the novel to its roots. We do not simply get to witness
again the birth of the individual as she navigates social constrictions
on her identity. Instead, we get to see the problems inherent in this
process for a contemporary postcolonial subject. Despite its arguments about subjectivity, *Brick Lane* cannot be read as an example of
what Wood describes as the "immigration of content" (29); the effect
of its use of realism is, in the end, identifiably different from the traditional novel of the nineteenth century. The relationship between
form and content in *Brick Lane* renders the form "visible." The idea
of liberal *Bildung* and the practice of mimesis (including the representation of consciousness) are estranged by the content: we see
them at work, when we are usually asked to take them for granted
in realist fiction. Thinking back to the skating scenes, we see how
the demands of representing different cultural signifying systems
render unstable the novel's transparency. The form is pulling in one
way—toward nineteenth-century liberalism—but the content won't
let it do its work without a struggle.

 Brick Lane does not bring back to the novel its old content; it asks
us to take the notions of universalism that were inherent in its traditional form and apply them to those who are often viewed as outside
this discourse. Undertaking this activity, as I hope I have shown,
entails gains and losses. A purposive narrative of liberation emerges.
Nevertheless, the very idea that, through narrative progress, what
was "other" will eventually find its place within an England where
"You can do whatever you like" implies that this other was not quite
ready before. However, those elements of postcolonial subjectivity
that are incommensurable with realism are not entirely discarded.

Instead, they are felt as a problem that stretches the novel's formal constraints. In a sense, we have the inverse of García Márquez: we have the freedom, but we feel the weight of the absent communal past. The part of Nazneen's consciousness that belongs to a more collective form of life remains interestingly unmappable by the realist narrative voice.

University of East Anglia

WORKS CITED

Afzal-Khan, Fawzia. "Post-Modernist Strategies of Liberation in the Works of Salman Rushdie." *Journal of South Asian Literature* 23 (1988): 137–45.

Ahmad, Aijaz. *In Theory: Classes, Nations, Literatures*. London: Verso, 1992.

Ali, Monica. *Brick Lane*. London: Doubleday, 2003.

Bakhtin, Mikhail. "From the Prehistory of Novelistic Discourse." Trans. Caryl Emerson and Michael Holquist. *Modern Criticism and Theory: A Reader*. Ed. David Lodge. London: Longman, 1988. 124–56.

Baucom, Ian. *Out of Place: Englishness, Empire, and the Locations of Identity*. Princeton, NJ: Princeton UP, 1999.

Belsey, Catherine. *Critical Practice*. London: Routledge, 1980.

Bhabha, Homi K. "DissemiNation: Time, Narrative, and the Margins of the Modern Nation." *Nation and Narration*. Ed. Homi K. Bhabha. London: Routledge, 1990. 291–322.

Brecht, Bertolt. "Against Georg Lukács." *Aesthetics and Politics: The Key Texts of the Classic Debate within German Marxism*. Trans. Stuart Hood. London: Verso, 1977. 68–85.

Brontë, Charlotte. *Villette*. 1853. Oxford: Oxford UP, 2001.

Edmundson, Mark. "Prophet of a New Postmodernism: The Greater Challenge of Salman Rushdie." *Harper's Magazine* Dec. 1989: 62–71.

Engblom, Philip. "A Multitude of Voices: Carnivalization and Dialogicality in the Novels of Salman Rushdie." *Reading Rushdie: Perspectives on the Fiction of Salman Rushdie*. Ed. D. M. Fletcher. Cross / Cultures 16. Amsterdam: Rodopi, 1994. 291–304.

Gąsiorek, Andrzej. *Post-War British Fiction: Realism and After*. London: Arnold, 1995.

Head, Dominic. *The Cambridge Introduction to Modern British Fiction, 1950–2000*. Cambridge: Cambridge UP, 2002.

Hiddleston, Jane. "Shapes and Shadows: (Un)veiling the Immigrant in Monica Ali's *Brick Lane*." *Journal of Commonwealth Literature* 40 (2005): 57–72.

Kristeva, Julia. "Word, Dialogue, Novel." *The Kristeva Reader*. Ed. Toril Moi. Trans. Sean Hand and Leon S. Roudiez. Oxford: Blackwell, 1986. 34–61.

Lukács, Georg. "The Ideology of Modernism." *The Meaning of Contemporary Realism*. Trans. John and Necke Mander. London: Merlin, 1963. 17–46.

MacCabe, Colin. *James Joyce and the Revolution of the Word*. London: MacMillan, 1979.

Rushdie, Salman. "Imaginary Homelands." *Imaginary Homelands*. London: Granta, 1991. 9–21.

—— *Midnight's Children*. London: Cape, 1981.

—— *The Satanic Verses*. London: Penguin, 1988.

Sage, Victor. "The Poetics of Mimesis: Aristotle, Tragedy, and Realism." *Theatre Theories: From Plato to Virtual Reality*. Ed. Anthony Frost. Norwich: Pen and Inc, 2000. 25–43.

Sangari, Kumkum. "The Politics of the Possible; Or the Perils of Reclassification." *The Politics of the Possible: Essays on Gender, History, Narratives, Colonial English*. London: Anthem, 2002. 1–28.

Wood, James. "Making It New." *New Republic* 8 Sept. 2003: 29–34.

CONTRIBUTORS

REBECCA L. WALKOWITZ is associate professor of English at the University of Wisconsin-Madison. She is the author of *Cosmopolitan Style: Modernism beyond the Nation* (Columbia, 2006) and the co-editor of six books, including *Bad Modernisms* (Duke, 2006), *The Turn to Ethics* (Routledge, 2000), and *Media Spectacles* (Routledge, 1993). She is now at work on a book-length study about the effects of globalization on national paradigms of literary culture, titled "After the National Paradigm: Translation, Comparison, and the New World Literature."

MATTHEW HART is assistant professor of English at the University of Illinois at Urbana-Champaign. He has published articles on T. S. Eliot, poetic modernism and postcolonial poetics, Tory Englishness after 9/11, and the cartographic drawings of Layla Curtis. He has two book projects underway, titled "Nations of Nothing but Poetry" and "Late Britain," and is a 2006-7 fellow at the Cornell University Society for the Humanities.

WEN JIN is assistant professor of English at Columbia University. She is working on a book manuscript on the ethics of comparison in post-World War II Chinese American transnational literature and culture.

ERIC HAYOT is associate professor of English at the University of Arizona. He is the author of *Chinese Dreams: Pound, Brecht, Tel quel* (Michigan, 2004) and the co-editor of two collections, *Sinographies: Writing China* (Minnesota, forthcoming in 2007) and *The EverQuest Reader* (Wallflower, forthcoming in 2007). He hopes to complete a book manuscript titled "On Chinese Pain" while a 2006-7 fellow at the UCLA International Institute.

VĚRA ELIÁŠOVÁ is a doctoral candidate in English at Rutgers University. Her dissertation is titled "Women in the City: Female Flânerie and the Modern Urban Imagination." She has also been working on female flânerie in transnational literary contexts. Her interview with Iva Pekárková appeared in the Summer 2006 issue of *Contemporary Literature*.

J. DILLON BROWN is assistant professor of English at Brooklyn College, City University of New York. He is at work on a book manuscript examining postwar West Indian novels and their relationship to the metropolitan site of production.

ALISTAIR CORMACK is a tutor at the University of East Anglia. He is the author of *Yeats and Joyce: Cyclical History and the Reprobate Tradition* (Ashgate, forthcoming). His current writing project is on colonialism and forms of narrative in Irish and British prose from *Ulysses* to *Brick Lane*.

• COMING IN •

CONTEMPORARY LITERATURE

◆ VOL. 48, NO. 1, SPRING 2007 ◆

"An Interview with Thane Rosenbaum," conducted by Derek Parker Royal

"Intellectualist Poetry in Eccentric Form: John Ashbery, French Critical Debate, and an American Raymond Roussel," by Charles M. Cooney

"The Imaginary Solution," by Craig Douglas Dworkin

"Other People's Holocausts: Trauma, Empathy, and Justice in Anna Deavere Smith's *Fires in the Mirror*," by Gregory Jay

"Memlik's House and Mountolive's Uniform: Orientalism, Ornamentalism, and Lawrence Durrell's *Alexandria Quartet*," by Donald P. Kaczvinsky

Reviews by Steven Belletto, Lee M. Jenkins, Brian May, and Adalaide Morris

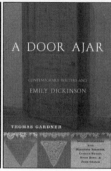
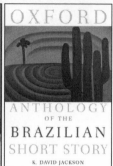

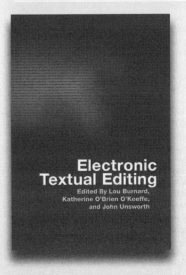

Somewhere in Germany

A Novel

Stefanie Zweig, translated by Marlies Comjean

Somewhere in Germany is the sequel to the acclaimed *Nowhere in Africa*, which was turned into the Oscar-winning film of the same name. It traces the return of the Redlich family to Germany after their nine-year exile in Kenya during World War II, and of their adaption to their new home amidst the ruins. TERRACE BOOKS **Cloth $24.95**

The Tree of Life: A Trilogy of Life in the Lodz Ghetto

Book Three: The Cattle Cars Are Waiting, 1942–1944

Chava Rosenfarb, translated from the Yiddish by the author in collaboration with Goldie Morgentaler

"A work that rises to the heights of the great creations of world literature and towers powerfully over the Jewish literature of the Holocaust."—Decision of the Jury for the Manger Prize for Yiddish Literature, 1979

This third volume in this powerful trilogy follows the tragic fate of the inhabitants of the ghetto. Rosenfarb, herself a survivor of the Lodz Ghetto, Auschwitz, and Bergen-Belsen, has created characters who struggle to retain a sense of humanity and dignity. LIBRARY OF WORLD FICTION/TERRACE BOOKS **Paper $21.95**

Ulysses in Black

Ralph Ellison, Classicism, and African American Literature

Patrice D. Rankine

"A powerful and pioneering study that creatively links the rich traditions of classical antiquity to contemporary black thought. I highly recommend it."—Cornel West, Princeton University

In this groundbreaking work, Rankine asserts that the classics need not be a mark of Eurocentrism. Instead, the classical tradition can be part of a self-conscious, prideful approach to African American culture and identity. WISCONSIN STUDIES IN CLASSICS **Cloth $45.00**

Butterfly Boy

Memories of a Chicano Mariposa

Rigoberto González

"In the tradition of Richard Rodriguez, this stirring memoir of a first-generation Mexican American's coming-of-age and coming out is wrenching, angry, passionate, ironic and always eloquent about conflicts of family, class and sexuality. . . . An unforgettable story of leaving home today."—*Booklist*

"Poignant, heartfelt memoir of a gay Latino immigrant's coming-of-age, played out against a relentless backdrop of abuse and neglect."—*Kirkus Reviews*

WRITING IN LATINIDAD: AUTOBIOGRAPHICAL VOICES OF U.S. LATINOS/AS **Cloth $24.95**

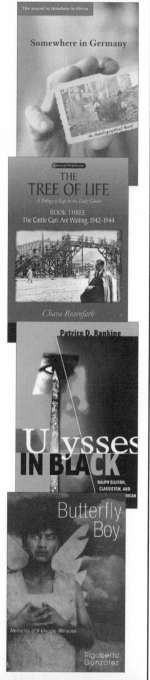

ᴔ The University of Wisconsin Press

At booksellers, or visit www.wisc.edu/wisconsinpress

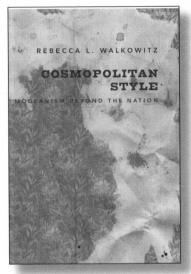
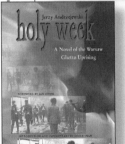

Mr. Ding's Chicken Feet
On a Slow Boat from Shanghai to Texas
Gillian Kendall

A funny, moving journey across the Pacific Ocean, told by the sole woman aboard a Chinese ship, employed to teach English to the Chinese crew. Suddenly thrust into an alien world, thick with cigarette smoke, sea creatures, and male sexuality she thoughtfully reflects on the variety of emotional landscapes she encounters, shifting as she explores her own culture, orientation, and heart. TERRACE BOOKS **Paper $22.95**

Death of a Department Chair
A Novel
Lynn C. Miller

"A tidy mystery with enough ambitious careerists and theorists to staff a dozen dysfunctional lit departments. Miller knows where the academic bodies are buried both literally and figuratively, and she touches up a traditional mystery with some lively, nontraditional angles."—Janice Law, author of *Nightbus*
TERRACE BOOKS **Paper $24.95**

Countering the Counterculture
Rereading Postwar American Dissent from Jack Kerouac to Tomás Rivera
Manuel L. Martinez

Rebelling against bourgeois vacuity and taking their countercultural critique on the road, the Beat writers and artists have long symbolized a spirit of freedom and radical democracy. Martinez offers an eye-opening challenge to this characterization of the Beats, juxtaposing them against Chicano nationalists like Raul Salinas, Jose Montoya, Luis Valdez, and Oscar Acosta and Mexican migrant writers in the United States, like Tomas Rivera and Ernesto Galarza. **Paper $29.95**

A World for Julius
A Novel
Alfredo Bryce Echenique, translated by Dick Gerdes, with a new foreword by Julio Ortega

Winner of the Outstanding Translation Award of the American Literary Translators Association and the Columbia University Translation Center Award

Julius was born in a mansion directly across from Lima's old San Felipe Hippodrome. Yet despite the soft shelter of family and money, hard realities overshadow Julius's expanding world. This lyrical, richly textured, postmodern novel charts the decline of an centuries-old aristocratic family faced with the invasion of foreign capital in the 1950s. THE AMERICAS **Paper $19.95**

See our Web site for other titles in the Americas series.

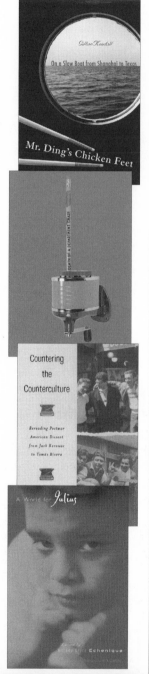

〰 The University of Wisconsin Press
At booksellers, or visit www.wisc.edu/wisconsinpress